Development and Social Action

**Selected essays from
*Development in Practice***

Introduced by **Miloon Kothari**

A Development in Practice Reader

Series Editor: **Deborah Eade**

Oxfam GB

Published by Oxfam GB
First published 1999

© Oxfam GB 1999

ISBN 0 85598 415 5

A catalogue record for this publication is available from the British Library.

Available from the following agents:
for the USA: Stylus Publishing, Inc., PO Box 605, Herndon, VA20172-0605
tel 703 661 1581/800 232 0223; fax 703 661 1501; email styluspub@aol.com
for Canada: Fernwood Books Ltd., PO Box 9409, Stn. A, Halifax, Nova Scotia B3K 5S3
tel 902 422 3302; fax 902 422 3179; email fernwood@istar.ca
for Southern Africa: David Philip Publishers, PO Box 23408, Claremont, Cape Town 7735,
South Africa; tel. 021 644136; fax 021 643358;
for Australia: Bush Books, PO Box 1370, Gosford South, NSW 2250, Australia;
tel. 043 23274; fax 029 212248
For the rest of the world, contact Oxfam Publishing, 274 Banbury Road, Oxford OX2 7DZ, UK.

The views expressed in this book are those of the individual contributors, and not necessarily
those of the publisher or editor.

Published by Oxfam GB, 274 Banbury Road, Oxford OX2 7DZ, UK

Oxfam GB is registered as a charity (no. 202918) and is a member of Oxfam International.

Designed by Oxfam Creative Services   Typeset in Melior   Printed by Oxfam Print Unit

Contents

Preface

Deborah Eade

For many progressive NGOs and civil society organisations (CSOs), social action — people's capacity to organise together for a common, social goal — lies at the heart of their understanding of development. Popular mobilisation, whether to defend existing rights that are under threat, or to protest against the denial of these rights, is seen to be just as critical to the development process as economic growth — if not more so. Without this kind of mass engagement in promoting and then defending these demands, even concrete gains may remain very fragile. A case in point is the closing of public child-care arrangements in Britain following World War II: although they evidently benefited working women and enabled more women to earn an income, they were able to be suspended with relatively little protest, partly because they had not been fought for by the women who used them, but were viewed as a service which the state needed to provide only as part of the war effort — an effort which entailed drafting women, temporarily, into the munitions factories. With potentially high male unemployment in the post-war period, it was perceived as a more pressing political priority to get men into jobs than to keep women in them. Arguably, had public nurseries originally been established in response to a mass lobby, the political price of closing them might have been prohibitive. Had this happened, generations of working parents (and their children) in Britain would have enjoyed a higher quality of life, and many inequalities between men and women would almost certainly have diminished or even disappeared.

People organise for altruistic motives, as for example in the anti-slavery movements of the nineteenth century or the international anti-apartheid campaign of our own times. In other cases, the motivation is to further their own perceived interests as a group — be these the rights of indigenous peoples or ethnic minorities to cultural self-expression or self-rule, or the demand for female suffrage or the rights of women to leave husbands who subject them to abuse. One might also view many of the national liberation wars of the last 50 years as a form of social action on a massive scale. While the claims of some of the armed opposition movements to represent 'the people' look somewhat inflated in retrospect, these movements were nevertheless often more representative than any other form of political expression available to ordinary citizens. (For instance, the fact that many peasant communities opted to remain in or return to the war zones during El Salvador's 12-year war does not necessarily imply, as the Salvadoran military then maintained, that they were therefore all signed-up members of the armed opposition, the FMLN. Nor does it mean that the FMLN was a model of democracy, transparency, and public accountability. Of course not: it was a guerrilla army which was fighting a prolonged war against far better-resourced and often brutal government forces. What it does mean is that many of the country's poorest people regarded the FMLN's overall project as representing their interests more effectively than the existing political system could ever do.)

What was common to the various forms of social mobilisation in the past, however, was the fact that campaigns, whether local or international, were generally grounded in time and place, and could be focused on an identifiable target or aimed at a tangible (albeit ambitious) goal. This might be to bring down a government or to reform a state institution — such as to disband a discredited branch of the public-security forces or to enact some form of legislation. Or it might be aimed at influencing an external body, such as a foreign government, the World Bank, or a private company.

What has changed today, as Miloon Kothari argues in his introduction, is that the locus of social action has changed, and will continue to change, in the context of rapid economic globalisation. While the gulf between rich and poor grows deeper and wider, as an inevitable by-product of the form that free-market ideologies are taking, it is ever harder to pin down in any precise way the institutions and policies that are ultimately responsible. Increasingly, these are governed by forces that originate beyond and operate across territorial borders. In a broad sense, one can place responsibility at the door of the international financial institutions, such as the World Bank or the International Monetary Fund (IMF), or of the World Trade Organisation (WTO); or of bodies such as the OECD, or the regional development banks such as the Inter-American Development

Bank (IDB). But these are essentially inter-government bodies, and although the individual power of, say, the G-7 nations versus the collective power of the G-77 member states is reflected in the economic policies of these institutions, there are nevertheless many international mechanisms that could be used to hold them accountable, to say nothing of the importance of lobbying one's own government.

For instance, there have been increasing calls since 1995 for the Bretton Woods institutions, as part of the UN system, as well as the WTO (which is not) to be formally accountable to the UN Economic and Social Council (ECOSOC), through its annual sessions. (Their refusal to be answerable to this inter-government body raises doubts, some would say, about whether their claims to transparency and openness to public scrutiny are more than rhetorical.) Miloon Kothari illustrates some of the creative ways in which existing human-rights machinery has been used by a range of CSOs to hold public institutions accountable to the values to which they are formally and legally committed. But he also illustrates that this is not the only root of the problem.

Blame is often attributed to those multinational enterprises which are most egregious in their disregard for human rights, or whose behaviour most threatens the well-being and livelihoods of millions of innocent people. Companies like Monsanto, Shell, and Nike are, at the very least, asking themselves how to avoid precipitating such public-relations disasters in the future: one hopes that this self-searching might be the beginning of a more responsible attitude towards business ethics. In a commoditised world, consumers also have an ethical responsibility to engage with the forces of economic globalisation. Consumer mobilisations such as the Clean Clothes Campaign have raised public awareness about the employment practices of companies whose workforces are mostly located in poor communities, usually in Third World countries. And fair-trade groups like the Max Havelaar Foundation have long promoted the interests of the producers of coffee and other commodities. The rights of children, and the rights of child workers, have assumed greater prominence in recent years, especially during the 1998 International March Against Child Labour. But most rights violations are of a far less spectacular nature — even banal, to quote the philosopher Hannah Arendt — and do not arouse international public indignation. More significantly, economic globalisation makes it increasingly difficult to identify and isolate 'the culprit'. Companies move their operations from one location to another, experience boardroom takeovers, undergo mergers and demergers across totally different sectors, and play the financial speculation games more quickly than we can scrutinise their behaviour and expose shady or harmful practices.

But as the processes of deregulation, of the 'marketisation' of public services, and of the liberalisation of international trade grind inexorably on, so the forces of popular resistance must take new shapes and forms. Struggles for social and economic justice are still experienced at the local level and in people's daily lives, and it is critical to promote social action at this level. But the levers of change are seldom within reach of the average citizen; or indeed of any single pressure group acting alone even at a national level, much less internationally. Making the links goes much further than variations on the old slogan of 'think global, act local'. The ways in which the same global forces now penetrate the lives of millions of individuals around the world both compel and allow for different forms of protest, and for different forms of transnational organisation and cross-cultural communication. The forces that oppress and divide contemporary societies are stronger, more widespread, and more diverse than they have ever been; but the potential to generate international solidarity across borders and frontiers has never been greater.

In the early 1990s, NGOs dedicated major intellectual energy to the question of how to 'scale up' their impact. The problem was that to the extent that they moved far outside their own little world of development projects and aid funding, they focused on what *they* could do to influence the wider policy environment. Ten years on from such debates, it is now obvious even to the most narcissistic NGO that its own influence on the world is insignificant. However vociferous its campaigns, however subtle or high-powered its advocacy work, however strong its public appeal, no NGO can hope to achieve very much if it works alone. The challenge facing NGOs today is that of determining the values and priorities that should shape their alliances with other CSOs (such as trade unions, human-rights organisations, or church-based groups), and then being self-effacing enough to work with a range of social actors in more effectively protesting against the violations and humiliations to which the prevailing world economic order condemns millions of women, men, and children. Only on the basis of making common cause among themselves will CSOs achieve political credibility in proposing more humane, more ethical, and more sustainable alternatives to 'development' as we now know it. The experiences gathered in this volume suggest that, despite their commitment to broad-based mobilisation for change (and many NGOs worldwide have their historical roots in such forms of expression), NGOs still have a lot to learn about new forms of social action.

Globalisation, social action, and human rights

Miloon Kothari

Introduction

The concern with social action and development dates back to the struggles for independence in the period following World War II. The original notion of development was to open up spaces for deprived social sectors who were themselves often deeply involved in the struggles for self-determination. In that context the Universal Declaration of Human Rights (UDHR) was conceived, and the United Nations (UN) was set up to promote processes which subsequently gave rise to the concept of development. The state was supposed to be, in its counter-imperial and post-colonial role, a catalyst for social action: a role that received serious attention from civil society organisations (CSOs).[1]

The state's role as a catalyst for social action was, however, subverted by monopolistic tendencies. Soon after the post-colonial phase, both the state and international agencies began to emphasise social and economic policies that focused on wealth-creation. 'Development' thus became tied to the creation of national market economies, to be integrated into a global economic system that was based on market principles. This approach, much accelerated by the deregulation of global markets from the 1980s, has led to growing disparity in the distribution of wealth, polarisation of social classes, and increasing dependence on foreign aid and international capital in many Third World countries. The most recent of these tendencies, especially after the collapse of the socialist states and the emergence of a unipolar world, is known as economic globalisation.[2]

This paper argues that there is a major crisis in the philosophy, the reality, and the very notion of development which, instead of being a *process* to create conditions for self-reliant, sustainable communities, has become simply a *project*. The misuse and atomisation of the original understanding of development, which was directly linked to the achievement of social justice, has led to deepening poverty, even in times of economic boom for investors and soaring stock-market indices. This misappropriation has left a painful legacy whose lexicon of acronyms — IMF, WB, SAPs, GATT, WTO, NAFTA — represent lost ideals, lost decades, and a consistent assault on the true development capacities of people and communities.

For those who advocate stable social institutions that can foster policies, laws, and programmes aimed at bringing about social justice, respect for human rights, and development, economic globalisation is already leaving pernicious and long-lasting effects. Further, the dismantling of socially conscious legislation, institutions and programmes, is eroding the social gains made through decades of civil-society struggle.

This paper also argues both that the onus is on CSOs to recapture the radical notion of development and that, ironically, the catalyst for doing so is to be found in the very processes that have been produced by economic globalisation.[3] Ever more intense collaborative transnational alliances are needed to restore what has been destroyed in recent decades. But the inability to understand the many dimensions, some quite technical, of globalisation, the reluctance to challenge the institutions that spearhead it, and a focus only on local-level action will serve to marginalise CSOs, and to consign many millions of people to further exclusion and poverty.

At the dawn of the twenty-first century, economic globalisation is the phenomenon that dominates the world stage. Its many manifestations are all around us, as are its manifold failures. The iniquitous outcomes of economic globalisation have been confirmed in numerous UN reports. Even the international economic policy forums now recognise that the so-called 'trickle down' effect, for long the social justification for economic liberalisation, is not occurring. Studies such as UNCTAD's *Trade and Development Report 1997* and UNDP's *Human Development Report 1997* (*HDR*) convincingly show that the opposite is true. UNCTAD demonstrates that since the early 1980s the world economy has been characterised by rising inequality, both among and within countries, that income gaps between North and South continue to widen, and that the income share of the richest 20 per cent has risen almost everywhere, while that of both the poorest 20 per cent and also the middle class has fallen.[4] The *HDR 1997* similarly shows that, although poverty has been dramatically reduced in many parts of the world, one-quarter of the human race remains in severe poverty; that the human development index (HDI) declined in the previous year in more than 30 countries — more than in any year since the *HDR* was first issued in 1990; and that economic globalisation had indeed helped to reduce poverty in some of the largest and strongest developing economies, but had also produced a widening gap between winners and losers among and within countries.[5]

The USA, whose ideology created and sustains the global architecture on which economic globalisation depends, is disgraced, both politically and in terms of its own domestic dispossession and poverty.[6] Poverty is now more widespread and extreme in the USA than in any other industrialised country. What right, then, does the USA have to dictate the world's economic ideology? Powerful voices are now emerging within the USA to question the 'Washington Consensus', the basis of economic globalisation as we know it, including such establishment figures as the Chief Economist of the World Bank, Dr Joseph Stiglitz.[7]

As if the adverse effects of the liberalisation of trade and investment were not enough, attempts are being made to create conditions which will allow for uncontrolled capital flows. The trend began with the establishment of global deregulated markets in the 1980s and 1990s. While massively increased financial mobility has become a primary danger to the health of national economies — as demonstrated by the crisis in Southeast Asia — the scale of such financial flows is astounding and indicates the exponential growth in this area.[8]

For those pushing for further liberalisation of investment, the past two years have witnessed the attempt to adopt a Multilateral Agreement on Investment (MAI). This was until recently being negotiated at the Organisation for Economic Co-operation and Development (OECD), the international club of the world's 29 richest countries. If adopted, the MAI would have contributed a significant chapter in what has been called the 'constitution of a single global economy', or 'a bill of rights and freedoms for transnational corporations ... a declaration of corporate rule'. Until February 1997, when a draft was leaked, it was for the most part negotiated in secret and was driven by the aggressive advocacy of the International Chamber of Commerce, the US Council on International Business, and other corporate-backed groups. Essentially, the MAI sought to complete the economic liberalisation agenda, favouring the rights of transnational investors and corporations over the rights of workers, consumers, communities, and the environment.

In December 1998, under intense pressure from CSOs (described below), and in response to the withdrawal of France from the negotiations, the OECD abandoned the MAI. However, the increased freedom for investment is very much on the agenda at various global and regional forums. Provisions that made the MAI notorious with the environment, human rights, and development NGOs are cropping up at the WTO, the IMF, the FTAA (the Free Trade Agreement of the Americas), and elsewhere. CSOs thus need to be more, and not less, vigilant.

It is against the background of attempts to liberalise finance, trade, and investment still further that we contemplate perhaps the greatest challenge to social action: how to sustain countervailing forces that challenge, expose, demystify, and discredit the lure of economic globalisation and blunt the power of those who are devising ways to push the world closer to the edge of economic and social disaster — processes already evident with the recent crises in Southeast Asia, Russia, and Brazil.

It is imperative that CSOs recognise this omnipresent threat and use all available international instruments and mechanisms, as well as government commitments from the recent series of UN conferences. For social actors and activists who want to remain relevant in a rapidly changing world, the pressing need is to grapple with the world's economic systems, at whatever level possible — from gathering information and gaining understanding to carrying out research on the impacts, from advocacy work aimed at reform of global institutions to staking claim to space during international and regional negotiations on economic treaties, and an increased role for the UN. Without such forthright countering of economic globalisation and without taking advantage of the spaces it has inadvertently opened up, social action and development have a bleak and fragmented future.

Approaches to social justice and sustainable development

While ever more people and institutions now acknowledge the problems with the economic liberalisation model, what is conveniently being overlooked is the framework within which economic policy needs to be formulated for the benefit of humankind. The existing international human-rights instruments[9] and UN monitoring mechanisms for compliance with these instruments already provide such a framework and confer upon states the legal obligations to protect, promote, and fulfil human rights. A number of instruments of a declamatory nature also exist. Together, these form useful points of departure in articulating and putting into practice *collective* rights, such as the right to development and to a clean environment. Certain instruments also promote the rights of specific population groups such as indigenous and tribal peoples, minorities, and disabled persons.[10] Collective rights are emerging as an important area of articulation and action among social movements and campaigns around the world for rights such as clean drinking water, or for the rights of women, indigenous peoples, peasant farmers, and so forth.[11]

Underpinning the human-rights instruments are the basic principles of non-discrimination, equality, and self-determination, and the right to political participation. Viewed from the perspective of people and communities fighting for adequate food, heath care, housing and living conditions, education, and a voice and representation on political bodies, these instruments provide a bulwark, a standard to aspire to, and, for civil-society groups, a set of rights to be claimed. A more forthright and comprehensive approach to human rights can provide for a sharper critique of government responsibility and provide benchmarks for interventions by all sectors of society, including those who are marginalised and suffer discrimination.

Human rights provide the perspective, the context, and the substance (through the entitlements contained in numerous instruments) to realise sustainable development and social justice for all. The holistic approach offered by the concept of human rights can strengthen (to take some examples) struggles for women's rights and for the environment. Viewed in such a light, the realisation of human rights for every woman, man, and child is the primary system through which international investment, finance, and trade regimes can be held accountable. For the policies, programmes, and instruments emanating from economic globalisation affect people at the local level, both directly through the acquisition of natural resources and indirectly through the influencing of national policies that undermine the capacity of people and communities, especially the marginalised, to control their own space and resources. Such impacts are clearly a violation of internationally accepted obligations under human-rights treaties.

The four fundamental principles that are under threat, as outlined by the International NGO Committee on Human Rights in Trade and Investment, form a useful framework to explain the all-encompassing scope of this approach, and also offer clear directions for gaining and retaining human rights:[12]

The primacy of human rights: The promotion and protection of human rights must be accepted as the fundamental framework for and goal of all multilateral and bilateral investment, trade, and financial agreements. Such agreements cannot exclude or ignore human-rights principles and objectives without losing their most fundamental claim to legitimacy.

Non-retrogression: All states have a duty to respect, protect, ensure and fulfil international human-rights obligations and cannot derogate from or limit them except as expressly provided for in the relevant human rights treaties. 'Rollback' and 'standstill' requirements, as formulated in the MAI, are incompatible with the requirement that economic, social and cultural rights be realised progressively, as explicitly stated in the International Covenant on Economic, Social and Cultural Rights (CESCR). Governments must demonstrate that they are taking concrete steps towards realisation of these rights. Moreover, state parties have a specific duty not to take retrogressive measures that would jeopardise economic, social, and cultural rights.

The right to an effective remedy in the appropriate forum: The right to an effective remedy for anyone whose rights have been violated cannot be contracted away by the state nor denied by the operations of intergovernmental institutions. Investment or trade bodies should not adjudicate concerns that fall firmly into the human-rights domain, as disputes between corporations and state actors, but these should be dealt with by appropriate domestic, regional, and international human-rights fora and enforcement mechanisms.

Rights of participation and recourse of affected individuals and groups: Human rights cannot be effectively realised unless the right of participation of the affected populations in planning, implementation, and seeking redress for violations is respected. The participation of women in all these processes is particularly important.

The new social movements which have adopted this holistic approach have done much not only to strengthen the pro-environment lobby and women's movements, but also to demonstrate the imperative of viewing human rights and development as complementary and mutually reinforcing means of achieving social justice for all.

There are also valuable insights and directions offered by the resolutions emanating from the UN human-rights programme. Take, for example, the resolution adopted on 20 August 1998 by the UN Sub-Commission for the Prevention of Discrimination and the Protection of Minorities and entitled:

'Human rights as the primary objective of trade, investment, and financial policy'. In this resolution the Sub-Commission emphasised that the realisation of the human rights and fundamental freedoms described in the international human-rights instruments is the 'first and most fundamental responsibility and objective of States in all areas of governance and development'.[13] This phrase reaffirms language adopted by the world's governments in the Declaration and Plan of Action from the 1993 World Conference on Human Rights.[14] The Sub-Commission also expressed concern about the human-rights implications of the MAI 'and particularly about the extent to which the Agreement might limit the capacity of States to take proactive steps to ensure the enjoyment of economic, social and cultural rights by all people, creating benefits for a small privileged minority at the expense of an increasingly disenfranchised majority'.

Taking these international instruments as point of departure, several international NGOs have mobilised at local, national, and international levels to promote economic, social, and cultural rights in the context of economic globalisation. Two examples will serve as illustration.

Habitat International Coalition (HIC): Basing its work on the right to housing and land, HIC works through its three committees: housing and land rights, women and shelter, and housing and environment.[15] The Coalition's work proceeds from a holistic perspective which seeks, through alliance building, training, use of the UN system, research and fact-finding, to counter the negative effects of economic globalisation through stressing the inviolability of the gaining and retaining of housing and land rights as essential to the realisation of all human rights.

FoodFirst International Action Network (FIAN): A global coalition promoting the human right to feed oneself, FIAN works through national chapters and urgent actions against violations of the right to food and land. FIAN has been the principal force, in collaboration with CSOs and NGOs across the world, behind the drafting of a Code of Conduct on the Right to Food, following successful advocacy at the 1997 Rome Food Summit to get the right to food into the formal Declaration. The Code contains particular provisions on the accountability of non-state actors.

Viewed from the perspective of entitlements offered by existing international instruments, it is clear that a system more sensitive to human rights and to environmental concerns would have afforded better protection to the vulnerable individuals and communities who are now bearing the brunt of the global economic crisis, through no fault of their own and with no opportunities to participate in shaping international economic structures and policies. It is also clear that, unless reforms to the international economic system explicitly incorporate respect for human rights and the environment at a structural level, they will not address the fundamental and practical concerns and suffering of the overwhelming majority of the world's people and communities, whose welfare and economic development they must surely be intended to promote.

New forms of social action

Recent years have witnessed some remarkable CSO initiatives, surmounting cultural, thematic, and language barriers, building solidarity, and successfully taking on powerful global institutions in the process.

The coalition in opposition to the MAI

One such is the global coalition which developed to counter the MAI. Over 650 CSOs and NGOs from 70 countries joined to steer a global campaign, using a variety of instruments, media, advocacy, alternative investment policies and treaties, and a range of collectively agreed strategies. The anti-MAI coalition consists of environment, development, human-rights, and church-based CSOs and NGOs, as well as local governments and parliamentarians. While the MAI was being debated at the OECD, the coalition also included national anti-MAI campaigns from more than half the OECD member countries and from a number of developing nations.

The anti-MAI coalition used electronic communication as a primary means of spreading information, building solidarity, and co-ordinating multi-level activities. Its strength was acknowledged in the report ('the Lalumiere Report') prepared for the French government which led to its decision to withdraw from the MAI negotiations.[16] The report refers to the surprise felt by the OECD member governments at the 'scale, strength and the speed with which the opposition appeared and developed' and goes on to say '[t]he MAI thus marks a stage in international negotiations. For the first time, one is seeing the emergence of a "global civil society" represented by NGOs which are often based in several states and communicate beyond their frontiers. This evolution is doubtless irreversible.'

The Lalumière report points to the Internet as a major source of power for the MAI opposition. The coalition's members used the e-mail to its maximum effect from the beginning of their campaign. In order to maintain contact and share strategies, they used e-mail listserves and websites, created and maintained by NGOs, and were able to inform millions of people worldwide about the MAI negotiations. Drafts of the text were circulated via the Internet, enabling large numbers of diverse groups to engage in critiques and analyses, which were then redistributed. The Internet has enabled groups from all over the world to work together, share knowledge and expertise, move towards becoming a global civil society — and gain credibility in the process.

The anti-MAI coalition is still vigilant, as the main provisions pushing financial liberalisation are emerging at regional and international economic forums and treaty-making processes such as the IMF, FTAA, and WTO. Since the principal resources in developing countries are in agriculture, mining, forestry, and fisheries, MAI-like provisions could considerably exacerbate existing pressures on these sectors, and on the often vulnerable people and communities whose livelihoods depend on them.

People's Global Action

Another example of spirited global opposition to economic globalisation is that of the People's Global Action (PGA). Over 300 representatives of people's movements from 70 countries met in February 1998 in Geneva to initiate an international popular movement against various aspects of globalisation. Uniquely, the PGA is primarily composed of social movements and people's organisations such as the National Alliance of People's Movements (India), the National Zapatista Liberation Front (Mexico), the Landless Peasant Movement (Brazil), the Peasant Movement of the Philippines, and the Canadian Postal Union.

This meeting resulted in a people's manifesto against global 'corporate rule' which argues that '[t]he WTO, the IMF, the World Bank, and other institutions that promote globalisation and liberalisation want us to believe in the beneficial effects of global competition. Their agreements and policies constitute direct violations of basic human rights (including civil, political, economic, social, labour and cultural rights) which are codified in international law and many national constitutions, and ingrained in people's understandings of human dignity.'[1]

During the May 1998 second ministerial meeting of the WTO, the PGA launched a series of co-ordinated protest actions across the world, including demonstrations in Geneva. The resulting negative publicity has caused much concern within the WTO. Among the actions planned for 1999 is an InterContinental Caravan, which will attempt to bring 500 Indian peasant farmers to Europe to protest before national parliaments, and the WTO, multinational companies, and banks that are pushing for global free-market policies.

International NGO Committee on Human Rights in Trade and Investment

Also worthy of mention is an alliance of development and human-rights NGOs which in May 1998 formed the International NGO Committee on Human Rights in Trade and Investment,[18] with the express goal of ensuring that human rights are no longer ignored in international economic policy and practice. In a policy statement quoted above, this Committee outlines four fundamental principles of human rights as being under threat from the way in which economic globalisation is proceeding and calls for these to be accepted as the 'organising principles for all bi-lateral and multi-lateral trade, investment and financial agreements, laws and policies'.

The statement also stresses the need for 'alternative international investment and trade agreements and processes that would genuinely seek to ensure that international investment and trade regimes are fully consistent with international obligations arising from standards relating to human rights, environmental protection and sustainable development', and goes on to observe that 'Such alternative measures, promoting the establishment of an integrated international agenda, would serve to strengthen democratic control of capital flows and to stimulate investments and commerce that would benefit disadvantaged groups especially women, children and vulnerable communities.'

The NGO Committee was also instrumental in convincing the UN Sub-Commission on Prevention of Discrimination and Protection of Minorities to adopt the resolution on trade, investment and financial policy alluded to earlier. In a press release on 21 October 1998, the NGO Committee stated:

> We are convinced that if international economic policy initiatives (including the WTO agreements and rulings, the policy prescriptions and structural adjustment provisions of the IMF and the World Bank, and the MAI under negotiation at the OECD) were genuinely tested against existing international legal human rights and environmental obligations, the international economic policy environment would be dramatically different, as would the institutional architecture of the system.

The principal message of such groups is that a reformed international economic architecture must necessarily be built upon the foundation of explicit recognition of obligations stemming from the key human-rights principles relating to self-determination, participation, non-discrimination, an adequate standard of living, food, housing, work, and education; and the specific rights of women, indigenous people, and children.

Space does not permit a summary of other initiatives against economic globalisation.[19] Over the past two years, however, it is clear that at national, regional, and international levels numerous initiatives have been taken which point towards a nascent movement of counter-globalisation led by CSOs and NGOs.

Challenges ahead

Although human rights offer a principle on which to base opposition to the challenges posed by economic globalisation, significant obstacles remain. At the same time, some existing CSO and NGO strategies point to recommendations for enhancing the struggle. These agencies must also overcome three inter-related obstacles of a somewhat different order. One is the need to define the nature of the state, faced as we are with opposing views, some calling for its withdrawal and others for it to play a more 'regulatory' role. Another is the need to revitalise the United Nations to play the role that was envisaged in its Charter and developed during the 1980s but then abandoned under the pressure of the forces of economic globalisation. A further crucial obstacle is the unwillingness of actors at all levels, including CSOs and NGOs, to understand and address the impact of economic globalisation on women.

Recasting the role of the state

With the onset of economic globalisation, much concern has been expressed by CSOs and NGOs about the withering away of the state. However, advocates of globalisation, pushing for the increasing privatisation and commodification of all spheres of life, have referred to the economic unviability of the welfare state and the need for states to 'harmonise' their economic priorities with their 'dependency-creating' social responsibilities. Such visions have contributed significantly to states' desperate search for better 'economic indicators' that are divorced from better 'social indicators'. The advocates of a strong state fear the bargaining away of state sovereignty under multilateral trade, investment, finance, and intellectual-property agreements, and under the regimes of structural adjustment and debt repayment.

It is essentially argued by the proponents of economic globalisation that the state can no longer (in fact needs no longer) play a proactive role in terms of guaranteeing the economic, social, and cultural rights of its citizens. The private sector (national and international) along with a vibrant NGO sector (primarily development and humanitarian agencies) can well handle these tasks. By the same logic, and when the state is itself found to violate these rights, the dissenting roles of the human-rights and environmental movements should be reinforced, to press the state to adopt an unequivocal pro-people stance and oppose its repressive tendencies. (Of course, it is not only the state that violates rights. There are cases of politicians and right-wing ideologues (often belonging to CSOs) using economic globalisation as a scapegoat for all ills, or whipping up anti-imperialist sentiments and appealing to religious identities to create a base for nationalistic policies on the economy, immigration, and other matters.)

It is critical to keep in mind that the struggle is not limited to blunting or reforming the forces of economic globalisation but also pertains to the recognition of existing violations of economic, social, and cultural rights and the need to improve the conditions in which a significant part of humanity lives.[20] The fundamental priority is to halt the worsening conditions that are directly linked to the growing disparity of wealth, whether due to the forces of economic globalisation or to socially unjust policies at national levels. This is all the more critical as it is now abundantly clear that the poor do *not* gain from periods of economic boom and stock-market euphoria. They had no part in planning the policies that led to economic globalisation and yet, when economic crisis strikes, they suffer disproportionately. The responses of the global institutions, such as the IMF's bailout loans, are designed to assist loss-making banks, not to help those who are caught in a downward spiral towards joblessness, homelessness, and destitution.

In the past year, however, the very voices which have ardently advocated a 'reduced' role for the state are now, in a dramatic overturn, calling urgently for it to recast its critical 'regulatory' role. These voices now want the state to be the arbiter, the protecting guardian for the social sectors against the ravages that are being wrought by an increasingly unbridled global economic system. They include well-known economists like Jagdish Bhagwati and Joseph Stiglitz, prominent businesspeople such as George Soros, and influential media organs including *The Financial Times* and *The Economist*. What is needed, then, is to strengthen the state to stand up to the forces of globalisation by reasserting its transformative role: not only to regulate but also to guarantee conditions for the sustenance and development of conditions that allow for the realisation of human rights for all its residents.

What should the role of the state be? And how should CSOs respond to state violations of human rights? Once again, existing human-rights instruments offer the most precise and sensitive framework, obliging the state 'first and foremost' to promote the human rights of the vulnerable sections of society and not to take any retrogressive steps (through policies, programmes, and laws) that would further dispossess these groups or marginalise other sectors. States have legal obligations to respect, promote, and protect human rights, including the right to political participation and the right to an adequate standard of living. If they were to follow these (voluntarily accepted) obligations, then much of what passes as the global economic regime would be in violation of the human rights of the all residents of these states. As pointed out by Yash Ghai:

> [t]he regime of rights provides the nearest thing to a coherent challenge to economic globalisation. It emphasises the importance of human dignity, the right to work in just conditions and in return for fair wages, the right to welfare, the care of the children, the equality of women, the respect for cultural and economic rights of indigenous peoples, the protection of the environment, the exercise of popular sovereignty through democratic constitutional orders, and the accountability of holders of power. It seeks to conserve natural resources for future generations while at the same time aiming to distribute the fruits of their contemporary exploitation on a more equitable principle, returning in some cases to the concept of communal ownership on a global basis, redefining the concept of property, the commons of the world. It promotes cosmopolitanism and respect for diversity. It has produced a greater consciousness of rights and provides an important foundation for networking (of individuals and NGOs) around rights and against the dehumanising effects of globalisation. Contemporary globalisation is self-evidently inconsistent with these objectives. [21]

While the state's transformative role is being reasserted by CSOs and within parts of the UN system, it is also important to find ways and means to sustain and increase the spaces for human-rights and development groups to collaborate with its more progressive elements. This is perhaps the most promising means by which to strengthen the state, both to stand up to the deleterious forces of globalisation, and to take advantage of the positive social benefits that can accrue from interacting with global institutions, legitimised by reference to international treaties, norms, and standards.

The need for a revitalised UN

If the international economic institutions are to be more accountable, then the UN has to play a central role and devise ways to create democratic structures (including participation of CSOs and NGOs) which will lead to the development of new multilateral treaties on trade, investment, and finance. This role is crucial, because all these issues have an impact on the social sphere.

The perspective and specific duties required to perform this role are already contained in numerous international human-rights instruments which, in the rush to push the 'market' solution, have been cast aside. Valuable provisions and guidance are offered, for instance, in addition to the international Covenants and Conventions, in the Declaration of Social Progress and Development, the Declaration and Programme of Action of a New International Economic Order, and the Charter of Economic Rights and Duties of States.

Various efforts were made in the 1980s to promote social justice in the process of economic liberalisation and the growth of transnational corporations (TNCs), by organisations and initiatives such as the UN Centre on Transnational Corporations (UNCTC), the UN Fund for Economic Development (SUNFED), the New International Information Order (NIIO), and the New International Economic Order (NIEO). However, these valuable efforts were systematically undermined by the proponents of wholesale liberalisation.

Subsequently, the UN has taken the lead in cautioning against unguided liberalisation and in highlighting the need to define the obligations of states, and equip them to meet their commitments. For instance, the 1993 Vienna Declaration and Programme of Action (PoA) confirmed that the protection and promotion of human rights and fundamental freedoms is the first responsibility of governments, and that the human person is the central subject of development. Similarly, the 1995 Copenhagen Declaration and PoA recommended that states should intervene in markets to prevent or counteract market failure, promote stability and long-term investment, ensure fair competition and ethical conduct, and harmonise economic and social development.

The development of a principled leadership within the UN is vital to counter three obstacles to implementing human rights, halting the negative affects of economic globalisation, and offering a framework for the reform of economic institutions so that these work together towards social-justice and economic goals:

1 Currently, the effectiveness of the enforcement mechanisms of institutions such as WTO and NAFTA is in stark contrast to the lack of attention given to developing similar mechanisms for the international human-rights instruments.

2 A major obstacle to the development of human rights, particularly economic, social, and cultural rights is, unsurprisingly, the USA. For example, in the 1998 UN General Assembly, the USA reneged on its endorsement of the 1993 Vienna Declaration and Programme of Action, and was the sole member-state to vote against a resolution recognising the Right to Development. Ways need to be found to rein in US power, even if that country is becoming more isolationist.

3 There is a need to restrain the UN Secretary-General's enthusiastic embrace of the global business community, represented by groups such as the International Chamber of Commerce (ICC), which is composed of many of the most powerful TNCs and is hardly the partner that the UN needs if it is seeking to 'promote and encourage respect for human rights and fundamental freedoms ...', as its Charter obliges it to do.

In tackling these obstacles, the UN can regain its leadership role through a serious commitment to the various Declarations, Covenants and Conventions to which its member-states have agreed, and by underpinning this with an approach based on respect for human rights: something that would be very much in keeping with the policy of 'mainstreaming human rights' being pursued by Kofi Annan.

Women and economic globalisation

Perhaps the most neglected aspect of the social dimensions of trade, investment, and financial policies and programmes is their impact on women.

The principal and lasting impact of a liberalised economy results in ever fewer controls protecting job security (for men as well as women), routine reductions in social expenditures, uncontrolled food prices due to the emphasis on agricultural export and the lack of protection for local food production and food-security regimes, the absence of safety-nets to prevent women having to take up casual labour and carry out multiple jobs, and the failure to protect women's access to land and credit. All these trends have an adverse impact on women. For example, a recent study of women workers in the electronics industry in India reveals their gradual displacement from secure jobs:

There is a two-step process of restructuring. The first step is casualisation of the workforce. The next step is redundancy of the existing workforce and relocation of units to lower wage areas with a temporary workforce. In fact, apart from transfer of jobs from permanent to temporary categories, companies also resorted to direct reduction of workers.[22]

Lacking opportunities for education and training, women are less well equipped than men to deal with the challenges and complexities of international trade. Their traditional reproductive and child-rearing responsibilities reduce the time they can devote to earning a living. The result is a reduction in household spending on education and health care. The stress on 'cash crops' for an export economy confines their access to land to marginal areas, which in turn curtails women's capacity to carry out subsistence agriculture and crop production for local markets. Combined with the fact that credit and extension services favour men, all these factors present obstacles to the productive role that women can play.

A study from Ghana presented at the parallel NGO Forum to the 1998 WTO Ministerial Conference concluded:

> Given women's disadvantaged situation and family responsibilities, trade and WTO rules do not provide women with as much income generating opportunities as men; or worse, they undermine women's trading activities and food production. Less income for women means less expenditure on education and health care, less purchasing power and productivity, and more reproductive work in the households. This moves the country away from raising standards of living and improving its production capacity. [23]

Economic globalisation has certainly brought about opportunities in the form of greater labour mobility. This has allowed some women to choose between agricultural labour and paid employment, and some studies suggest that women may sometimes prefer independent wage employment to the oppressive social structures and isolation in which they live, and the arduous, often erratic agricultural labour on which they depend. Of course, the objective working conditions are exploitative, as the jobs are generally insecure, badly paid, and part-time, denying employees their trade-union rights, and exposing women to sexual harassment and other threats. Given the global economic scenario, without changes that are sensitive to women's needs, the long-term prospects are bleak, because capital always seeks to reduce labour costs and to avoid stringent environmental and human-rights standards. This approach is all too evident, for example, in the proliferating export-processing zones (EPZs) which characterise economic globalisation worldwide, and whose principal workforce is young women.

A major reason for the failure of the global financial architecture in achieving even a modicum of social progress for vulnerable social sectors has been its failure to take into account or even acknowledge the role that women play in everyday development activities. It is critical, therefore, that all attempts to blunt the impact of economic globalisation and to offer alternative economic or legal frameworks recognise and develop benchmarks to assess to what extent women's role is being taken into account in 'designing development'. The few groups that have taken on the task of disaggregating the impact of economic globalisation and its associated processes have offered a number of recommendations that are useful starting points for further advocacy work to ensure gender-sensitive policy-making within the global trade, investment, and finance bodies (see below).

Opportunities for growth

Only recently has it become clear that economic globalisation offers opportunities as well as posing problems. International campaigns for limits to economic globalisation, such as the anti-MAI and Jubilee 2000 debt campaigns, have opened up the possibility for creating alliances across national boundaries, based on common values and objectives and a common perception of the power of solidarity to halt or at least gain time through delaying potentially harmful international economic initiatives stemming from the economic institutions that drive globalisation.

One clear advantage of such collectivities is that they are informally linked and non-hierarchical, and are organised around multiple focal points, each with its own programme, structured around national campaigns, yet all coalescing into a formidable whole. We might even say that economic globalisation provides a platform from which to launch a hundred transnational movements. It should now be possible, through the spaces opened up for international action and the confidence gained by knowing of and working with hundreds of like-minded people and communities across the world, for these transnational movements to tackle local problems that may not even have originated in, and are not perpetuated by, global processes.

The transnational solidarity created by the collective opposition to economic globalisation is bringing multiple benefits. Formerly diffused initiatives have joined together to promote common causes, and local struggles have gained the confidence that comes from the knowledge of support from other CSO and NGO sources. We should now look to develop strategies to counter local violations of economic, social, and cultural rights, and processes of exclusion and dispossession. The horizontal and vertical solidarity that has been built from these transnational initiatives needs now to be harnessed to promote local change.

The opportunity is then enhanced for CSOs to push at local, national, and international levels, sometimes simultaneously, for states to be accountable and representative — to fulfil the promise of the post-colonial phase. The devolution of power that was to come from above must now be demanded from below, in collaboration with global forces such as transnational collectivities of CSOs, as well as within institutions such as the UN, where opportunities exist or can be created for the support of local struggles for human rights and social justice.

This creation of new political spaces, carved out by cross-border, transnational initiatives, nevertheless raises a number of questions which need deep reflection and action. What is needed to sustain these collective transnational actions, campaigns, and movements (processes)? What are the limits of such initiatives? The human-rights regime provides a sufficient approach and a set of organising and intertwined principles, as this paper has argued, to gain and sustain social justice, equality, and democracy. What steps are necessary to move towards a wider adoption of this approach and to enhance its effectiveness? Can these forces continue to show positive results in the face of the simultaneous phenomena of fragmentation (often at the local levels) and integration inherent in globalising processes?[24] Can these collectivities, which work from a basis of a multi-centric world, constructively rival the traditional state-centric global system? What are the preconditions for these processes to reinforce local solidarities to counter local violations of economic, social, and cultural rights stemming from exclusion, discrimination, and dispossession?

A cursory overview of the national and international actions taken to date by CSOs in confronting globalisation, and a review of the opportunities and challenges in terms of existing and potential multilateral instruments within the economic globalisation mould reveal actions and directions that must be pursued by CSOs if they are to remain relevant and true to the task of both countering and offering alternatives to the forces of economic globalisation. These need to focus on hitherto neglected issues such as the impact of economic globalisation on women as well as on children, indigenous peoples, and poor peasant communities. Other valuable starting points are examples from India, Canada, and Mexico, where CSOs have developed useful local strategies and transnational alliances to expose and counter the negative tendencies of globalisation. One useful lesson from work done thus far is that it is important to keep breaking down the North–South barriers. Essentially, CSOs, particularly those working at the local level, must break loose from the isolationism that can mar local efforts and join national and transnational efforts to hold economic globalisation accountable to people's processes. This is critical to the formation of a global civil society.

Deepening knowledge

CSOs and NGOs need to know about and deal with the processes and institutions that are driving economic globalisation — for example, the forces of financial liberalisation — and to seek relevant information and collaborate with CSOs that are dealing with hitherto low-profile institutions such as the Bank of International Settlements (BIS) and the International Organisation of Securities Commission (IOSCO).[25]

North–South barriers need to be broken down. The consequences of economic globalisation show clearly that everyone is in the same boat and that transnational alliances are of benefit to all CSOs. If anything, there is a need for far greater knowledge in the Third World countries of the scale of poverty, material and cultural, existing and growing in the First and Second Worlds.

Research and analysis

Given the paucity of case studies which examine the impact of economic globalisation on human rights and on the environment, there is an urgent need to develop appropriate methodology and research plans; search for available data, case studies and legal materials; analyse and compile data into succinct case studies on the specific, verifiable effects of trade and investment treaties; and prepare and disseminate materials in plain language as well as technical publications. Such work must include a gender-sensitive assessment of the impact of trade policy on women workers, farmers, entrepreneurs, and traders. There is a need for disaggregated data from reviews of trade policy and rules, without which it is difficult fully to assess the different impacts of economic globalisation on women and men.

It is also important to collaborate, for instance in joint research activities, with 'progressive' UN institutions that are seeking to counter economic globalisation — UNCTAD, UNRISD, OHCHR, ILO — to suggest how the UN could play a more active role on economic issues, including through the formation of democratic and representative bodies to examine issues and draft instruments likely to have an impact on millions of impoverished people across the world.

Joining alliances in solidarity work

Joining the active global coalitions such as the anti-MAI coalition or the International NGO Committee on Trade and Investment will bolster their strength and contribute to the growth of a movement towards the creation of a global civil society. We need platforms where 'horizontal' exchange can take place. For example, it is far easier to get information on what struggles are being waged against the WTO in industrialised countries than to get this information from countries in the South. This also illustrates the need within the South for more information-exchange, strategy-sharing, and solidarity-building.

Developing alternatives

It is important to learn about, publicise, and develop campaigns premised on valuable ideas such as the Tobin Tax[26] and the alternative agreement on investment proposed by some of the groups that are part of the global anti-MAI campaign. We need to learn from, test, and develop further alternatives.

Some groups are also proposing alternative means of judging the human-rights and environmental impact of economic globalisation forces such as TNCs. Joining these groups and participating in efforts such as People's Tribunals (such as the Permanent People's Tribunal, the PPT) and the tribunal on TNCs and human rights currently being planned is a way to increase the accountability of the proponents of globalisation.

In some countries, such as India, groups like Social Watch are proposing alternative economic surveys and alternative indicators and benchmarks to assess the state of the world's people. Social activists need to learn from, contribute to, and attempt similar exercises, particularly at national levels.

Advocacy, intelligence, and gaining new allies

Advocacy work aimed at global economic institutions is critical to make these institutions (~~such as WTO,~~ NAFTA, and IMF) democratic and sensitive to human rights, development, and environmental concerns. Use should be made of the working paper being prepared by the UN Sub-Commission for the Prevention of Discrimination and the Protection of Minorities 'on ways and means by which the primacy of human rights norms and standards could be better reflected in, and could better inform, international and regional trade, investment and financial policies, agreements and practices, and how the United Nations human rights bodies and mechanisms could play a central role in this regard'.

It is also important to call for the development of in-house capacity in gender analysis and to stress the need to mainstream gender analysis in all sectors within the purview of the IMF, WTO, and NAFTA. In the case of the latter two, it is equally vital to call for women's participation in all negotiations and dispute-resolution mechanisms, and more generally to assist in tracking MAI-like provisions in emerging multilateral and regional economic instruments.

All advocacy work needs to push organisations such as the WTO to adopt human-rights and environmental instruments as the basis of their work, for example in drafting new instruments and in dispute-settlement processes, and to respect the obligations placed upon states by these regimes.

It is also necessary to make alliances with the new converts, such as the economists and media cited earlier, which until recently were in favour of reducing the role of the state and are now calling for it to play a regulatory role.

Calling the state to account

In addition to the points made on this earlier, there is a need to push states to act in accordance with the human-rights and environmental instruments that they have ratified and also to respect the provisions agreed to in the Declarations and PoAs signed at the UN conferences in Rio, Vienna, Beijing, Cairo, Copenhagen, Istanbul, and Rome. At Beijing, for example, governments recognised that they should take account of women's contributions and concerns in economic structures. They also committed themselves to adopting a gender perspective in all policies and programmes by making an analysis of the effects on women and men respectively 'before decisions are taken'. Obviously states have failed to do this. Specifically, governments should be called on to explain the adoption of any new obligations, such as many instruments that drive economic globalisation, if they conflict with their existing ones.

At the national level, governments and multilateral institutions should be called on to ensure that technical assistance is gender-sensitive and that it promotes the upgrading of technology and skills, including opportunities to acquire new skills, for women as well as for men. Governments must also ensure the adequate flow of information and technological transfer between the North and the South, and between men and women, and must ensure that women have access to land and credit.[27] To this can be added the need for women to have access and inheritance rights to housing and land.

Conclusion

Despite all the counter-evidence, countries across the world continue to be lured by the false promises of free-market ideology, privatisation, and the withdrawal of the state from basic responsibilities to its citizens. The lure seems so great and the pressures so intense that states are willing to pursue the free-market agenda no matter what the social cost. Tragically, the harsh lessons from the lost decades of structural adjustment and debt seem not to have registered in the minds of the decision-makers.

The developing global economy urgently needs to be informed and guided by the principles and the imperatives inherent in the international human-rights regime. Such a task is critical to the revival of the leadership exercised by the UN in the 1980s and for the consolidation of peace and justice worldwide. Conditions need to be created for the harmonisation of international trade, investment, and financial regimes with existing human-rights obligations. This would ultimately lead to the establishment of an integrated international agenda which would cover not merely agreements, policies, and practices in international trade and investment, but also (more importantly) international obligations and standards relating to human rights, environmental protection, and sustainable development. Focusing merely on the former will only undermine the far more basic obligations underscored by the latter.

In order for this to happen, it is again the task of CSOs to hold international and regional economic actors accountable for respecting human rights as the primary basis for global economic policies and programmes. In the process, it is essential for CSOs to use the UN, to press for international democratic forums, and to push the UN to work primarily for the world's downtrodden peoples. By establishing such an overarching framework, national governments can also be pushed in the same direction. Engagement in social action for achieving just and humane development involves such an all-encompassing approach, particularly keeping in mind the well-being of the deprived and the oppressed.

The challenge is for all of us to keep moving forwards and to keep taking advantage of the tremendous solidarity that now exists among groups representing or consisting of marginalised and oppressed people and communities across the world. The struggle in which these groups are engaged is for the sovereignty (self-determination) of people and communities, beyond national borders, against the forces of economic globalisation, using as their principal basis international instruments concerning human rights, the environment, and development. If economic globalisation signifies a breaking down of national borders and controls, then the answer that is being given by civil society is also transnational and inspired by fundamental human values based on the belief in solidarity and comradeship that is missing in the technology-driven, hierarchy-based system of economic globalisation. The struggle is between those working for dignity and justice for all and those bent on creating a world driven by mechanistic and profit-driven motives that benefit a small minority only. Nothing more or less.

The overriding challenge is to find ways of getting people to mobilise politically so that the ownership of the existing instruments and of the process of refining and developing them is democratised, and the states and the international economic agents and forums are held accountable for our human rights and our fundamental freedoms.

Notes

1 In this paper, the term 'CSOs' includes community-based organisations, social movements, issue-based campaigns, and NGOs. For clarity, the term 'NGO' is sometimes used to connote an intermediary support organisation.

2 For a discussion on the post-colonial hijacking of the development agenda in Africa, see Firoze Manji: 'The depoliticisation of poverty' in Deborah Eade (ed.) (1998) *Development and Rights*, Oxford: Oxfam.

3 The term 'economic globalisation', as used in this paper, encompasses institutional processes that deal with trade, investment, finance, intellectual property, structural adjustment, and debt, within an ideology of economic liberalisation.

4 UNCTAD: *Trade and Development Report 1997*, Geneva: UNCTAD, 1997.

5 UNDP: *Human Development Report 1997*, New York: Oxford University Press, 1997.

6 63.8 million people (one in four US residents) live below the poverty line, and there are 2 million homeless people, of whom 500,000 are children. From 1979 to 1994, real family income for the top tenth of the US population increased by 83 per cent, while the bottom tenth lost 14 per cent, and the next tenth lost 5 per cent. Figures taken from the Congressional Hearing on Hunger and Homelessness in the US, 23 September 1998.

7 See for example Dr Joseph Stiglitz, Ninth Prebisch Lecture, 19 November 1998, UNCTAD, Geneva. Stiglitz stated that the Washington Consensus had failed to foster development because it 'all too often confused means with ends — taking means such as privatisation, "getting the price right" and trade liberalisation as ends in themselves'. His alternative development paradigm is, however, disappointing, because it falls short of recognising the valuable process already in place in the form of numerous CSO and NGO initiatives and through the international instruments on human rights, environment, and development.

8 In 1980, foreign-exchange trading alone was US$80 billion on average per day, and the ratio of such trading to world trade was about 10:1. In 1995, daily trading averaged US$1260 billion, and the ratio to world trade was nearly 70:1. This is equal to the entire world's official gold and foreign-exchange reserves.

9 See in particular the International Covenant on Civil and Political Rights (CCPR), the International Covenant on Economic, Social, and Cultural Rights (CESCR), the Convention on the Elimination of All Forms of Discrimination against Women (CEDAW), and the Convention on the Rights of the Child (CRC), texts available in *Human Rights — A Compilation of Instruments* (1994) Vol.1 (First and Second Parts), New York and Geneva: UN. The texts are also available at: <www.unhchr.org>

10 See in particular the Declaration on the Right to Development, the Declaration on Social Progress and Development, and the Charter of Economic Rights and Duties of States. CEDAW is also a powerful instrument promoting the collective human rights of women. Also see regional instruments such as the African Charter on Human and People's Rights, and NGO instruments such as the Universal Declaration of the Rights of People (Algiers).

11 Numerous UN mechanisms exist, from Special Rapporteurs to treaty bodies to technical assistance intended to guide and facilitate the implementation of the human-rights instruments.

12 See Policy Statement of the International NGO Committee on Human Rights in Trade and Investment, *Investment, Trade and Finance: the Human Rights Framework: Focusing on the Multilateral Agreement on Investment (MAI)*, September 1998.

13 UN Sub-Commission resolution 1998/12, adopted on 20 August 1998.

14 'Human rights and fundamental freedoms are the birthright of all human beings; their protection and promotion is the first responsibility of Governments' (Paragraph 1 of the Vienna Declaration and Programme of Action. Adopted at the Vienna World Conference on Human Rights, June 1993).

15 HIC is a global alliance of 350 CSOs and NGOs from 70 countries. For a description of its work on housing and land rights, see Miloon Kothari: 'The global struggle for the right to a place to live', *Development in Practice*, 7(1), reprinted in Deborah Eade (ed.): *Development and Rights*, Oxford: Oxfam, 1998. See also Miloon Kothari: 'Homelessness and the right to adequate housing: confronting exclusion, sustaining change' in *The Universal Declaration of Human Rights: Fifty Years and Beyond*, Amityville, NY: Baywood Publishing Company for the United Nations, 1998.

16 Lalumière Report , October 1998, commissioned by the French Government and prepared, after consultation with negotiators of the MAI and civil-society representatives, by MEP Catherine Lalumière, Inspector General for Finance Jean-Pierre Landua, and Advisor at the Court of Auditors Emmanuel Glimet.

17 People's Global Action Manifesto, People's Global Action (PGA) February 1998.

18 The NGO Committee includes Habitat International Coalition, the People's Decade on Human Rights Education, Lutheran World Federation, the Latin American and Caribbean Committee for the Defence of Women's Rights, Youth for Unity of Voluntary Action, the Centre for Equality in Rights and Accommodation, and the Mazingira Institute. See the annotated bibliography in this volume for contact details.

19 See, for example, the work of the Third World Network (Malaysia), Public Citizens Centre (USA), Polaris Institute (Canada), Focus on the Global South (Thailand), Informal Working Group on Gender and Trade (Sweden), National Alliance of People's Movements (India), ATAC (France), and the Jubilee 2000 Debt Campaign (UK), among many others. See Annotated Bibliography for further details.

20 See, for example, *HDR 1997*, which calculates a series of measures, comprising the Human Poverty Index, against which countries are annually ranked. They include the prevalence of illiteracy, life expectancy, degree of malnourishment, and access to health services and safe water. In 1996 over one billion people fell below this index, a figure reflecting a deteriorating position in 30 countries.

21 Yash Ghai: 'Rights, social justice and globalisation', in Joanne Bauer and Daniel Bell (eds.): *The East Asian Challenge to Human Rights*, Cambridge: Cambridge University Press, 1998.

22 Amrita Chachchi 'The new labour market', quoted in Bharat Dogra 'Women are shouldering the burden of liberalisation in India', InterPress Third World News Agency (IPS) 7 December 1998.

23 Informal Working Group on Gender and Trade: 'The Need for a Gender Analysis of the WTO: Ghana Case Study', leaflet distributed during the WTO Ministerial Conference, Geneva 1998.

24 The tension between 'the fragmenting consequences of conflict and the integrative effects of co-operation' has been called *fragmegration*. See James Rosenau, 'States and Sovereignty in a Globalising World', paper presented at the seminar 'International Solidarity and Globalisation: In Search of New Strategies', Columbia Presidency of the Non-Aligned Movement and the Swedish Government, Stockholm 27-28 October 1997.

25 For a useful discussion on this issue and other ideas for action from CSOs, see Kavaljit Singh 'New challenges for People's Movement', *Mainstream*, 12 December 1998.

26 The Tobin tax is named after the economist and Nobel Prize laureate, James Tobin. He proposed a low-rate uniform tax on transboundary short-term speculative investment flows to raise several hundred billion dollars a year for development purposes.

27 See Angela Hale (ed.): *Trade Myths and Gender Reality: Trade Liberalisation and Women's Lives*, Uppsala: Global Publications Foundation and International Coalition for Development Action (ICDA), 1998.

■ **Miloon Kothari** *is the Convener of Habitat International Coalition's Housing and Land Rights Committee and the Joint-Convener of the International NGO Committee on Human Rights in Trade and Investment.*

Inclusive, just, plural, dynamic: building a 'civil' society in the Third World

Smitu Kothari

Introduction: six popular movements

I shall begin by briefly citing six among thousands of recent events which highlight the efforts of civil society in the Third World[1] to reaffirm its democratic and political potential and which underscore the endemic problems in the dominant economic and political processes — problems which are severely constraining and, in many cases, destroying, the very basis of survival on the planet. These events give us a profound insight into the struggle to build a 'civil' society in the Third World.

Pakistan: the Alternative Development Network

Some three years ago, 40 representatives of Pakistani NGOs gathered in Islamabad to discuss how their various activities could be restructured and better coordinated, in order to move from being conventional development or social-action groups to becoming a social and political movement that could redefine and democratise the relationship between the state and civil society. They represented a cross-section of a new national alliance — the Alternative Development Network — an initiative with the powerful potential to recover politics from politicians and political brokers and establish a more egalitarian and democratic order in Pakistan. Part of the agenda of this gathering was to discuss ways to strengthen the Pakistan–India People-to-People Initiative which had evolved a year before in a climate of mistrust and hostility between the political élites (including religious hard-liners) of the two countries. This climate had adversely affected both the realisation of a more democratic and peaceful interrelationship between the peoples on both sides of the border and the restoration of democratic and tolerant societies within each country.

Since the Islamabad gathering, participants worked to establish the critiques and strategies that they had discussed in several further meetings. The Pakistan–India People-to-People Initiative for Peace and Democracy has since been institutionalised and has subsequently gathered in Delhi, Lahore, and Calcutta and in smaller meetings. The next event was held in November 1998 at Peshawar. Its significance was marked by the courage and perseverance of citizens' groups in Pakistan in inviting 200 Indians from vastly diverse backgrounds, at a time of growing cynicism and mistrust among the political élites in both countries. That the implications of the recently exploded nuclear devices were among the central elements of the agenda underlined the importance of this initiative.

Nepal: The People's Plan for the Twenty-first Century

The second example is the convergence in the Nepalese capital of Kathmandu of over 500 representatives of women's organisations, trade unions, fishing communities, indigenous and tribal peoples, farmers, child workers, human-rights organisations, and support groups working among and with them. The occasion was the third General Assembly of the People's Plan for the Twenty-first Century (PP21), an 'alliance of hope', an Asia-wide loose association of citizens' groups. The participants shared the lessons learned from their long struggles to establish more accountable governance, as well as their own autonomous initiatives towards building a 'society which is gender just, culturally plural, socially equitable, politically participatory, peaceful, democratic and ecologically sane ... based on life-centred values — compassion, caring, nurturing and sharing'. The resulting Sagarmatha Declaration[2] outlines both a powerful critique of the dominant economic and political system and the vision towards which the members will be collectively working as they move into the next millennium (PP21 1996).

Mexico: the Zapatista rebellion

The third example arises from the years that have passed since the extraordinary revolt of peasants — 'Zapatistas' — in the Chiapas region of Mexico, a revolt that took virtually everyone by surprise. Subsequent developments in 1995–96 point to the evolution of a radical new politics that is being simultaneously articulated by the local peasants, and by numerous other Mexican movements and groups, as well as their supporters around the world. In their call to all Mexicans to participate in a broad movement for 'jobs, land, housing, food, health, education, independence, freedom, democracy, justice, and peace', the Zapatistas gave primacy to resisting anti-democratic trends and developments (like the abrogation of agrarian reform or their forcible 'integration' — via the North American Free Trade Area (NAFTA) — into the world economy on terms over which they had no control; or against the ruling trends in the Mexican economy which had resulted in the rapid extraction of the oil, timber, minerals, and labour of Chiapas, with the benefits and profits predominantly accruing to large landowners, ranchers, merchants, and politicians; or the continuing human-rights-violations, including massacres, by representatives of large landowners, often supported by the Mexican army). They also helped to place popular and democratic movements at the centre of Mexico's political process. In essence, the movement and its widespread support highlighted the central importance of democracy, justice, and dignity. A government that initially responded with military force eventually backed down and engaged in a series of crucial public dialogues, thus accepting a majority of the Zapatistas' demands. Though there is still far to go before the radical agenda is implemented (the negotiations keep being stalled by official intransigence or violence), the revolt and its aftermath have had an exceptional impact in Mexico and beyond. In doing so, it has strengthened civil society in Mexico (Collier 1994).

India: the National Front for Tribal Self-rule

The fourth event involved people belonging to tribal groups and movements from all over India representing the recently formed National Front for Tribal Self-rule, who converged in Delhi to seek the implementation of an official commission's report on tribal self-governance. They were also asserting their primary rights over productive natural resources and an end to the state's treating them as trespassers in their own lands and forests. For, since 1865, the forests of the Indian sub-continent had been placed under state control 'for reasons of empire' — a policy process that was adopted with minimal changes by post-independence governments.

Three years earlier, responding to widespread protests by tribals against continued violations of their customary and resource rights by state and non-state actors, the Indian parliament had set up a committee headed by a tribal. His report argued that tribal society had been marked by its own representative systems of governance through the *Gram Sabha* (village council), which should be legally recognised as the primary centre of tribal governance. He also argued that the long-standing demand for tribal control over productive land and forests should be conceded, and that administrative interference in tribal affairs should be minimised. The government largely ignored his report—hence the mass gathering.

The tribals' assertions were powerfully summed up in the slogan, 'Our Rule in Our Villages'. This declaration did not imply secession from India but, rather, the assertion of relative autonomy from what was experienced as an intrusive and exploitative state apparatus and the unjust social and economic order that it legitimised at the expense of their livelihoods, identities, and systems of self-governance (Kothari 1994). The demonstration partially achieved its goal after a week in Delhi: the central government acceded to the demand to recognise the primacy of the *Gram Sabha* and in December 1996 cleared the way for an historic amendment to the Constitution, recognising the tribal right to self-rule. Significant activities are now underway to give substance to the promise of greater political autonomy in tribal areas. The movement has also influenced the views of civil society as a whole about the need to rethink democratic institutions, so that they nurture greater control by local communities over their resources and over external decisions that affect their lives and livelihoods.

Similar mobilisations have been witnessed in indigenous and tribal regions world-wide, and several major global alliances have been formed. These, coupled with the efforts of many groups to articulate their concerns before a special sub-commission and the human-rights committee of the UN, can also be seen as part of an effort to build a global civil society that is firmly rooted in local democratic processes.

India: People's Global Action

The fifth example is of farmers in the Indian state of Karnataka, who laid siege to the first Indian franchise of Kentucky Fried Chicken (KFC) in Bangalore. KFC, operated by Pepsi Cola Co., was forced temporarily to shut down. The action was symbolic of protest in different parts of the country against handing over control to transnational corporations (TNCs) in critical areas like food supply. It specifically opposed the mass marketing of chicken by a centrally controlled corporation using, it was alleged, chemical additives that were in violation of national standards. These farmers had earlier successfully protested against the US-based Cargill Corporation for aggressively marketing hybrid seeds at the expense of locally controlled and produced food crops. Cargill was forced to withdraw from Karnataka. Recently, farmers' movements across India have been protesting against Monsanto Corporation's plans to introduce its 'terminator' seeds, which would inhibit the new crops' germination, thus compelling the farmer to buy fresh seeds. The Indian government had to assure parliament that it was officially banning Monsanto from importing any such seed. The concerns underlying these protests are central to the building of a civil society, a major issue being that of who should have rights over resources that are critical to the lives and livelihoods of a majority of people on the planet. Should these rights rest with private corporations and an international institutional system that privileges private accumulation and profit, or should they be under the primary protection and care of communities whose economic and cultural systems are so integrally linked to access to those resources? How justified is an international patent regime that permits the private patenting of the blood-line of indigenous peoples and of seeds and medicinal plants that are an integral part of their knowledge and culture? (Brush and Stabinsky 1996). The mobilisation in Karnataka goes to the heart of these questions of justice and democracy.

Similar mobilisations against the loss of control over productive natural resources and the victimisation caused by economically unjust processes have taken place across the less industrialised world. Hundreds of groups, coalitions, and alliances have linked together not only to hold multilateral banks and TNCs accountable, but also to evolve alternatives to centralised economic decision-making and the spread of monoculture, where the needs of the market predominate over concerns for democratic control of productive resources and the respect for crop and biological diversity. One such forum is the People's Global Action, which draws together hundreds of grassroots movements and groups working for a more democratic, just, and transparent international and global system.

For the past decade, groups from all over the 'South' have linked with support groups in the G-7 countries and held parallel meetings during the annual Aid Consortium and World Bank–International Monetary Fund (IMF) meetings. More importantly, they have outlined an alternative structural adjustment which leads to the wider realisation of social justice and ecological sanity. In mid-1998, a People's Summit was organised during the G-7 meeting to celebrate the numerous ways in which local communities are recovering control over their economies and their lives.

The farmers of Karnataka are one part of this global effort not only to hold corporations and states more accountable, but also to question who should control intellectual property with respect to genetic resources, and to highlight the need to rethink the very basis of centralised corporate control over the seeds of life.

Beijing: the fourth World Conference on Women

The final example is of the popular mobilisation before the Beijing women's conference in 1995. On an unprecedented scale, the preparatory process moved beyond urban-based activists and scholars to involve tens of thousands of women who had hitherto rarely moved out of their communities and villages. The voices and concerns of these women 'from the margins' influenced both independent national agendas and the popular agenda in Beijing. In numerous countries, women vocally contested the official government presentation. In almost all cases, they achieved an impact on the content and thrust of their respective governments' submissions, and also contributed to the development of alternatives to the dominant economic, religious, cultural, and political institutions and processes, widening the critique of their repercussions on the families, communities, areas, countries and regions in which they lived. They gave voice to a growing realisation that all over the world — from the spaces of inter-personal relationships to the global economy — the democratic process was itself under threat (*Lokayan Bulletin* 1998).

A diverse and innovative struggle for a democratic polity and a humane society

The six events or movements highlighted above represent something of the vast outpouring of democratic activity in the civil society of the Third World.[3] It encompasses a staggering diversity of innovative endeavour which ranges from democratic control over local governments and productive resources to building transnational alliances; from hitherto subjugated communities and minorities asserting their democratic rights to the struggles of women to recover their dignity and rights over productive resources; from efforts to nurture folk and indigenous traditions of song and theatre to alternative networks of decentralised communication; from local actions seeking prohibition of the production, sale and consumption of alcohol to collective efforts to ban joint-venture licences to domestic and TNC enterprises; from building democratic producer cooperatives to collective actions against the privatisation of profitable public corporations; from campaigns against the use of amniocentesis tests to identify and abort female foetuses to regional campaigns against permitting Western drug corporations to patent and penetrate a low-cost and indigenous medicine system; from campaigns against irresponsible and destructive tourism to struggles against 'destructive' development projects; from prolonged local agitation against corrupt officials to massive national support to weed out corruption in public life; from initiatives to restore control over local forests to massive collective effort to draft 'people's' policies; from people's tribunals to 'try' those guilty of violating human rights and the environment to efforts to form joint management systems to conserve and nurture fragile ecosystems; from efforts to educate farmers and workers about the impact of the World Trade Organisation (WTO) or NAFTA to mass public demonstrations against the policies and conditionalities of the international financial institutions (IFIs).

These diverse activities indicate the potential of civil society coming into its own but, more importantly, they teach us lessons about the limits of representative democracy, the adverse implications of the current patterns of development, and the responsibility of citizens in contemporary society — lessons that are fundamental to the building of a democratic polity and a humane society.[4]

Triumphant capitalism and civil strife as threats to civil society

In the best sense, then, a 'successful' and dynamic civil society would build democratic relational networks to nurture or protect diverse religions, belief systems, communities, families, and political and economic pursuits. The greater the success in democratically developing and sustaining this diversity, the more mature a civil society would be. Given today's juncture of triumphalist capitalism, homogenising cultural and consumerist values, highly inegalitarian societies, the steady withdrawal of the state from its democratic and welfarist roles, and the explosion of civil strife and ethnic conflict, such a conception of civil society may seem utopian. While there is undoubtedly some truth in this, it is in understanding and contesting the structures which legitimise inequality, undemocratic practices, and ecological destruction — as well as in celebrating the diverse attempts to sustain ethical, democratic, and ecological spaces — that our defence of civil society should lie. It is to that end that I make the following observations.

There was significant expectation, in the immediate post-war decades and the successful anti-colonial struggles, that modernising, benevolent states in most of the Third World would usher in a more just and democratic society; and that, in the process, they would create conditions which would gradually facilitate a democratic and self-confident civil society — a civic space that would in turn keep the state in check, ensure its role as a non-partisan arbiter, and progressively nurture plural social, cultural, and economic activities.

Almost without exception, this expectation lies in tatters. Society today is arguably more conflict-ridden, more thoroughly penetrated by intrusive and exploitative economic and political interests, and more replete with extremist and reactionary forces than at any point in the past 50 years (if not more). Witness the complex conflicts in Bosnia, Angola or Rwanda, or in large swathes of Latin America, South Asia and Africa. The social movements of reactionary and culturally violent forces are pervasive in many countries. For instance, one of the most successful social movements in post-colonial history in India does not represent women or subjugated communities but the forces of Hindu right-wing reaction—a movement that has mobilised millions of people across caste and class (though primarily among the upper and middle classes) and whose efforts generated the groundswell that led to the destruction of the Babri mosque at Ayodhya in 1991 (Kothari 1994). The movement draws its strength and in return sustains some of its social force in a complex web of local and national level relationships with the state, and with political parties like the ruling Bhartiya Janata Party (BJP) (Indian People's Party) and the Shiv Sena (The Army of Shiva, based primarily in the state of Maharashtra, where it rules with the BJP).

So, while democratic struggles attempt to give content to building a civil society, numerous forces, nationally and internationally, are rapidly thwarting the potential of Third World nations to become relatively self-reliant, intor-dependent polities which nurture the democratic interests of diverse communities living within them. These forces can be characterised as a 'regressive' mobilisation: this ranges from religious extremists mobilising mass support to undermine the peaceful coexistence of different religious and ethnic groups, often fuelling inter- or intra-country conflict, hatred, and 'cleansing', to the use of 'land armies' to protect the interests of large landowners against demands for economic justice and land redistribution; from the whipping up of hate against poorer classes and minorities to numerous forms of violence against women and other vulnerable communities; from armed gangs ruling neighbourhoods and unleashing a wave of terror on local citizens to public announcements that call on supporters to participate in pogroms or to purge areas of particular communities; from forcible eviction of city residents by land sharks to networks that benefit from the trafficking in women and children; from civilian support for military action against democratic and non-violent protest to support for investments and technologies that are clearly undermining the economic and ecological endowments of poor countries. The list is long and represents forces and trends that inhibit the longer-term realisation of a democratic polity.

These forces of democratic closure, if I may call them that, have arisen in contexts that are rooted in complex historical, colonial, and developmental factors. They are also both fed by, and are often a reaction to, the perpetuation of a homogeneous consumer culture and desires kindled by a homogenising popular media. While the initial fascination for the John Wayne–Dynasty–Baywatch type of Western programme is waning in favour of 'indigenous' content, let us not be fooled. Overwhelmingly, what dominate are soap operas, grossly simplified and distorted religious teleplays, escapist song-and-dance, fist-and-gun cinema, and official propaganda—much of it interspersed with advertising which promotes aspirations for the magic of consumer choices. Papanek was right when he wrote, over a quarter of a century ago, that advertising 'makes you buy what you don't want with money that you don't have' (Papanek 1971). Global corporate spending for advertising, packaging, and promotions totals over US$500 billion annually. That so many of us so uncritically accept this climate of psychological persuasion is itself a contributing factor in keeping civil society weak and fragmented.

The myths of 'free choices' and 'free markets'

Many, however, argue that the best judge of good civil society is how 'freely' the market-place functions: the primary indicator of the good life then becomes the range of choices available to the individual consumer. Societies where these choices are limited are then, by definition, 'lesser' societies. It does not particularly matter if a just and plural political order prevails, or even if the country concerned sinks ever deeper into external debt. Maximising production and maximising profits almost become ends in themselves. The market is given greater value than the building of democratic political community and a cooperative economy that privileges both producer and consumer in a relationship of mutual responsibility (Ichiyo and Kothari 1996). It does not particularly matter that neither the market nor international trade is really 'free', or that choices of material objects are not equally accessible and available. It does not particularly matter if market processes pollute and violate the natural regenerative capacities and sustainability of the earth's ecosystems — ecosystems that are themselves the immediate life-source of a majority of the world's population (Durning 1992). It is indeed sad that we have moved to a point where even democracy is equated with consumer choices and not with political freedoms and social justice, and far less with ecological justice (Kothari and Parajuli 1993).

The problem is not one of distribution. Even if some goods and foods were subsidised and made accessible to the poor and the lower-middle classes (as with India's state-run ration shops), the lack of purchasing power for hundreds of millions of people means that they cannot buy those products. Again, what rarely gets questioned is that the production of commodities is itself iniquitous, with benefits accruing unequally and with labour so undervalued. For instance, the daily wage of a hard-working marginal peasant with deep knowledge of the complex cycles of life is thousands of times less than the hourly fee of a city lawyer.

What is hidden in the assumptions of 'free choice' and 'free trade' is that capitalist development itself inhibits the realisation of a vibrant and democratic civil society. For instance, it engenders displacement, dispossession, and marginalisation of millions of people annually. In India alone, over half a million people each year are forcibly displaced by planned development projects. Even if the displacement were justifiable, most do not even get adequate cash compensation (which is itself so demeaning to culturally and ecologically rooted communities) (Kothari 1996).

Economic centralisation, ecological degradation, and civil society

Further, since so much modern industrial production and commercial activity is contingent on the intensive and extensive extraction of natural resources, and since a majority of Third World people still depend for their subsistence on the regenerative capacities of their natural resource base — whether land, forests, rivers or the ocean — ecological degradation, misuse, and despoliation inevitably force them to live an increasingly untenable life on the periphery of society.

Yet, even in these margins, they are evolving complex new forms of economic and social subsistence. Even from the margins, many of them contribute more to developing civil society than do those with privilege and power. However, their capacity to play an active role as full participants in building a vibrant civil society is discounted by the centralisation of economic and political power, primarily because of the critical loss (and lack) of control over productive resources.[5]

In fact, most of the Third World has experienced a process whereby economic decision-making is shifting from the hands of primary producers to national governments, private entrepreneurs or TNCs. Indeed, control is even slipping away from national governments as faceless financial bureaucrats, economists, and TNC executives increasingly decide the direction of national and global economies (Kothari 1994; Cavanagh and Barnet 1994). For instance, TNCs today control 70 per cent of all the land in the Third World that grows export crops. They control 80 per cent of international trade and are the prime beneficiaries of this control. Not only are local (particularly small) producers more vulnerable as a result, but the capacities of national governments to monitor and regulate these corporate activities are inevitably inadequate (Korten 1995).[6] Even this level of hegemony does not seem to satisfy the dominant economic actors: witness the pressure they exerted on the OECD countries to draft and approve the Multilateral Agreement on Investment (MAI). If not for a remarkable global mobilisation that included concerned legislators, the draconian MAI would have become international 'law'. In October 1998, campaigners from all over the world met at a major workshop in Paris to ensure that instruments like MAI should not become a reality (*Lokayan Bulletin* 1998, 14(4):6).

A democratic civil society cannot be built without holding corporate activity accountable to a framework of democratic rights, including those enshrined by the UN, and to transparent public processes in whichever country that they operate. It is no exaggeration to say that governments which permit rapacious corporate activity (including the financial institutions which support this activity) are guilty of undermining both their own sovereignty and the security of present and future generations.

The state stepping back?

Across much of the Third World, the pressure from TNCs, IFIs, and others who directly and indirectly support their agenda is to 'roll back the state' and permit free access to markets, resources, and labour. Even in relatively strong democratic societies like India, with strong internal legislation to protect the interests of national production and patents, pro-privatisation and 'free market' voices call for a 'stepping back' of the state. Western governments and IFIs concur. There are clear double standards here, since the pressure on the Third World to open its borders to powerful corporations and other financial interests is not reciprocated in the form of reduced protectionism at home. Countries like the USA and France impose stringent barriers against the entry of goods and services from the Third World. Ironically, while no effort is spared to assist TNCs and other economic interests to 'open up the Third World' in order to gain access to its resources, markets, labour, and sites to dump industrial waste, there is no counter-mobility granted to the workforce. Capital and goods must be free, and labour must be kept bounded inside national frontiers unless selectively required by the industrial, agricultural, or service sectors or as domestic labour.

In country after country, business interests are being equated with national interests, while social and cultural interests are demoted to a secondary position, if not sacrificed altogether. Further, states go out of their way to use their military, police or other coercive means to facilitate the entry of entrepreneurs carrying foreign exchange. A few years ago, India's ex-Finance Minister, echoing this spirit of deregulation, stated that power should increasingly move from the state to 'the Boardroom', following an earlier announcement that the Indian police would be trained by Western security experts to protect the 'life and property of foreign investors'. Sustaining this status quo is antithetical to the building of a democratic civil society.

The goal of building a civil society is for all people to have modest economic and social security. This inevitably means that the top-down, welfarist, waged-employment option looks less and less attractive. Strategies which address both structural inequalities and the lack of rights over productive resources will have to be mainstreamed. The wholly abominable polarisation of wealth — which has doubled almost everywhere in the past 30 years (UNDP 1995, 1997) — and the grossly inequitable sharing of economic and political power will have to be transformed. Only then will an egalitarian order, which is a prerequisite of a 'successful' civil society, come into being. Economic democracy implies an acknowledgement that state safety-nets and temporary entitlements merely serve to hide the dominant economic ethos which is rapidly colonising much of the world, and alienating ever more people from their sources of subsistence and meaning. For instance, most credit and reform programmes have primarily benefited intermediate classes and rarely provided poorer producers with sustainable livelihoods. True democratisation demands a restructuring and socialising of the economy and its embedding in the values of social responsibility and ecological sustainability (Robertson 1990; Daly and Cobb 1989).

It is precisely towards that end that the initiatives outlined at the beginning of this essay were focused. These and similar voices within civil society are part of an important political expression that argues against a unipolar vision of the world, in which the market must define economic behaviour and where the state should facilitate the 'freeing' of the market and intervene only minimally in the immediate and longer-term interests of its citizens — particularly those who are vulnerable and poor. Markets cannot guarantee equitable distribution, nor should states be reduced to promoting the interests of national and global capital. These voices argue that states must have the ability to hand over and defend the control of local communities (with mutually agreed norms of conservation and use) over biological and genetic resources within its bounds. They also argue that there is no single linear process of development and that there are diverse ways of working towards a preferred society. The numerous efforts world-wide — from producer–consumer cooperatives to alternative agricultural movements to worker-controlled production systems — point to growing efforts to build alternatives to the dominant unsustainable institutional and production processes.

Situating civil society and the state

It is evidently crucial to strengthen and build associations and alliances through which civil society can be nurtured, where socially and politically committed individuals organise themselves in democratic forums, institutions, and associations within a democratic state, almost harking back to Rousseau's portrayal of a moral citizen striving for a truly democratic goal. Many of the efforts of hitherto neglected or excluded communities (such as those with which this essay began) can be seen as part of this endeavour. At a time when there is so much fragmentation and mistrust in society, the ideal of becoming responsible citizens with rights and obligations seems particularly relevant.

However, the modern state, particularly in the Third World, has not only grown substantially, but remains to a considerable degree outside the control of its citizens. States have acted coercively to oppress and contain sections of civil society. Societies also continue to witness the persisting power of both traditional feudal and upper-class networks as well as of predatory and polluting industrial and economic élites.

In the complex societies in which we all live, it is inconceivable that the state will wither away. While global (and some national) economic forces would like less state intervention in the functioning of the 'free market', in reality the state continues to be intrusive. This is precisely why it is an important political challenge to build a democratic state that can act as a buffer against predatory capital (domestic and transnational) and as a non-partisan arbiter in domestic conflicts. Simultaneously, civil society must continue to engage in democratic struggles for justice and ecological sustainability.

In some of these struggles, it has been suggested that the state has become irrelevant or too deeply embedded in the dominating system. Thus, if governance were to be truly de-centred (in fact, non-centred), with a complex array of representative mediating institutions, there would be no need for a state. At present, however, it is dangerous to think of a state-less society, since whatever regulatory institutions are formed would play roles that the preferred state would perform anyway. Given national and global inequity and injustice, it would be better to struggle towards a democratic state than to delegitimise it further.

Nevertheless, it is the failure of the state to democratise itself, to make itself into a neutral arbiter in civilian affairs, to intervene in favour of the underprivileged, and to contain predatory economic interests that has impelled the creation of a wide variety of popular movements seeking democratic control over their resources and their lives. In numerous cases, from Peru to Mexico to India, communities and culturally defined groups are increasingly demanding democratic autonomy from the state and greater control over their own affairs. These campaigns have taken two major forms:

■ *Movements for redefining the internal boundaries of the nation (either for the redrawing of internal boundaries of provinces, states or regions, or for the creation of a new territory comprising parts or wholes of existing geographical entities).* The underlying logic of such movements is that internal boundaries were defined by the colonisers or in the post-colonial period, on the basis of the dominant language and culture, thus discriminating against 'other' cultures and identities. Examples are the struggle in Chiapas or the campaigns of several tribal groups in Africa who were divided or forced into territorial boundaries created by colonial powers, or the demand for the past 40 years to carve out a new state in India — Jharkhand — based on predominantly tribal identities. In 1997, the government recognised demands for the formation of an autonomous Jharkhand Council to govern a new territory which cuts across the older internal boundaries. Similar demands had already been conceded to the Gorkha National Liberation Front (Gorkhaland) and to the Bodo community.

■ *Movements to secede from the nation-state.* These movements can be witnessed within Kashmir, Punjab, and Mizoram in India, within Sindh in Pakistan, within Northern Ireland in the UK, and among the Tamils in Sri Lanka, and the Catalans and in Basques in Spain. Such movements have usually faced brutal repression by the state (which often allows the movements to exhaust themselves, while simultaneously encouraging its own militant groups and waging an active propaganda war). In many cases, these movements have never enjoyed majority support. Eventually, under state repression, selective accommodation of their demands, the sustained generation of a climate of fear, as well as declining popular support have weakened their effectiveness and reach.

Such movements are obviously not always distinct from one another. Secessionist groups may accept compromises with the state and, conversely, movements for autonomy may become secessionist. What is important is that most of these movements are direct consequences of undemocratic economic and political processes.

So, where does all this leave us? We must acknowledge that in much of the Third World, civil society is still nascent. In addition to all the external actors who constrain and restrict it, civil society is full of passive clients of the state and the market. In an aggregate sense, these forces induce or support the closure of democratic political space. They inhibit (through fear, coercion, or ideology) the realisation of the full democratic potential of members of society in the pursuit of a democratic polity. They inhibit or destroy the strength of civil society that lies in inclusiveness, in pluralism, in the numerous efforts to foster associations, institutions, groups, and alliances that can nurture and democratise a pluralist ethos (Walzer 1995; Keane 1988). Thus, the real task of democracy has just begun — from building democratic relations in the family, the community, and the workplace to democratisation of global institutions.

Portents and challenges for the future

It is precisely this challenge that communities all over the Third World have taken up. Refusing to become 'victims' of undemocratic political and economic processes, they are asserting greater autonomy as well as mobilising themselves to confront the processes that marginalise them.

Crucially, for many, the primary goal is no longer the 'seizure' of the state. Like the tribals affiliated to the Indian National Forum for Tribal Self-rule or the peasants of Chiapas, they assert that in their demand for greater control over their productive resources and for their own political and social institutions they are fighting not just for their livelihoods but also for their identity. In that respect, they seek to strengthen plural institutions. However, the questions of what processes of democratic functioning they evolve internally, and how they define intra-group relationships towards a democratic civil society, are challenges that they and others like them must increasingly face.

These are issues that encompass all of humanity. The pursuit of wider public freedoms in civil society also requires a reciprocal responsibility to contribute to the 'larger good'. For instance, those seeking greater autonomy also have to give up some of their own freedom of action, for the sake of what I would call responsible autonomy — an autonomy where rights are coupled with sacrifices and duties.

In fact, the challenge in creating a dynamic civil society is to accept that any collective endeavour which pursues both the interests of the specific community or group or association as well as the 'larger good' will have to make compromises. If a truly plural and democratic civil society and state is the goal, then creative methods of accommodation as well as inclusive (rather than exclusive) strategies will be needed. This will require collective endeavour that both democratises the state and rule-making initiatives in civil society and formulates monitoring and mediating institutions. Any process that generates or legitimises iniquitous relationships or consequences — between classes, women and men, communities, associations, nations and regions — will have to be contested. So, for instance, if a new national or international legal regime (like the WTO) were established, comprehensive national and international debate would be mandatory. Even after this debate, if the new regime is shown to be affecting a given group, community, or country adversely, mechanisms for generating correctives will be required. (For a positive approach to protectionism see, for instance, Lang and Hines 1993.) Extractive processes that exploit natural resources without the consent of the communities that primarily depend on them and without a wider public debate would not be permitted to go ahead. Even here, principles will have to be evolved that test developmental interventions on the basis of their cost to present and future generations. All this points to the massive possibilities available to all those committed to the building of a democratic polity.

Political and economic democracy

These challenges sound daunting. The task of creating a socially just, ecologically sane, and politically democratic polity demands that we accept nothing less. The dominant myths of the market and of 'development' and the claims for capitalist paradigms of growth will have to be confronted and alternatives devised within thousands of democratic and culturally plural popular forums. Much of this will also need creative responses to the conflicts that will inevitably ensue as dominant interests are made to relinquish their undemocratic controls. As countless struggles for justice, whether in the family or in the workplace, have shown, rarely do those in power willingly surrender it to those they have dominated. But the more the forces of domination and divisiveness are permitted to prevail, the more they will succeed in controlling society for their narrow economic and political ends. Without challenging dominant patterns of economic development and the individuals, institutions, and corporations which justify them — nationally and internationally — it will not be possible to strengthen and build truly democratic societies. The present patterns of industrial and capitalist development are not just unsustainable but also inhibit the realisation of a politically active and vigilant civil society, since the colonisation and the destruction of livelihoods and ecosystems are inherent in them.

There has been a relatively recent trend to involve representatives of NGOs (rarely social and political movements) in joint forums with government or IFIs. While accountable and transparent joint committees have an important function in democratising the policy-making processes, increasingly loud voices among civil society actors in the South are arguing that efforts like, for instance, the World Bank–NGO Committee (set up almost a decade ago) have done more to legitimise the Bank than to yield significant changes in Bank practice in countries and in national policy processes (Rich 1994). And, while the Bank has moderately reformed itself (more because of sustained social protest than because of the work of the Committee), it continues to propagate a world-view of economic development which is antithetical to evolving effective strategies to use natural resources in a sustainable fashion, to democratise control over these resources, to reduce substantially the polarisation of wealth, and to make corporate activity transparent and accountable. In addition, so many of the activities of daily life are not driven by the state or the market. These are precisely the spaces where creative and innovative initiatives (that are neither governmental nor economic) are struggling for political and human rights, seeking to influence policy-making processes and public opinion, as well as working to transform the system itself. Women have played and will have to play an even more central role in challenging dominant economic and cultural systems and in safeguarding sustainable livelihoods.

Unless groups in civil society as well as sensitive politicians, policy-makers, and representatives of donor agencies and IFIs heed the call from the margins (where they will discover a flourishing civil society) and their alliances, the planet will continue to hurtle towards greater turmoil, exclusion, injustice, social conflict, and ecological collapse. This is not a doomsday prediction. It is an appeal to listen to the voices from the movements of the Third World (including the Third World in the First World) and to the growing evidence from countless studies that underscores the implications of the dominant patterns of economic development. Only a democratic civil society and a democratic state can provide an alternative. Pointing to the success of East Asian economies is not a solution, since those 'successes' have been achieved under largely authoritarian governments and by the colonisation of millions of people whose forests, lands, and rivers have been taken over to provide for these engines of growth. According to an official 'Taiwan 2000' report, the lower reaches of all 44 of Taiwan's rivers are biologically dead.

Despite some environmental awareness, much of the earth's resources continue to be exploited beyond their capacities for natural regeneration, thus undermining the very future of life on earth. So much of the world and so many of its peoples continue to be colonised and exploited, with the justification that these are necessary sacrifices for growth. Is this the legacy we want to leave for our future generations? Or do we want to challenge the forces of power and privilege and join hands with those who, often against overwhelming odds, are showing the way towards a society that is marked by gender and social justice and ecological sustainability? The choice seems to be an easy one. The tasks are at once profound, essential, and imperative.

Acknowledgement

This is a revised version of an article first published in *Development* 12(3) 1996.

Notes

1 I use the term 'Third World' (or 'less industrialised nations') instead of 'South' or 'developing countries' for two main reasons. Firstly, because there is a growing 'South in the North' and vice versa. The two Norths look increasingly similar and have similar aspirations, while the Souths are being victimised by and organising resistance to dominant developmental paths. Secondly, the term 'developing countries' is insulting to the peoples of the Third World, since it denotes a linear path to development, with the 'developed' as the end model to which to aspire.

2 The Sagarmatha Declaration was published in *Lokayan Bulletin* (March–April 1996).

3 The brief description of these six events entails some simplification. For instance, many activists are also raising significant issues concerning internal democracy — either along property and class lines, or in their families, communities, organisations, and associations. This process of internal democratisation is also a crucial element of the 'thickening' of civil society.

4 Other controversial and important Third World actors are militant political groups like the New People's Army in the Philippines or the Communist Party of India (Marxist-Leninist) in India — many of whom enjoy substantial public empathy among oppressed and subjugated peoples in the context of sustained repression by state forces, upper-class/caste groups, and predatory economic interests.

5 In addition to (and often compounded by) this corporate onslaught, what has also declined are the complex ways in which voluntary action was sustained among communities across the Third World. Communities had evolved codes which provided an ethical and normative framework for themselves, governing how individuals within it related to each other and to the 'outside world' or with nature. Undoubtedly, communities were also sites of other forms of oppression and exclusions. But the fact that collectives and collectivities in civil society, through a process of what I call mutual accountability, can provide ethical and democratic norms for a just and ecologically sane interaction with others is crucial in the long struggles ahead.

6 As so clearly evidenced in the Uruguay Round of the General Agreement on Tariffs and Trade (GATT) and powerfully highlighted in the first case adjudicated by the WTO in April 1996.

References

Brush, Stephen B. and D. Stabinsky (1996) *Valuing Local Knowledge*, Washington DC: New Island Press.

Cavanagh, J. and R. J. Barnet (1994) *Global Dreams: Imperial Corporations and the New World Order*, New York: Simon and Schuster.

Collier, G. A. (1994) 'Roots of the rebellion in Chiapas', *Cultural Survival Quarterly*.

Daly, H.E. and John B. Cobb (1989) *For the Common Good: Redirecting the Economy Toward Community, the Environment and a Sustainable Future*, Boston: Beacon Press.

Durning, A. (1992) *How Much is Enough: The Consumer Society and the Future of the Earth*, New York: W. W. Norton.

Ichiyo, M. and S. Kothari (1996) 'Towards Sustainable Systems', paper prepared for the General Assembly of the People's Plan for the 21st Century, Kathmandu.

Keane, J. (1988) *Democracy and Civil Society*, London: Verso.

Korten, D. (1995) *When Corporations Rule the World*, West Hartford: Kumarian Press.

Kothari, S. (1994) 'Global economic institutions and democracy: a view from India', in Cavanagh et al. (eds.) *Beyond Bretton Woods*, London: Pluto Press.

Kothari, S. (1995) 'Social movements and the redefinition of democracy', in P. Oldenburg (ed.) *India Briefing*, Armonk, NY: M.E. Sharpe.

Kothari, S. (1996) 'Whose nation is it? The displaced as victims of development', *Economic and Political Weekly* XXXI(24) (15 June 1996).

Kothari, S. and P. Parajuli (1993) 'No nature without social justice', in W. Sachs (ed.) *Global Ecology: A New Arena of Political Conflict*, London : Zed.

Lang, T. and C. Hines (1993) *The New Protectionism: Protecting the Future Against Free Trade*, New York: New Press.

Lokayan Bulletin (1998) special issue on 'Globalisation and the MAI', 14(4).

Papanek, V. (1971) *Design for a Small Planet*, New York: Pantheon.

Postel, S. (1994) 'Carrying capacity: earth's bottom line', in L. Brown (ed.) *The State of the World*, New York: W. W. Norton.

PP21 (1996) *People's Plans for the 21st Century, Shaping our Future: Asia-Pacific People's Convergence*, Hong Kong: PP21.

Rich, B. (1994) *Mortgaging the Earth: The World Bank, Global Impoverishment and the Crisis of Development*, Boston: Beacon Press.

Robertson, J. (1990) *Future Wealth: A New Economics for the 21st Century*, London: Cassell.

UNDP (1995 and 1997) *Human Development Report*, Oxford: OUP.

Walzer, M. (1995) *Pluralism, Justice and Equality*, Oxford: OUP.

■ **Smitu Kothari** *is co-founder of* Lokayan *('Dialogue of the People'), which promotes exchange between non-party political formations and concerned citizens in India and beyond. He is Editor of* Lokayan Bulletin *and a political organiser involved in ecological, cultural, and human-rights issues for a socially just and ecologically sane alternative, nationally and globally. He was recently a Visiting Professor at the Universities of Cornell and of Princeton, is President of the International Group for Grassroots Initiatives, a Contributing Editor of* The Ecologist *and* Development, *and a founding member of* Jan Vikas Andolan *('Movement for People's Development'). This paper was first published in* Development in Practice, *Volume 9 number 3, in 1999.*

Civil society and substantive democracy: governance and the state of law in Belgium

Koenraad Van Brabant

Governance and international development co-operation

Governance and the role of civil society in achieving good governance have received much attention in mainstream development thinking in the 1990s. Power and politics are thus introduced into the discussion.

The good-governance agenda follows an earlier focus on the state as economic actor. Just as governments were formerly advised to allow more space for private economic actors, they are now supposed to allow more players on to the scene in which power is wielded. Room must be given to citizens to organise themselves independently and to influence politics and government policies. Where it was not yet in place, the strong advice was to introduce 'democracy' with a multi-party system and elections as its most prominent manifestations.

Governance and civil society have also entered the humanitarian sector. The post-conflict reconstruction agenda has expanded from the rehabilitation of physical and social infrastructure to, ambitiously, the (re)construction of viable societies with power-sharing politics and an assertive civil society. Elections, as in Cambodia and Mozambique, have often been the culmination and goal of substantial UN peace-support operations. Significantly, the focus of international attention has been mostly on government and the executive, to a much lesser degree on the judiciary, and hardly at all on Parliament as the legislative body.[1]

Democratic institutions and an active civil society are thus seen as important basic frameworks and preconditions to reduce poverty, social exclusion, and violent civil strife. They form the basic ingredients of the recipes prescribed for post-communist and post-conflict societies.

'Democratisation', however, poses intellectual and pragmatic questions for development activists:

1. It brings into the picture the role of the state as regulator and protector, after an earlier emphasis on the state as producer and service-provider. In the development sphere, this expanded attention has been spearheaded by the campaigns for human rights, for the rights of women, children, and asylum seekers. More recently in the humanitarian field, the proliferation of small arms and the concerns about breaking the cycle of impunity are focusing minds on the state as a source of security and justice.

2. The recent interest in civil society has often centred very much on the promotion and capacity of NGOs. Other forms of social organisation, such as the churches, labour unions, professional associations etc., have received far less attention. One criticism has been that this negates, and may even undermine, more broad-based social activism and people's movements (e.g. Stubbs 1997).

3. Identifying the absence of formal democracy is relatively easy: one-party states, no elections, military rule, open repression are all clear indicators. But the concerns do not stop with the introduction of formal democracy. There are variations in the democratic model: different electoral systems, degrees of decentralisation, and forms of political accountability. Moreover, some democratic glitter does not mean one has struck gold. Has Kenya become a democratic society since multi-party politics were introduced? How substantive is the democracy in Sri Lanka, where there are many parties and regular elections but where there have also been violent insurgencies against the state, by both Tamils and Sinhalese? How democratic was the opposition against Milosevic in Serbia that in late 1996 occupied the streets for weeks but is now silent about the repression of the Kosovars?

How much intellectual understanding do we, as development activists, have about 'democracies'; and how do we practically engage with 'democratisation'? Does development assistance stop with supporting the emergence of a general organisational capacity in civil society, as is the case for many NGOs? Does it involve itself with the structures of formal democracy, as is sometimes the case of bilateral and multilateral donors? Or does it engage with the more complex, legal-political machinery that turns a social vision into reality, and that determines how substantive a democracy really is?

Elsewhere I have questioned the implicit North-South division in the discourse on conflict, development, and good governance in the European Union (EU) (Van Brabant 1998). EU countries are implicitly seen as democratic and developed. Yet the EU suffers from an appalling democratic deficit, and its ruling institutions oppose a strengthening of the European Parliament. There are also very different 'democratic' practices among its aid-providing member states.

This paper explores some of these questions, taking as an example the crisis of governance in Belgium. What is striking is that the crisis was caused not by social or political issues, but by a perceived dysfunctioning of the institutions of law and order. The paper first reviews the nature of what has been the largest ever popular mobilisation in Belgium and its fundamental weaknesses: organisation, civic education, and the translation of widespread discontent into an agenda that can be politically operationalised. Further analysis shows how the very mechanisms for successful conflict management developed in Belgium have given rise to a political culture that has now come to be seen as the obstacle to better governance. That culture is carried by an exclusive 'political society' whose functioning has frustrated the development of an active civil society, notwithstanding indications that Belgium disposes of much social capital. That raises the fundamental question of what relationship social movements can have with established political parties in furtherance of their aims.

Child abuse and the crisis of governance

Politics in Belgium tends to be referred to in three ways. It is wrongly equated with 'Brussels', the seat of the European Commission. It is regularly and more correctly cited as a model of the peaceful transformation of a unitary system into a federal state along ethnic lines. And it has been seen as remarkable for its post-World War II stability. Since mid-1996, however, the country has been experiencing an acute crisis of governance, often expressed in two key phrases: 'the gap between the politician and the citizen' and 'the crisis of confidence in the institutions'.

The immediate cause of this crisis was not the constitution or the economy, but child abuse. In mid-1996, two men, 'D' and an accomplice, were arrested for the abduction, sexual abuse, and murder of several children. Two abducted girls were found alive and four other victims murdered, while other children remain missing. In March 1997, another man, 'PD', was arrested for similar offences against another girl.

Horrible in themselves, the tragedies generated a crisis of governance for two reasons. First, it quickly became obvious that had it not been for major failings in the institutions of law and order, notably the *gendarmerie* [2] and the judiciary, the perpetrators, who had earlier been convicted for child abuse, could have been stopped much earlier. More problematic, however, were the persistent rumours that at least 'D' was part of an organised criminal network that abducted children for abuse by wealthy paedophiles. Speculation continued that unidentified individuals in elite circles had interfered with the police inquiries in order to protect themselves. Fuelling that suspicion were other recent high-profile cases of terrorist gang murders, a political murder, and corruption scandals in political circles. That none of these cases had apparently been resolved had already given rise to a public perception of a malicious lack of political will. At best, therefore, the institutions of law and order appeared incompetent. At worst, their effective functioning was impeded by criminal elements in the highest circles of power.

Citizen and civil-servant mobilisation

This crisis generated unprecedented levels and forms of citizen mobilisation. The most dramatic occurred in October 1996. The trigger was the decision by the highest judicial authority, following the request of 'D's' defence lawyer, to remove from the case the district attorney whose investigations had finally led to his arrest. The defence had argued that the presence of the district attorney at a thanksgiving dinner, given by the parents of the two girls who had been found alive, cast a doubt of 'partiality' on his inquiry, which violated the rights of his client. Predictably, the high-level acceptance of this argument created public outrage. Factory workers and school children went out on the streets, and blocked motorways and city centres. Harbour workers went on strike, some prisons were on the brink of mutiny, and fire brigades symbolically hosed the court buildings 'clean'. Belgium was brought to a standstill. The commotion culminated in a 'White March' demonstration in the capital, in which over 300,000 people — some 3.5 per cent of the population — participated, the largest mobilisation in Belgian history.

Less attention has been devoted to the no less unprecedented mobilisation of sections of the civil service. During the height of the turmoil, members of the magistracy, normally aloof and distant, not only engaged in televised debates but, in an *ad hoc* and belated attempt at civic education, went out to address audiences in schools and universities to explain the functioning of the judicial system and, sometimes, to argue their case. A year later, when an official inquiry had confirmed structural problems, but also individual failings in especially the *gendarmerie* and the judiciary, personnel of both these institutions held strikes both to express their sense of demoralisation but also to protest against their colleagues and their institutions being held accountable. The crisis of governance focused on the institutions of law and order more than on the government.

Mobilising for rights and governance: who sets the agenda?

In retrospect, it is possible to see how the agenda, initially carried and defined by ordinary citizens, was gradually taken over by career politicians. It could be argued that, as such, Belgium has shown itself to be a functioning democracy. What raises doubts about this assertion is the crucial role of events, and of the press in enlarging these events, to sustain the momentum for reform.

Between mid-1996 and mid-1997 the mobilisation was essentially driven by some of the parents of missing children. In the years prior to the arrest of 'D', a few small 'self-help' groups had come into being in support of individual afflicted parents. In 1991, a national Support Fund for Abducted and Missing Children had been set up. In the face of perceived indifference and ineffectiveness in the law-and-order institutions, some parents continued various activities in the search for their children: putting up posters, searching certain areas, making inquiries. Importantly, they kept arguing their right to have access to the files on the inquiry into the disappearance of their children, a right seldom granted in Belgium, on the grounds of having to safeguard the 'confidentiality' and 'impartiality' of the inquiry. The discovery of some missing children in August 1996 gave the parents unprecedented media attention. Some of these began to politicise their personal tragedy by publicly criticising the failings of the institutions of law and order. It was again six sets of parents who transformed the spontaneous outrage over the removal of the district attorney into a nascent people's movement. Using the now international media attention, they called for, and defined, the White March 'for truth'.

This March channelled the popular outrage that had started to turn more violent, and transformed it into a set of symbolic and dignified actions. The momentum of the White March led to the spontaneous creation of some local grassroots activist groups, the 'White Committees', which rapidly expanded when the parents called for this to happen. These Committees continued to organise many local actions and mobilisations, in the same spirit as the White March.

This has been established as the largest social mobilisation in Belgium's history (Walgrave and Rihouz 1997:113). Yet by summer 1997, the movement was running out of steam amid widespread pessimism. Very little impact appeared to have been achieved. Most distressing, however, were the tensions created by its fundamental internal weakness: lack of organisation. Indeed, this major mobilisation of Belgian citizens had happened almost spontaneously, virtually without organisational underpinning. The White Committees came into being in much the same way, functioning more as informal networks than as an organised movement. In January 1997, the six parent groups created the 'White March Foundation', with a national secretariat formed as the interface between the parents and the White Committees. A self-appointed daily committee started running the secretariat. It derived its mandate from the trust of the parents, but had no formal legitimacy in its relationship with the White Committees. When the need arose to create 'regional co-ordinators', the question of whether these would be nominated and mandated by the self-appointed 'national co-ordinators', or bottom-up from the White Committees, highlighted the problem of legitimate leadership. Friction and tension also arose between the original self-help groups based around individual parents and the new 'white movement'. Not until a series of plenary meetings in mid-1997 did the outline of an acceptable decision-making forum take shape, and could questions of strategy, objectives, and organisational structure be constructively addressed. By then, however, differences of opinion between some of the parents had become public, and some of the more outspoken parents had stepped back from an official involvement with the movement.

The second fundamental weakness of the 'white movement' was its lack of clear objectives. An impressive, but problematic, characteristic of the White March was its silence. More than 300,000 people marched in silence, without slogans or demands. Expressive of the widespread unease with the 'state of the nation', the March and the 'white movement' lacked political objectives. Symbolising purity, the demonstrators had no (political) colour; but also no claims.

Virtually simultaneously with the White March came the first reactions of 'political society'. Significantly, the first publicly to admit that the institutions had failed was the King. Constitutionally, the King of Belgium stands above the institutions and has only moral authority. This he exercised in a timely and constructive manner. But it was the Prime Minister, receiving the parents at the end of the White March, who, in making four concrete promises, defined an agenda that the silent demonstrators had left open: a European Centre for Missing Children — after the American model — located in Belgium; access for victims to the files concerning their case; the depoliticisation of the civil service and the judiciary; and a parliamentary commission of inquiry to investigate the failings of the institutions of law and order.

That parliamentary commission formally started its work a few days after the White March. It was composed of parliamentarians from the governing and opposition parties, and virtually all its hearings were broadcast live on television. Its inquiry revealed structural problems in the institutions of law and order. Crucial appeared to be the multiplicity of structures with policing roles. There is the criminal police force (*recherche*), part of the judiciary and under the authority of the Minister of Justice. But there are also the municipal police and the national *gendarmerie*, responsible for general order, under the authority of the Minister of the Interior. Each can play a role in investigating a crime, but in doing so they should be directed, controlled, and co-ordinated by a district attorney (*juge d'instruction*), who prepares the dossier for the prosecutor's office. In practice, the three forces with policing authority act fairly autonomously with regard to the district attorney, and often do not communicate with each other; at times they even actively compete with each other. The situation is further aggravated by the lack of communication and co-operation between police units and districts attorneys in different administrative zones. The weak supervision and direction provided by district attorneys is partly a result of an overburdened and under-resourced judiciary, a consequence of years of political neglect; but also of a lack of pro-active policies within the judiciary. Finally, the structural problems can be compounded by a lack of professional competence, management experience, and basic motivation and sense of responsibility. This, in turn, is partly the result of a long-standing 'politicisation' of the civil service, whereby nominations and promotions have been more influenced by party-politics than by merit. The report also draws attention to the need for better support for victims and their right to information about the progress of the inquiry, a right formally granted to the defendant.

Through its report, the Parliamentary Commission developed and to a degree re-focused the agenda. At a structural level, it recommended the creation of a unified police force. Some legal reform was suggested, along with a better-resourced judiciary. Crucially, however, a more independent mechanism of quality control had to be introduced into the judiciary, since its internal mechanisms were clearly failing. The report also identified a number of individuals who had shown unacceptable indifference or incompetence in the inquiries into the missing children, or whose conduct raised even more serious questions about their motives (Chambre des Representants 1997).

Responsibility for the follow-up of these findings lay with the Ministers of Justice and of the Interior. In the following year, these came under increasing criticism, especially from some of the parents. The discussions about the reform of the police and the judiciary appeared to be bogged down in party-politicking. Even more embitterment was created by the fact that none of those individuals singled out for their professional failings had been sanctioned. Some had taken early retirement, a few had been suspended, while others had just been advised to take 'a step aside' voluntarily. This only fuelled the public perception of lack of accountability for politicians and the senior civil service.

Eventually a 'breakthrough' was triggered by a most unexpected occurrence. In April 1998 'D', Belgium's 'number one criminal', while being taken by two *gendarmes* from prison to the court-house in order to consult the files on his case — a right denied to the parents of the missing children — managed to escape for a few hours. Sensing the public mood, the Ministers of Justice and of the Interior immediately resigned and were followed, after some pressure, by the commander of the *gendarmerie*. Within days, the governing and most opposition parties suddenly reached agreement on the reform of the police and the judiciary. Problematically, the reforms are now more driven by rapid responses to a political crisis, while there had been ample time to base them on an in-depth management review (see Glidewell 1998).

By mid-1998 then, there was a European Centre for Missing Children, there had been a Parliamentary Inquiry, there was a new law giving victims access to the files, and reform of the institutions could start. The questions of individual responsibilities and of the depoliticisation of the civil service remained pending. By mid-1998 too, the agenda was no longer being carried by the 'white movement' but by the mainstream political parties. That shift was further underlined by the fact that some of the parents had established a formal distance between themselves and the 'white movement' which they helped to initiate; they publicly expressed their support for the Green Party, because of its perceived alternative vision and political integrity. At the same time, the most vocally critical parent started a new 'white party'.

Maintaining momentum: the role of events and of the press

The White March and the 'white movement' were essentially an expression of unease, distrust, and protest against the continual failings of the relevant institutions in Belgium. Without effective organisational underpinning or clear objectives, however, it remained a reactive mobilisation, unable to choose its own timing and themes (Walgrave and Rihoux 1997:55).

The political institutions, notably the executive, showed themselves capable of identifying concrete objectives, but as far as substantive measures and changes were required, they appeared obstructed by party-political positioning and procedural inertia. Time and again, momentum in this established democracy had to be obtained from dramatic events. First came the discovery of some missing and murdered children, followed by their funerals. Then came the decision to remove the successful district attorney from the case. Subsequently, momentum was re-generated by the discovery of another murdered child. Later followed public 'revelations' about sadistic and satanic networks of paedophiles in elite circles, from young women who had undoubtedly suffered abuse but whose stories appeared ultimately to be the product of troubled minds. Finally, there was the temporary escape of 'D'. Repeatedly, events recreated the sense of crisis that provided what seemed to be the only effective incentive for reform.

Yet there would not have been that degree of popular mobilisation and public pressure had it not been for the media. The media substituted for a virtually non-existent organisation in mobilising the population for the White March. In the first six months of the crisis, the media generally took the side of the parents and, through their support, partially helped to create the 'white movement'. The Parliamentary Commission would not have had the same appeal without the high media attention. Significantly, its report is not readily accessible to the general public. Its substance is mostly disseminated in press reports and in books written by journalists.

In the early days, the media took on the role of the channel *par excellence* of the new, mobilised, citizen. Some media workers explicitly saw themselves as part of the school of 'civil' or 'public journalism' (Merritt 1995), according to which the role of the media is not to mirror society but to mobilise civil society and so become a major instrument of participative democracy. The risks are that, poorly practised, this becomes a journalism of emotions rather than of facts, and that the media catch on to a topic for marketing rather than for political purposes (Grevisse 1997). Certainly as of mid-1997, parts of the written press began to carry sharper criticism of the more vocal parents and of the Parliamentary Commission. By and large, the media played a crucial role in civil mobilisation, but failed in civic education.

Civic education: the rights of children and the state of law

In so far as the events in Belgium have given rise to the claim that a 'new citizen' has come into being, the public debate is interesting as much for what it focused upon as for what it ignored.

Throughout, the crisis has been more about the state of law than about the rights of the child. Child abuse has only been a secondary theme, and then only in the context of the non-related paedophile. In October 1996, some 25 per cent of the population signed a petition demanding more severe punishment for convicted paedophiles. Belgian social-service institutions already have a fairly developed awareness of child abuse, and there exist a number of services specifically for children. The recent nomination of an Ombudsperson for Children strengthens this network. The public debate about paedophilia and child pornography, however, never really extended 'inwards' to include incest, nor 'outwards' to sex tourism and international trafficking in children and women. Inasmuch as the child stood central in the public debate, the key issue was the need for the law-and-order forces actively to respond to 'unusual disappearances' rather than shrugging them off as yet another case of a child 'running off for a few days'.

Mostly, the spotlight was on the functioning of the institutions of law and order. The ineffectiveness of the various police forces appeared essentially a matter of organisation, management, and competence. The debates about the judiciary, however, raised far more fundamental questions.

Only briefly, following the decision to remove the district attorney from the case, did the public debate touch upon the philosophy of law. At its heart was the discussion about a formalistic or a substantive approach to law. The formalists kept repeating the theory of the state of law: independence of the judiciary, the need for procedures to ensure consistency and impartiality, the protection of the right of the defendant, and the respect for the letter of the law and for a verdict.

Underlying this position is a positivistic philosophy that equates legal reasoning with formal logic. In that view, the removal of the district attorney from the case represented a situation in which the application of a sound principle unfortunately went against public opinion. The formalists strongly resented the public hearings of the Parliamentary Commission as a formally deficient 'trial in the court of the press'. The substantivists, by contrast, accept that the law does not exist outside and above society and must adapt to changes in that society. They concede that the application of the law always involves interpretation and judgement, so that argument and debate are an inherent aspect of doing justice. Procedures are necessary rules of the game, but if procedures take precedence over judgement, they can impede justice. The application of the law is, therefore, legitimately open to debate (see Perelman 1978: part II).

The challenge for a legal system is to avoid being led by public opinion, while also being sensitive to the society in which it is embedded. There is a widespread perception in Belgium that justice is often obstructed by defence lawyers, who skilfully play procedural games to delay a case until it legally expires, or to have it dismissed on procedural grounds: 'Justice delayed is justice denied' and 'justice must not only be done, it must also be seen to be done'. The problem is not only in Rwanda (Vandeginste 1997), but also in Belgium. The Belgian, like most Western legal systems, focuses heavily on the defendant, to the point of neglecting the rights of the victims. That may lead to an increasing loss of confidence.

Hardly touched upon, but no less important, was the question of legislative reform. Unlike the systems in Britain or the USA, for example, the whole Belgian legal system is codified, and derived from the French *Code Napoléon*, with no use of case law. Over the course of the years, new laws may be added, but old and now superfluous laws and procedures are seldom deleted. The result is a bureaucratic and sometimes outdated penal code which maintains many now irrelevant clauses and stipulations that hamper rather than facilitate the course of justice. This is essentially a long-standing failing of the legislative, i.e. parliament.

No less fundamental was the independence of the judiciary. A basic premise of democratic constitutions is the separation of legislative, executive, and judiciary powers. In the 1990s, international development agencies have correctly been emphasising in transitional (post-communist or post-conflict) societies the importance of the independence of the judiciary. Here, however, the question was: to whom are individual magistrates, and the judiciary as an institution, accountable? What mechanism of quality control exists? The highest judicial authority in Belgium deplored the creation of a supervisory High Council for Justice, which will include a number of experts from outside the magistracy. Their view is that the magistracy must supervise itself. One corporate association of magistrates has resisted the blame cast on colleagues by the Parliamentary Commission as a form of political interference. The counter-argument has been that the long-standing influence of party-politics in the nomination and promotion of magistrates has jeopardised the independence of the judiciary far more, and that there is an urgent need to restore its independence through such de-politicisation.

Finally, the resignation of the Ministers of Justice and of the Interior highlighted the question of political accountability. It contrasted sharply with the on-going bitter demand for the voluntary resignation of a previous Minister of Justice, now a judge in the European Court, who in 1992 had, against advice to the contrary, signed for the release of 'D' from prison, subject to monitoring by a social worker. It has also been argued that the past and the current Prime Minister, as heads of government, who together and for over a decade have neglected the judiciary in favour of the financial and economic agenda of the EU, should be held accountable. That raises the question whether political accountability attaches to a post or to a person; and, if the latter, can someone be held accountable for mistakes made in a public office s/he no longer holds? No less problematic was the call for a high-level magistrate to resign over the escape of 'D'. This was not necessarily because of any sanctionable failing, but because of a need for 'symbolic sacrifices', to restore public confidence. Such cosmetic symbolism, however, does nothing to improve the state of law or the quality of governance.

A noticeable weakness of the 'white movement' was its inability clearly to articulate a perspective and a position on these fundamental issues of a well-functioning democracy. Legal-aid or child-rights organisations did not play any significant role in the 'white movement' or help it to clarify its arguments and its demands. The vagueness and the confusion in the debate over these issues illustrated the absence of any real civic education as part of mainstream schooling, even about the basic premises and institutions of one's own society, let alone about variants in other countries that share a generally democratic framework. That these issues are confidently discussed only by some lawyers and political scientists is itself an indication of a 'democratic deficit'.

Democracy and social capital

Especially since the publication of *Making Democracy Work* (Putnam 1993), 'social capital' has become a key concept in social-development theory, notably in the thinking about governance and the role of civil society. In essence, social capital refers to the presence of multiple networks of civic engagement that, through upholding norms and generating trust, facilitate co-operation for mutual benefit. Putnam's thesis is that where there is a strong civic tradition, expressed for example by a vibrant associational life, high newspaper readership, and forms of political participation, those in power will be more responsive and accountable to citizens, and more ready to seek pragmatic compromise with political opponents.

As such, Belgium appears to have an abundance of social capital. There is plenty of associational life, fairly high news consumption, and obligatory voting. Moreover, compromise has been the hallmark of what are inevitably coalition governments with seldom fewer than four partners. And yet, in Belgium it appears to be precisely these characteristics that obstruct good governance. This has to be understood in the light of the existing political culture.

Since the nineteenth century, Belgium has been vulnerable to three structural conflicts. First, the potential conflict from the existence of three major worldviews: catholic, socialist, and liberal. The potential flash-point was education. Second, the potential conflict between organised labour and capital. Finally, the communal tension between Flemish and Walloons. The high degree of associational life allows for a rapid mobilisation and acute confrontation on any of these break-points.

The stability of Belgium is the result of successful conflict-management. First, all three major break-points were contained through pacts, the 'socio-economic pact' (1944), the 'school pact' (1958), and the 'communal pact' that inaugurated a gradual transformation from a unitary to a federal state (1971). Simultaneously, a political culture for effective conflict-management was developed, the major tools of which were proportional representation, 'particracy', and compromise.

Proportional representation rather than majority rule ensures that no major segment of society is excluded from power. Particracy indicates that the political parties have come to dominate the web of associations and social services that can cover a Belgian from cradle to grave. The catholic, socialist, and liberal blocks have developed associational 'cloaks' for their own members, in what has been called a system of 'confessional apartheid' (Stouthuysen 1997: 54). Particracy thus means that the political parties have come to behave as the monopoly expression of political will. This, mixed with proportionality, has given rise to 'proportional distribution'. In other words, public resources — from civil-service positions, subsidies, representation on boards and committees to literary prizes — get shared out 'proportionally' by the political parties to their constituents, not always on the basis of merit. Finally, coalition politics inevitably requires much negotiation to reach pragmatic compromises. Particracy alongside compromise politics, however, has resulted in party-politicking. Often, the purpose of a deal between the admitted interest groups is to manage conflict and to maintain the balance of power, not to solve the problem. Governance then becomes a question of political power-games without concern for managerial effectiveness.

Much of the political wheeling and dealing is highly discreet, not to say secretive, and removed from public scrutiny. Over the years, this 'sofa politics' (Huyse 1973: 28) has created a shadowy political society, an elite which with its technocrats, civil servants, and selected interest groups is more pervasive in its influence than the visible, elected, politicians, and whose actions and transactions are not transparent. The citizen inevitably gets frustrated, distrustful, and apathetic. Belgium was thus a stable but also an elitist democracy.

The system was tolerated as long as the public resources that were distributed through political clientelism generated pay-offs and benefits to enough people. But the need for fiscal rectitude and leaner government since the mid-1970s meant that there were fewer spoils to be had. Over time, citizens became more critical of a political culture that for decades had avoided many conflicts but not fundamentally resolved many problems.

One critique of Putnam is that he overlooked 'political society'. There are forms of elite politics whose networks generate not social capital for the public good but 'political capital' that benefits restricted interest groups (Harris and De Renzio 1997: 926). It is worth remembering that democracy in classical Greece, the cradle of democracy, only extended to an elite of 'citizens'. The strength and persistency of the rumours about high-level 'protection' for 'D' and his associates, whether true or not, indicates the contempt and distrust that the secretive 'old political culture' of Belgium has generated. The Belgian case also supports another critique of Putnam's thesis. Putnam holds that high levels of civic engagement will stimulate good governance. The concepts of a 'political society' and of a 'political culture' indicate that a reverse influence may also obtain: some forms of political culture stimulate more civic engagement and generalised trust than others. The Belgian political culture essentially generates apathy and disengagement. A strong and active civil society may, therefore, require political society's commitment to efficient and transparent governance (Harris and De Renzio 1997: 927). The difficulty faced by the 'white movement' was that demands that could be achieved within the existing political culture were not enough. The problem was that of the existing political culture itself. But what mechanism can turn an elitist democracy into a more participative one?

Other countries have experienced events comparable to those in Belgium: for instance, the police inefficiencies in the West murders case in the UK, or the popular reactions against the release of convicted child abusers into the community. Yet these have not led to a major crisis of governance. The depth of the crisis in Belgium, and the focus on the functioning of key institutions of governance rather than, for example, on child abuse, can be understood only in the light of the resentment against the 'old political culture' that had been building up for many years. Both Belgium and the UK are considered democracies, but their political cultures differ. In the UK, for example, citizens are socially and politically more active, and appeal more to their MPs to voice their views. British MPs can, therefore, experience stronger tension between having to accept the party-whip and being responsive to their constituents, something virtually non-existent in Belgium. In the UK there is not a tradition of coalition governments, there are more independent regulators and ombudsperson functions, and there is stronger pressure for inquiries to be made public.[3] And the use of case law in the British legal system allows more room for the consideration of arguments than codified law.

Political parties and social movements: towards a new political culture?

Since the late 1960s, new social movements have arisen in Belgium in the context of the old party-political culture. Of the 'internationalist' ones, solidarity with the Third World movement was non-confrontational, whereas that for peace and nuclear disarmament was much more so.

None of these made much impact on the existing political topography. The women's movement and the environmental movement have to a large degree been absorbed by the mainstream political parties. Although there are Green Parties in both Flanders and Wallonia, these are under pressure to demonstrate relevance and competence on all social and economic issues, not just environmental ones.

More explicit mobilisations for more substantive and inclusive democracy have come from the 'March against Racism' (1992 to 1994), in response to electoral gains of the nationalist right, and the 'white movement'. The latter was the first, implicitly more than explicitly, to challenge the dominant political culture and the poor governance that results from it. Simultaneous with the birth of a 'new citizen' is a concomitant demand for a 'new political culture' that would deal competently with substantive issues, over and across the party divide.

In early 1997, a few career politicians from different parties briefly articulated a vision and a manifesto for a 'new political culture' — an initiative that broke down in the first formal inter-party meetings to discuss it. Where the nature of party-politics and the reigning political culture are increasingly perceived as an obstacle rather than a channel for substantive democracy, as in Belgium (and other places too, such as Sri Lanka), a social movement faces a major problem. Elections may alter the balance of power between parties but will not lead to radical changes in the system.

It is these new social movements that have been highlighting values and demands for solidarity, gender equality, sustainable development, and a more participatory democracy. But they face structural difficulties. They are generally characterised by local, grassroots units of organisation. One challenge is, therefore, to realise and sustain popular mobilisation in the absence of strong national and integrated structures, particularly if it cannot count on the support of the media. Another is that of transforming emotion into political demands, an area in which there is a clear need for civic education. Then comes the challenge of translating a popular demand into a political agenda. This requires legal-political expertise and experience with the functioning of government. Here the crucial question becomes: what tactical or strategic relationship will a social movement develop with political parties?[4]

Obviously, then, the democracy and good governance that the Northern powers prescribe to Southern and Eastern governments are not as straightforward and unproblematic as they may appear. And those who are working for 'democratisation' need significant legal-political expertise and tactical and strategic acumen.

Notes

1 Nor is much attention paid to the variable importance given to the referendum in different democracies (see *The Economist*, 21 December 1996).

2 A national police force with a military-style training and organisation.

3 Belgium, on the other hand, has been better at managing the relationship between labour and capital and between the nationalities on its territory.

4 Whether a political party belongs more to the sphere of the state or more to civil society may be a contextual question rather than a definitional one.

References

Chambre des Représentants de Belgique (1997) *Enquête sur la manière dont l'enquête, dans ses volets policiers et judiciaires a été menée dans "l'affaire Dutroux-Nihoul et consorts"*, Brussels.

Glidewell, I. (1998) *The Review of the Crown Prosecution Office*, London: HMSO.

Grevisse, B. (1997) 'Het klankbord van de straat', interview in *KNACK*, Brussels (15 January 1997).

Harris, J. and P. De Renzio (1997) '"Missing Link" or analytically missing? The concept of social capital', *Journal of International Development* 9/7: 919-37.

Merritt, D. (1995) *Public Journalism and Public Life: Why Telling the News is Not Enough*, Hove: Lawrence Erlbaum Associates.

Putnam, R. (1993) *Making Democracy Work: Civic Traditions in Modern Italy*, Princeton: Princeton University Press.

Perelman, C. (1978) *Juridische Logica als Leer van de Argumentatie*, Antwerpen: Standaard.

Stouthuysen, P. (1997) 'De nieuwe burger en de crisis van de oude politiek', in C. Eliaerts (ed.) *Kritische Refleties omtrent de zaak Dutroux*, Brussels: VUB Press.

Stubbs, P. (1997) 'The role of NGOs in social reconstruction in Post-Yugoslav countries', *Relief and Rehabilitation Network Newsletter* 8: 7-9.

Van Brabant, K. (1998) 'Analysis and advocacy on a European policy on conflict prevention', *Development in Practice 8/2*: 217-20.

Vandeginste, S. (1997) *Justice for Rwanda and International Cooperation*, Antwerpen: Centre for the Study of the Great Lakes Region of Africa.

Walgrave, S. and B. Rihoux (1997*) Van Emotie tot Politieke Commotie: De Witte Mars een Jaar Later*, Leuven: Van Halewyck.

The Economist (1996) 'A survey of democracy', London (21 December 1996).

■ **Koenraad Van Brabant** *is the Co-ordinator of the Relief and Rehabilitation Network at the Overseas Development Institute, London. This paper was first published in* Development in Practice, *Volume 8, number 4 in 1998.*

EURODAD's campaign on multilateral debt: the 1996 HIPC debt initiative and beyond

Sasja Bökkerink and Ted van Hees

Introduction

'Multilateral debt is not a widespread problem for Severely Indebted Low Income Countries', wrote the World Bank in September 1994.[1] Ten months later, an internal World Bank document called for the establishment of a 'Multilateral Debt Facility' to reduce the multilateral debt burden of 24 likely candidates.[2] This would be part of a co-ordinated effort of bilateral, multilateral, and commercial creditors to bring the debt burden of developing countries to a sustainable level. Six months on, the IMF joined the World Bank in proposals to resolve the debt problem of Heavily Indebted Poor Countries (HIPCs), including the multilateral debt problem.[3]

In other words the World Bank, and to a degree the IMF, made a U-turn. Having initially denied the multilateral debt problem, they slowly started to recognise it and then came up with a proposal to deal with it. Although imperfect, this proposal reflects to some extent the demands made by NGOs which, together with progressive forces within the Bank and certain creditor countries, have played a crucial role in this process. While the multilateral debt problem is now too great to ignore, it is the persistent pressure of these players that has been responsible for the enormous progress made by the International Financial Institutions (IFIs).

This article analyses this progress and focuses on the contribution of the European Network on Debt and Development (EURODAD).[4] It must be emphasised that the major strength of EURODAD's work derives from its close links with NGOs inside and outside its network. Specifically, without the support and co-operation of Oxfam International's Advocacy

Office and the Center of Concern (both based in Washington), EURODAD's activities would have had less impact.

Background to the multilateral debt campaign

Multilateral debt is an increasing part of the overall debt problem of developing countries, comprising 30 per cent of the total long-term debt stock of HIPCs in 1994. Multilateral creditors received half of these countries' debt repayments. This debt is a major impediment to social and economic development. It also has indirect negative consequences, since the preferred-creditor status of the IFIs means that multilateral debt is serviced prior to other debt.[5] Consequently, arrears to (mainly) bilateral creditors have been accumulating. In addition, aid resources intended for social development and poverty alleviation are being diverted to service the multilateral debt.

Stimulated by discussions with debt experts such as Percy Mistry and Matthey Martin, EURODAD began work on advocating a comprehensive and concerted approach to the problem. It entails taking all aspects of the debt problem into account — commercial, bilateral, and multilateral debt — encouraging all major players to take responsible action.

EURODAD's first work on multilateral debt is represented in its campaigning document 'Target 1992'. After a slow start, the December 1993 seminar on multilateral debt organised by EURODAD and the Dutch NGO Novib acted as a major incentive for further discussion on the issue of multilateral debt. Early the following year, EURODAD and its colleagues formulated its 'Appeal for a just solution of the multilateral debt problem', which was signed by several hundreds of NGOs and used in lobbying. However, some major European NGOs were reluctant to sign. Evidently, more discussion on a specific or sophisticated approach (particularly on the credit-rating problem) was needed. At their July 1994 conference on multilateral debt — two months after an official conference on the issue organised by the governments of Sweden and Switzerland — NGOs tried to resolve their differences and to agree a policy based upon equal treatment of all creditors. NGOs agreed to accept the preferred, but not the exempt, creditor status of the IFIs.[6]

On 3 October 1994, the multilateral debt campaign was launched officially. Over the next two years, hundreds of NGOs worldwide became involved. The interest of the NGO community in the issue is reflected in the growth of EURODAD's multilateral debt network, which by the end of 1996 comprised over 150 NGOs, NGO networks, academics, debt experts, representatives from the UN, UNCTAD, UNDP, the Non-Aligned

Movement (NAM), the Commonwealth Secretariat, and other interested institutions and people, on both the debtors' and the creditors' side.

EURODAD's main function in the campaign was, and still is, analysing major developments, sharing information, stimulating discussion, and giving strategic guidance. In terms of lobbying and press work, the other two main elements of the campaign, EURODAD played a role at certain key moments in relation to specific fora and events such as G7 meetings, the Spring and Annual Meetings of World Bank and IMF, and their Interim and Development Committees.

Towards a recognition of the multilateral debt problem

In 1995, after a long period of consistently denying the existence of a multilateral debt problem, the World Bank and the IMF slowly started to change their position. The first signs of this change were their joint papers of February and March 1995. According to the first paper, about eight countries might experience problems in servicing their multilateral debt obligations.[7] This projection was based on the assumption of an annual nominal export growth rate of six per cent and an annual nominal three per cent growth rate for new concessional lending. It was also assumed that a multilateral debt-service to export ratio of 10 to 12 per cent would be unsustainable.

EURODAD argued that these assumptions were far too optimistic. In letters to Executive Directors of the World Bank and the IMF, as well as to various members of their staff, EURODAD pointed out that export growth projections were highly unrealistic, that a constant real level of new concessional loans was equally unlikely, and that the debt-service ratios were far too high. Further, EURODAD stressed that the debt problem was underestimated, because several countries were excluded from the analysis, including four countries in arrears to the IMF. Finally, the analysis assumed the full application of Naples Terms[8] and similar reductions of commercial debt, while there was no indication that such reductions would take place. EURODAD's concerns were shared by many other NGOs.[9]

Thanks to the pressure exerted by EURODAD and others, as well as the progressive attitude of some Executive Directors and Development Ministry officials, the staff of the World Bank and the IMF were asked by their Boards to prepare a second paper. At a World Bank Board meeting in March 1995, the Dutch, British, Canadian, US, Swiss, French, and Swedish governments were generally positive about the need to do something about the debt problem, including multilateral debt, emphasising that the World Bank report was too optimistic about export growth and resource flows. The Italian, Australian, and Japanese governments, however, were still unwilling to take any action.

The second joint paper showed that changing the assumptions regarding export growth and the amounts of new concessional lending significantly altered the projections.[10] For example, if three per cent nominal export growth was assumed, there would be not eight but 23 problem countries. Nevertheless, the paper's conclusion did not differ from the earlier one: provided that sufficient new and concessional loans were made, multilateral debt would not be a widespread problem.

As it gradually dawned upon the IFIs that a multilateral debt problem *did* exist (at least for a few countries), they started to discuss options for dealing with it that went beyond existing mechanisms.[11] These included making the IMF's major structural adjustment lending instrument, the Enhanced Structural Adjustment Facility (ESAF), permanent; and using gold sales for this purpose, softening the terms of lending of ESAF and IDA (International Development Assistance), and extending IDA's 'fifth dimension'.[12]

As EURODAD pointed out, the problem with the two IDA options was that they would divert these resources from aid purposes to debt relief. Moreover, EURODAD stressed that gold sales should be used not to replenish the ESAF but to relieve the debt burden. It pressed the IFIs to come up with more realistic solutions and asked for genuine burden-sharing: the IFIs need not give up their preferred creditor status, but they should abandon their 'exempt' creditor status and reduce the multilateral debt burden of the poorest, most indebted countries. This could be financed by an optimal policy mix which would aim to protect the financial standing of IMF gold sales and other IMF reserves, the special SDR allocation for debt relief, and World Bank reserves and profits. It was also stressed that resources should be *additional*: debt relief should not divert aid money.

During the Spring Meetings of the World Bank and the IMF in April 1995, it became evident that there was some tension between them. While the Bank seemed to be open to NGOs' comments and ideas, the Fund stuck to its analysis and downplayed the multilateral debt problem to one of a 'small handful of countries'. In a letter sent to the G7 countries before their Halifax meeting in June 1995, EURODAD called for a comprehensive approach to the debt problem and stressed the flaws in the international debt strategy. EURODAD thus asked the G7 to increase Naples Terms from 67 per cent to 90-95 per cent, to urge the IFIs to reduce multilateral debt, and to delink debt relief from current (and in many respects failing) structural adjustment programmes.

This meeting was a small victory for the multilateral debt campaign. For the first time, the problem was explicitly acknowledged, with the G7 calling for a comprehensive and co-ordinated debt approach, asserting that:

> There is general agreement that measures have to be taken to ensure that the burden of multilateral debt does not impede the growth prospects for the poorest countries. Exit strategies need to be found for countries with particularly high levels of multilateral debt, but with good track records. The IMF and the World Bank should take the lead in developing a comprehensive multilateral approach to assist countries with multilateral debt and debt service ratio's above prudent levels in addressing their debt burdens, through the flexible implementation of existing instruments, and new mechanisms where necessary. Thought should be given to the better use of all existing IMF and World Bank resources.[13]

The promise of a genuine resolution of the multilateral debt problem

The G7 call for a comprehensive approach to the debt problem was picked up by the IFIs. Finally, the World Bank (and later the IMF) started to come up with solutions. In July 1995, a Special Task Force at the Bank prepared a proposal to create a Multilateral Debt Facility (MDF). James Wolfensohn, who had been elected president of the World Bank on 1 June 1995, was to some extent behind this quick response of the World Bank to the call of the G7.

The MDF proposal was leaked to the *Financial Times* in September 1995. The idea was to create a facility which would pay, over a period of 15 years, the multilateral debt-service of a selected group of 20 HIPCs, with the aim of achieving a sustainable debt level. All aspects of the debt burden would be taken into account. Completed debt-reduction agreements with bilateral and commercial creditors as well as a good track record would be a condition for multilateral debt relief. To avoid the perception that the Bank would be recycling its own money, the facility would be created as an 'arm's length' mechanism outside the Bank's control, and at least half of the funding would have to come from other bilateral and multilateral donors. The Bank would contribute to the fund from its own resources, mainly through unexpected income from 1995 as well as future net income.

EURODAD and many other NGOs welcomed the MDF proposal as an important step towards a genuine resolution of the multilateral debt problem. For the first time, the World Bank had acknowledged explicitly that the problem affected more than just a few countries. Another new element was the proposal to reduce multilateral debt-service payments, while the MDF could offer a forum to deal with the entire debt of the poorest and most indebted countries in a comprehensive and concerted way. Moreover, it met two objections that the IFIs had raised against multilateral debt. These had maintained that multilateral debt reduction carried the risk of 'moral hazard', and feared that it could affect their credit-rating. However, as EURODAD had stressed before, these fears were poorly founded.

EURODAD and other NGOs realised that although the proposal was something of a breakthrough, it also had some important shortcomings. In its first reaction to it, EURODAD asked other NGOs to endorse the framework, while also commenting on the following flaws:

1 The debt problem was underestimated, as the choice of debt indicators was rather narrow, while the ratios chosen were too high. Moreover, four countries in arrears to the IMF were not included in the calculations.

2 The assumption of completed bilateral and commercial debt reduction was rather optimistic.

3 Bilateral donors were expected to contribute disproportionately: through bilateral debt relief and through contributions to the multilateral debt fund. The contributions of the IMF as well as the World Bank could be increased.

4 Debt relief remained linked to failing structural adjustment programmes.

Several countries opposed the proposal: Germany, Japan, and to a certain extent Italy and France. Others had problems with the financing of debt reduction — namely, the Nordic countries, the Netherlands, and Belgium — fearing that the facility would divert money from IDA. The most supportive countries were the USA and the UK. It should be noted that neither of these linked their support for the MDF to making bilateral contributions to it, though this irritated the smaller European countries that were prepared to contribute bilaterally. Bilateral contributions were also seen as a means to get a grip on the facility, instead of leaving it all to the IFIs.

Partially due to the opposition of the IMF, no consensus was reached on the proposal during the Annual Meetings of the World Bank and the IMF. The two institutions stated that the existing policy framework of strong adjustment in combination with appropriate debt-relief measures by bilateral and commercial creditors, and the provision of adequate new concessional funding, should be sufficient to bring debt and debt-service for most countries down to manageable levels. The major result of the Annual Meeting was the decision that the World Bank and the IMF should present a concrete joint proposal at the Spring Meetings in April 1996.

After consultations with NGOs from both North and South during its Annual General Meeting and at EURODAD's annual consultation in November 1995, EURODAD prepared a position paper reflecting their views and which could be used for lobbying purposes.[14] The main points were similar to the ones already mentioned.

A new analysis and the first joint proposals

In early 1996, the World Bank and the IMF presented three new papers.[15] The first defined debt sustainability and evaluated several studies on the link between debt and economic performance. The key criteria to assess debt sustainability were firstly, a net present value of debt-to-export ratio of between 200 and 250 per cent; and secondly, a debt-service-to-export ratio of between 20 and 25 per cent. Certain risk factors or vulnerability indicators would also be taken into account. The second paper detailed a debt sustainability analysis of 23 countries. On the basis of country studies and preliminary analysis of a further 16 countries, the paper concluded that eight countries would have an unsustainable debt level, 12 would be 'possibly stressed', and 19 would have a sustainable debt level within five years. This analysis was not restricted to multilateral debt, but aimed to determine whether the overall debt situation was unbearable. The third paper entailed a proposal to deal with the debt problem.

While EURODAD and other NGOs welcomed this first effort of the Bank and the Fund to present a thorough analysis of the (multilateral) debt problem, it was felt that it exhibited some major shortcomings and that the IFIs had underestimated the debt problem for the following reasons:

1 The threshold ranges were arbitrary. Moreover, the use of net present value of debt was questionable, given that investors look at nominal value. The discount rate to determine the NPV was also probably too high. In addition, it was future rather than present debt sustainability that was calculated.
2 Debt sustainability should be based on a broader range of criteria. It should be linked to the budget, and in particular to expenditures on social development. Also, as many HIPCs have large trade deficits, it would make more sense to link debt sustainability to net exports

(exports minus necessary imports). Moreover, the amount of arrears should be taken into account. Finally, fiscal indicators should be measured adequately.

3 The margins used in the calculations of the risk factors were too small; and several risk factors were not included, such as political instability, external shocks, the effect of the debt overhang, and adverse climatic changes.

4 Three countries excluded from the analysis (Liberia, Somalia, and Nicaragua) have unsustainable debt burdens.

5 The assumptions regarding export growth and new aid inflows, as well as the assumed sharp rise in private investments, were too optimistic.

Drawing on Matthew Martin's analysis,[16] EURODAD argued that at least 32 countries would face a debt problem if a broader range of more realistic debt indicators was taken. In addition, it stressed its preference for debt-reduction (as opposed to re-financing) as well as the need for a comprehensive approach to the whole problem. Finally, it urged the IFIs to delink debt reduction from current structural adjustment programmes. Many NGOs adopted EURODAD's criticism.

The third joint paper was sent to the Boards of the Bank and the Fund in early March 1996. This entailed a proposal to deal with the debt problem of HIPCs: the HIPC Initiative. The proposed mechanism for multilateral debt relief — the Multilateral Debt Trust Fund — was rather similar to the Multilateral Debt Facility, but far fewer countries would be eligible to use it.

This HIPC Initiative was divided into two phases of three years each, during which the country would implement a World Bank/IMF-supported adjustment programme. The first phase was based on existing debt-reduction mechanisms. Paris Club creditors, and other bilateral and commercial creditors, would grant up to 67 per cent debt-service relief during the first phase. At the end of the period, at the so-called decision point, they would give up to 67 per cent debt stock relief, if this would lead to a sustainable debt level. If not, the country could apply for the second phase, during which the reduction by bilateral and commercial creditors would be increased to 90 per cent. If debt stock reductions by bilateral and commercial creditors at the end of the second phase, at the so-called completion point, were not sufficient for the country to reach a sustainable debt level, then multilateral creditors should finally provide debt relief. A Trust Fund would be created to pre-pay a portion of the multilateral debts of these countries.

In a letter accompanying the joint paper, James Wolfensohn mentioned the possibility of using World Bank net income and surplus as possible sources to co-finance the Trust Fund, to which the IMF would not contribute directly — though it was suggested that it might do so through its ESAF.

In a letter to James Wolfensohn of the Bank and Michel Camdessus of the IMF, as well as to the respective Executive Directors, EURODAD responded to the proposed HIPC Initiative. It agreed with the need for a concerted and comprehensive approach, and with the need for a broad and equitable participation of all creditors, in order to achieve debt sustainability. But it was felt that the effectiveness of the proposal was restricted, for several reasons. First, the debt problem was underestimated and the timeframe of three-plus three years too long. Second, while action by the Paris Club and other bilateral and commercial creditors was a condition for multilateral debt relief, the amount of debt eligible for relief under Paris Club rules was too limited. Third, debt stock relief was not mentioned as an option. Fourth, the IMF would not be contributing to the Trust Fund. And finally, debt relief was linked to failing structural adjustment programmes.

However, NGOs disagreed among themselves on the continuation of the ESAF. Some believed that it should be abandoned, and others that it should be continued, though the adjustment programmes should be changed. At a NGO meeting in March 1996, consensus was reached on the following:

1 that the IMF option of extending the ESAF would not contribute to debt relief;
2 that the IMF should have no say in the Trust Fund if it did not contribute to it;
3 that governments should not contribute to the ESAF if the IMF was not contributing to debt relief; and
4 that gold sales should be used for debt relief, not for the ESAF.

At the IFIs' Spring Meetings, the framework for dealing with the debt problem was accepted. A major disappointment was the position of the IMF since it agreed to contribute to the Initiative only through a continuation of the ESAF. There was a discussion within the IMF on the possibility of softening the ESAF by extending the maturities, though EURODAD pointed out that this would hardly contribute to debt relief: re-financing old loans with new, softer loans would reduce the net present value, but would not solve the problem of a debt overhang. This re-financing strategy had proven unsuccessful in the past. EURODAD felt that the IMF had (ab)used the debate on multilateral debt relief to gather support for its permanent ESAF, as a way to remain involved in this group of developing countries. EURODAD and other NGOs suggested that the IMF should sell part of its gold stock to co-finance the Trust Fund.

Before their June 1996 Summit in Lyon, EURODAD urged G7 governments to endorse the Initiative, and to agree to topping up the Naples Terms to 90 per cent as well as broadening the amount of debt eligible for bilateral debt reduction.[17] The outcome of the Summit was rather disappointing. The G7 countries did not agree on an extension of the Naples Terms, but merely urged the Paris Club creditor countries to go beyond these where they deemed it appropriate to do so, on a case by case basis. This implied that the G7 had abandoned the consensus approach, enabling individual creditors to go beyond the agreed terms on their own. It proved how inappropriate and inadequate common action had become in the context of the Paris Club. The G7 endorsed the continuation of the ESAF and possibly a more concessional version of this as the IMF's contribution. The idea of reaching a consensus on gold sales was abandoned. To avoid an open conflict, the G7 stated that 'we will examine ... the options for financing the needed subsidies, using primarily resources held by the IMF'. It was also stated that the IMF should 'optimise its reserve management', which was in fact a reference to gold sales.

Small improvements

After the Spring Meetings in April 1996, the joint Bank/IMF proposal was further refined, and improvements made that met some of the concerns raised by EURODAD and other NGOs.[18]

The IMF's most likely contribution to the initiative would be a combination of escrowed (softer) ESAF loans and grants. The IMF staff preferred the grant option, because it was cheaper and would not increase the debt (while the loan option would increase the face value of the debt). The contribution to the Initiative and the continuation of the ESAF were to be financed by bilateral contributions and, if necessary, up to five per cent of the IMF's gold stock. (Essentially, the gold would be sold, the proceeds invested, and the profits on the investments used for the ESAF.) Remarkably, the IMF now admitted that new loans *would* increase the debt stock.

The IMF proposal to issue grants instead of loans was an improvement. Nevertheless, a direct contribution to the Trust Fund would have been better, since this could be used for stock reduction, not only to service relief. In addition, a separate mechanism for the IMF was inconsistent with the idea of a concerted approach. It was also possible that the IMF and the World Bank would have to contribute beyond their exact share, as some multilateral creditors, such as the African Development Bank, would not have sufficient resources to contribute. And finally, the proposed grants would still be directly linked to adjustment programmes.

The World Bank was prepared to undertake action during the second phase by providing supplemental IDA allocations and IDA grants, and committed itself to contributing US$500 million surplus income up to a total of US$2 billion for a period of four years. At the same time it expected that for the next five years annual allocations of its net income of between US$200 million and US$250 million would be needed. The Bank expected that other multilateral banks and bilateral donors would also contribute.

These proposals met some of EURODAD's concerns. Debtor countries would be involved in assessing financing needs; and the possibility of debt-stock relief (as opposed to debt-service relief) was mentioned. Remarkably, the IMF had mentioned grants as an option, as well as gold sales as a way to finance the ESAF. However, several of the concerns raised by EURODAD and other NGOs remained unanswered, such as the limited contribution of the IMF, the under-estimation of the debt problem, the long timeframe, and the conditionality involved.

The total costs of the Initiative were estimated at US$5.6 billion in net present value (excluding Liberia, Somalia, and Sudan), of which the multilaterals would pay US$2 billion. If bilateral and commercial creditors were to provide 80 per cent instead of 90 per cent debt relief, the costs for multilaterals would increase to US$3.2 billion. Eighteen countries would have sustainable debt burdens, and only 10 were expected to need multilateral debt relief.[19]

In August 1996, the IMF and the World Bank presented new details of the HIPC Initiative, which included the following improvements:

- Participation of the debtor country in the analysis was adopted.
- Vulnerability indicators were explicitly included in determining the 'target debt ratio' to be achieved by the end of the programme. The burden of external debt service on the government budget was introduced as an indicator.
- Social development was mentioned as a performance criterion.

- Some flexibility regarding uneven performance under an ESAF programme was introduced: if a country risked going off track, credit might be given for implementation prior to doing so.
- If after the first phase it was unclear whether a country would have a sustainable debt level after six years, the country would have the right to choose whether to continue with the second phase or to opt for a 67 per cent stock operation of bilateral and commercial debt.

In spite of such progress, however, several of EURODAD's concerns remained unresolved. At a meeting of several NGO networks in mid-September 1996, it was agreed that the HIPC Initiative had the potential to provide a comprehensive exit strategy towards debt sustainability. However, its flaws meant that it could only be seen as a first step. The following five points were brought to the attention of IFI policy-makers and government officials in the weeks before the Annual Meetings of the Bank and the Fund:

1 The proposal offered too little, too late, due to strict eligibility criteria and the long timeframe.
2 Multilateral as well as bilateral creditors should respect the principle of burden-sharing. The Bank and the Fund should not expect the Paris Club to go beyond present debt-relief measures if they were not prepared to take responsibility for their share.
3 The IMF should contribute to the multilateral debt Trust Fund from its own resources.
4 The Paris Club should commit itself to deferring early cut-off dates, cancelling all ODA debt, and increasing debt reduction to 90 per cent.
5 Structural adjustment programmes should not remain the key condition for debt relief.

At the 1996 Annual Meetings, the IFIs endorsed the initiative with no major changes, except that the Bank seemed to be prepared to be more flexible on the timeframe. The Paris Club agreed to an 80 per cent reduction of eligible Paris Club debt, on a case by case basis — less than the 90 per cent asked for by the World Bank and the IMF. But, as EURODAD pointed out, the actual effect of 67, 80, or 90 per cent debt reduction under Paris Club rules is much smaller than the percentages suggest, because of the early cut-off dates and because of the exclusion of ODA debt by large creditors such as the USA and Japan. The World Bank had calculated that for the 13 countries that would probably go to the second phase, an 80-90 per cent reduction under Paris Club rules would lead to an actual reduction of Paris Club debt of only 16.7 per cent and 24.7 per cent respectively.

NGOs had different opinions on the Initiative. Some, including EURODAD and most of its members, welcomed the framework, stressing that, in relation to the position of the Bank and the Fund two years before, much progress had been made. However, even these NGOs expressed concerns regarding the implementation of the Initiative (in particular by the IMF and the Paris Club) and criticised three major issues. First, the limited effect of Naples Terms, due to the exclusion of a large extent of Paris Club debt from treatment. Second, the fact that the IMF's contribution was insufficient, and depended too much on bilateral contributions rather than its own resources. And third, that the timeframe was still too long.

Other NGOs saw the Initiative as a means to continue imposing structural adjustment programmes on developing countries and so essentially rejected it. In particular, they criticised the IMF for abdicating responsibility for its own role in the debt crisis, stating that the ESAF should be discontinued.

EURODAD believes that these two NGO positions are less contradictory than might seem at first sight. Both imply serious doubts about the effect of ESAF programmes. Both criticise the contribution of the IMF and the Paris Club. The main difference is that EURODAD believes that the fight for changing adjustment should not take place at the expense of a debt framework which has many good elements. Moreover, once a sustainable debt level has been reached, debtor countries will be less dependent upon conditionalities from the IMF and related agencies for accessing foreign assistance to finance sustainable development and growth.

EURODAD has set itself two main tasks for the near future. First, it is necessary to keep pushing for improvements in the general framework, in particular regarding the three points mentioned above. Second, the implementation of the Initiative must be closely monitored. For this purpose, EURODAD and partner NGOs have agreed to set up a network to exchange information on the Initiative, and to build capacity in following its implementation. This network would consist of NGOs and debt experts from the HIPC countries as well as from the North.

Conclusion

As the global multilateral debt campaign has shown, lobbying can be very effective. In this case, major changes were made possible by the hard work of a coalition of NGOs, debt experts, and some progressive governments, as well as enlightened forces within the World Bank, in particular the World Bank Task Force on multilateral debt.

EURODAD played a central role in this global campaign by 'keeping so many people informed and in helping build a global network', as an NGO colleague commented in an internal report. Although EURODAD's main tasks were information-sharing, providing strategic guidance, and building a global network, other aspects of its work were important too: in particular, lobbying at national and international levels, and press work.

The global campaign on multilateral debt can be viewed as a success. The IFIs and governments have finally acknowledged the existence of a multilateral debt problem, and have come up with a proposal to deal with it in a concerted and comprehensive way. Moreover, in the course of 1996, small changes have been introduced to the HIPC Initiative. For instance, a developing country is allowed to participate in the assessment of its debt situation; and debt-sustainability analyses are based on a broader range of criteria, including government spending on social development. However, instead of what NGOs fought for and were promised by the World Bank HIPC team — namely, to include debt repayment compared with expenditures on social development from the national budget as an indicator in the debt analysis — the IMF and World Bank staff as well as some creditor governments have put social development as an extra conditionality, and thus another performance criterion in the HIPC framework.

This and other points presented above show that the present HIPC Initiative is far from perfect. The IFIs continue to under-estimate the problem, the timeframe of the Initiative is much too long, the contribution of the IMF is too small, the Paris Club offers too little, and current structural adjustment programmes remain the key criterion for debt relief. The biggest threat to its success is that the objective of minimal debt sustainability will be sacrificed for what some major creditors believe they can afford. Nevertheless, the Initiative is a good start. The task of NGOs is to keep lobbying for improvements to remove its major flaws, and monitor its implementation, by stepping up the pressure on the major players and also by assisting Southern NGOs to build their own capacity.

Notes

1 World Bank, *Reducing the debt burden of Poor Countries. A framework for Action*, Washington: World Bank, September 1994: 48.

2 World Bank Task Force, 'The Multilateral Debt Facility'. Unpublished paper. Washington, July 1995.

3 Forty-one countries are classified as HIPCs.

4 Throughout this article, EURODAD (European Network on Debt and Development) refers to the EURODAD Secretariat and not to the EURODAD network, which consists of NGOs in 16

European Countries. EURODAD has been working on the multilateral debt campaign with several active NGOs of the network as well as with NGOs outside it and other players, including governments in the USA, Canada, Japan, and the South.

5 To protect the credit rating of the IFIs, it is an unwritten rule that obligations to these institutions are serviced prior to other obligations. For the same reason, the IFIs have always refused to grant debt relief. Percy Mistry and others have argued that acknowledging the existence of bad debts and acting accordingly would not affect the credit rating. See, for instance, Percy Mistry (1994), *Multilateral Debt: An Emerging Crisis?* The Hague: Fondad. EURODAD believes that the IFIs should not be exempt from offering debt relief.

6 The NGO position was reflected in a letter from the global network of NGOs working on debt (the Global Debt Treaty Movement) to the G7 in Naples. This became the major guideline for NGOs working on multilateral debt.

7 World Bank/IMF, 'Multilateral Debt of the Heavily Indebted Poor Countries'. Unpublished. Washington, 6 February 1995.

8 Naples Terms are the latest terms for debt relief offered by the Paris Club, the group of bilateral creditors (mainly OECD countries). The maximum debt relief offered according to Naples Terms is a 67 per cent reduction of eligible debt stock. For details, see: *Naples Terms: Not what they appear to be.* EURODAD briefing paper, Brussels, 1995.

9 For a summary of EURODAD's comments, see: *Multilateral Debt: A Problem to be Acknowledged and Resolved.* EURODAD Briefing Paper, Brussels, March 1995.

10 World Bank/IMF, 'Issues and Developments in Multilateral Debt and Financing for the Heavily Indebted poor Countries — Further Consideration'. Unpublished paper, Washington, March 30, 1995.

11 These are the IMF's 'Right Accumulation Programme', the World Bank's 'Additional Support for Workout Programmes in Countries with Protracted Arrears', and IDA's 'Fifth Dimension'. For More information, see EURODAD World Credit Tables 1994/95.

12 See for an overview of these options EURODAD: *EURODAD World Credit Tables 1997*, Brussels, September 1996, 17-18.

13 G7: 'G7 Background Document to the Economic Communiqué'. Unpublished paper, June 1995.

14 EURODAD: 'Multilateral Debt and a Multilateral Debt Facility. Comments and Recommendations'. Brussels, 22 December 1995.

15 These were: World Bank, 'Analytical Aspects of the Debt Problems of Heavily Indebted Poor Countries', unpublished, January 1996; World Bank/IMF, 'Debt Sustainability Analysis for the Heavily Indebted Poor Countries', unpublished, 31 January 1996; World Bank/IMF, 'Proposed Action to Resolve the Debt Problems of Heavily Indebted Poor Countries', unpublished, March 6, 1996.

16 Matthew Martin, 'A Multilateral Debt Facility. Global or National'. Paper prepared for the G24, March 1996.

17 This could be done by including all debt generated from loans after a debtor government's first appearance at the Paris Club — the so-called 'cut-off date', which thus far is not eligible for debt relief.

18 See: IMF, 'ESAF Financing Modalities. Further Consideration', unpublished paper, 15 May 1996; World Bank, 'Status Report on World Bank Participation in the HIPC Initiative' , unpublished paper, 4 June 1996; IMF, 'Financing a continuation of ESAF and the Fund's participation in the HIPC Initiative', unpublished paper, 23 August 1996; World Bank: *World Bank Participation in the HIPC Debt Initiative*, 26 August 1996.

19 Four of the 41 HIPCs — Liberia, Somalia, Sudan, and Nigeria — were excluded from the analysis. The 19 remaining countries were potential candidates. For six of them, 67 per cent bilateral and commercial debt stock relief would be sufficient, while 13 countries would need to go to the second phase. For three of them, bilateral and commercial debt relief would be sufficient, while the remaining ten countries would also need multilateral debt relief.

■ **Ted van Hees** *is co-ordinator of EURODAD, where* **Sasja Bökkerink**, *who is now an independent consultant, worked on the multilateral debt campaign during 1995-96. This paper was first published in* Development in Practice, *Volume 8 Number 3, in 1998.*

A new age of social movements: a fifth generation of non-governmental development organisations in the making?

Ignacio de Senillosa

Introduction

It is easier to write about what to do than to do it. Writing does not require courage, but courage can be needed for action ... [and action] involves conflicts of interest where the weak are dominated, exploited and cheated by the powerful ... There are times for confrontation and big reversal: there are critical periods when small pushes can move major decisions, resources or systems one way or another: but most common are the times for patient work on small things. (Chambers, 1983: 193 and 216)

What we have in common with the situation in the developing countries is that in both cases the interests of the majority are disregarded ... while the interests of a minority are strongly promoted ... The political roots and mechanisms of such parallel situations, where a minority manages to make its interests prevail over those of a majority, show close similarities between the developing and industrial countries. (Singer, 1988: 2-3)

How can NGOs remain independent and radical in their approaches and avoid being 'sucked into the system'? (Harris, in Poulton and Harris (eds), 1988:5)

Non-governmental development organisations (NGDOs) have now peaked in their reputation as credible channels for 'delivering social development' to the most needy, and as agents who can mobilise ordinary people around challenging the forces that are blocking the fight against the poverty to which large sectors of the world's population are condemned to live. Despite many critical — and perhaps more balanced — studies on the practical effectiveness of NGDOs (and particularly Northern agencies), their supposed capacity to act as social and educational catalysts of public opinion remains almost unchallenged: it is simply assumed that they have the potential to propose a new paradigm in North–South relations. Hence, it is important to pull together our accumulated knowledge as well as subjecting this area of work to systematic evaluation.

Such evaluation is even more vital in a period of economic crisis and budget cuts such as we are now facing, when an implicit 'pact of silence' could be forged between bilateral and multilateral donors and NGDOs —- a mutually beneficial pact in which NGDOs are so keen to maintain their reputation that even the better ones risk becoming complacent and even co-opted by the very system they currently criticise. Indeed, some NGDOs have already flown so close to the neo-liberal sun that they have melted the wings of their utopian aspirations. Others are constrained by forms of sectarian, partisan or religious exclusion; or simply by wanting to defend their *modus vivendi*. However, many NGDOs — North and South — have fully integrated into what, following Korten (1990), we shall call the Fourth Generation, and are maturing and co-operating with each other to create a Fifth. These NGDOs are in a prime position to collaborate with social movements or grassroots organisations, and work with them for the structural transformation of society both locally and nationally. 'Think local and global, and act local and global' is the motto of NGDOs that are seeking to promote a more equitable society and sustainable environment.

Framework for NGDOs

Worldwide, there has been growing participation of civil society in public life, particularly in the last 30 years. We can identify four basic reasons for this phenomenon. Firstly, the disenchantment with and mistrust of officialdom. Secondly, a greater awareness of certain problems that have both a local and a global dimension — principally the increase in poverty and environmental degradation. Thirdly, the rapid globalisation of the world economy in the last two decades, as a consequence of deregulation and privatisation policies. And lastly, largely due to the spread of neo-liberalism, declining living standards among large sectors of the North —

a situation that lends itself to unsupportive or even racist attitudes towards the South, and a denial of the shared causes linking *their* poverty with *ours*.

Further, the ideological orientation of civil participation is as diverse as the many kinds of groups, their objectives, and the ways in which they organise and plan their activities. These range from local mutual assistance initiatives — with the potential to act as the instruments of democratisation, as much in the South as in the North and the East — to the mass mobilisations seen, for instance, in the 1995 public demonstrations against the French government's economic programme; the spontaneous eruptions of social violence in reaction to deteriorating living conditions, such as happened in Los Angeles in 1991; the 1989 'Caracazo' in Venezuela, the 1985 riots in Khartoum, or the 1984 Tunisian 'Bread Revolt'; various emancipatory or organised pressure groups (environmental, pacifist, and feminist, among others); and associations for social change of all kinds, including NGDOs.

Within the NGDO sector, we shall refer especially to those organisations that are tied to social movements, and which:

- influence private and public decision-making that affects them directly, or affects third parties whose interests they defend (by delegation);
- rely on a wide social base;
- claim to hold alternative ideologies or values;
- do advocacy and lobbying on behalf of people or communities whose human rights are infringed by the despotic exercise of economic and political power, both locally and internationally.

For instance, various ecological, pacifist, human-rights, ethnic-minority, feminist, and international solidarity organisations belong to this kind of 'anti-system movement' (Wallerstein, 1984). In some cases, they can be defined as New Social Movements (NSMs), sharing many obvious similarities with the trade-union movement of the nineteenth-century industrial revolution.

However, for organisations that are involved in the social field, the welfare and rights-based campaigning aspects of their work often go on simultaneously, and there are frequently ideological and institutional tensions in trying to harmonise these. This tension is particularly prevalent among NGDOs, an unfortunately imprecise term (perhaps 'International Solidarity Organisations' — ISOs — as used in Francophone areas, would be a better alternative?).

NGDOs: diversity, expansion, North–South co-operation

NGDOs are like a kaleidoscope of national, regional and international institutions of development co-operation (we use the term 'development' with all its conceptual ambiguity, assuming that readers will sense what we mean). The OECD calculated in 1988 that there were between two and three times as many NGDOs and similar organisations in the South as in the North (8-12,000 and 4,000 respectively). A major expansion occurred in the 1960s in the North, while in the South it took place in the 1970s, especially in countries like Peru and Mexico, India and Bangladesh, Senegal and Burkina Faso. These Southern NGDOs collaborate in turn with local groups.

By 1994, the number of local NGOs in the South had grown to 50,000. Unlike the earlier OECD calculation, this figure includes small NGDOs, but gives hardly an idea of the actual number of grassroots organisations. For instance, UNDP claims that there are 18,000 NGOs registered in the Philippines, while in the single Indian state of Tamil Nadu there are 25,000, two-thirds of which could be described as grassroots organisations (UNDP, 1993).

An interesting phenomenon is the proliferation of different kinds of networks: national and regional — for example, the NGDO Co-ordinating Committee in Spain, the 'Conseil des ONG d'Appui au Développement' (CONGAD) in Senegal, or the Asian NGO Coalition (ANGOC); North–North umbrella groups, such as CIDSE, EURODAD, or EUROSTEP; North–South umbrella groups, like IRED or ICVA; and South–South umbrella groups such as the Latin American Forum for Debt and Development, or Third World Network, which has offices in Malaysia, Uruguay, and Senegal.

As to what constitutes a desirable relationship between Northern and Southern NGDOs in terms of co-operation — an issue not covered here — we believe that the principal objective continues to be that Northern agencies should seek to withdraw from the scene, leaving the field entirely to the indigenous agencies (Gill ,1988: 172). The most important role for northern NGDOs is in their own countries. This withdrawal from the scene implies a process of decentralisation both in financial matters and in decision-making on the part of the Northern NGDO, but without losing direct contact with the situation on the ground, or with the analysis and campaigning activities of Southern people, their organisations and grassroots movements.

A point worth emphasising is that many NGDOs worldwide are companions in a continual learning and evolutionary process, whose two chief goals are, on the one hand, to give power and voice to those who are socially, economically, and culturally oppressed; and, on the other, to create a new model of relationships between the peoples of the North and the South.

Northern NGDOs

Schematically, we can define organisations of international co-operation which act in and from the North as non-profit organisations that are economically independent of official funding, have strong popular support, and emerge from private efforts to improve the living conditions of the poorest groups in the South and increase their social and political participation; while, at the same time, raising the awareness of their fellow citizens about the causes and nature of their (and increasingly our) impoverishment, and challenging those public and private authorities whose decisions are standing in the way of establishing a global society in which human rights are respected.

Of course, even if most NGDOs are politically non-partisan, none, irrespective of their ideological persuasion, can avoid the fact that development co-operation is itself unequivocally political and that it demands 'putting oneself on the side of' some, or even 'against' third parties, as Chambers puts it.

However, it is worrying to see the emergence of two strictly limited types of NGDO in recent years:

- those tied to fundamentalist groups or sects based on fundraising, proselytising, or gaining political influence. These have been active in Latin America since the mid-1970s through the infiltration of evangelical churches and ultra-conservative US-funded NGOs that served to demobilise the popular sectors;
- those which appear to be non-profit solidarity organisations, but in reality are profit-seeking.

As regards their funding, Northern NGDOs have seen their private funds quadruple in real terms between 1975 and 1993, rising from US$1.3 to US$5.7 billion (DAC/OECD, 1996). This now represents 9.2 per cent of total aid, that is official development aid plus private donations to NGDOs. According to the latest available data (1987), these donations are concentrated in the USA and Germany, which together represent 66 per cent of the total. However, if we take the estimates of the Development Aid Committee (DAC) of the OECD, while there are notable differences between countries, the total amount raised by NGDOs from their fellow citizens has practically stagnated in the last four years.

The same is not true of the amounts received from public sources, since despite representing only 14 per cent of the total funds channelled through NGDOs in 1993, these amounts increased 30-fold between 1983/84 and 1993, reaching US$956 million. Lastly, while no firm figures are available, direct bilateral funding to Southern NGDOs is increasingly significant.

Northern NGDOs: generations and areas of work

Generations of NGDOs

Largely inspired by Korten's classification, we can speak of four generations of Northern NGDOs (also applicable to an extent to those in the South) according to their overall orientation (Korten, 1990) (see Table 1).

- **First generation:** *welfarist* and characterised by emergency activities that began around 1945, the year in which the Nuclear Era began (with the bombing of Hiroshima and Nagasaki), the Second World War ended, and the United Nations was created; one year before the signing of the Bretton Woods Agreements from which the World Bank for Reconstruction and Development was born, and whose most important institutions are the World Bank, the International Monetary Fund (IMF),and the General Agreement on Tariffs and Trade (GATT).

- **Second generation** — *developmental*, in that they promote local development in the South and raise public awareness in the North, taking 1960 — the year in which 17 African countries gained their independence — as their starting point: the beginning of the neo-colonial dependency era.

- **Third generation:** based on *partnership* with the South and protest in the North, and for which 1973 can be taken as their starting point, the year in which the non-aligned countries proclaimed a New International Economic Order (NIEO) and which, paradoxically, thanks to higher petrol prices, which gave rise to the abundance of petro-dollars, began the period of Southern indebtedness that resulted in the so-called debt crisis of 1982 when Mexico claimed that it could no longer service its foreign debt.

Table 1: Generations of Northern Non-Governmental Organisations (NGDOs)

Orientation in North (N) and South (S)	First Welfarist (S)	Second Local development (S) Awareness-raising (N)	Third Partnership (S) and Critique (N)	Fourth Empowerment (S) and Political pressure (N)
Year of reference	1945	1960	1973	1982
Dominant mind-set	Emergency assistance, eg Catholic Relief Services (CRS), Save the Children (UK), BRAC (Bangladesh)	Development (North as development model; belief in 'trickle-down' effect)	Development as self-reliant political process (New International Economic Order seen to be possible)	Development must be socially equitable, and ecologically sustainable at local and global level. Gender analysis and empowerment of excluded groups.
Definition of the problem	Lack of goods and services	Lack of economic and technological resources. Basic needs not met. Under-development and neo-colonialism.	Institutional limitations, as well as local, national, and international policies. Role of local elites and transnational economic groups.	Local, national, and international limitations. Non-development in South, mal-development in North. Poverty as denial of basic human rights.
Timeframe for action	Immediate	As long as the project continues	Indefinite, long-term	Indefinite future
Scope	Individual or household	Community or people	Regional or national	National or global
Main actor	NGO donor	NGDOs in North and South, base/grassroots groups and beneficiary communities	All public and private institutions comprising the relevant system	Formal and informal networks of people and organisations at local and international level
Relations with NGDOs in North and South	—	Transfer of economic and other resources	Northern NGDOs: from funding to partnership	Concerted action and mutual support; decentralisation
Development education	Starving babies	Community self-help initiatives	Polities and institutions that impede local self-reliant development	Planetary community. Social, economic, political, and ecological inter-dependence.
Political strategy	—	Awareness-raising among general public about living conditions in the South. Emerging conflict between this and fundraising capacity.	Protest phase, directed at the interests and organisations that prevent the alleviation of poverty in the South. Denunciation of hunger and unequal terms of trade; lobbying for 0.7% of GNP for development aid.	Protest plus proposal phase. Denunciation and action: political pressure, public mobilisation, strategic alliances, growing use of social and telecommunications; encouragement for research.

Source: based on Korten (1990:117). The original version has been significantly modified and expanded.

- **Fourth generation** — based on *empowerment* in the South and *lobbying* in the North, and emerging from 1982. Obviously, this overlaps with the previous generations and shares many of their characteristics. It is formed by those NGDOs who, without abandoning their close co-operation with their Southern counterparts, prioritise the lobbying of opinion-makers and powerful groups as well as research and public awareness-raising in their own countries.

While 'generation' is a useful concept, it does have its limitations: the overlapping of different generations, the co-existence in many NGDOs of characteristics that fit into more than one generation, the marked differences in how these have evolved in different countries, and so on. But the term nevertheless implies evolution and adaptation to the socio-economic context, and assumes that certain central decisions will be taken in order to meet a given organisation's central objectives.

The change processes of established NGDOs and the emergence of new players likewise assume increasing diversity within the sector, and the growing specialisation of its members as well as ideological diversity among them. While the first generation is no worse than the fourth — it is vital to work for people's survival in situations of real need — we believe that certain characteristics and objectives of the latter make them better able to:

- contribute to bringing about structural economic and political changes in favour of those who are marginalised and impoverished throughout the world, in the belief that, as Jon Sobrino SJ argues, they frequently offer 'community against individualism, service against selfishness, simplicity against opulence', and can learn from their own efforts and others' 'struggles for freedom' (Sobrino, 1992:32); and
- contribute to bringing about structural economic and political changes in favour of the environment to which we are inextricably linked, in that 'everything that happens to the earth will happen to the earth's children' (letter to Ulysses Grant from Chief Seattle of the Dwasmish and Suquamish Tribes in 1855).

Areas of activity

Northern NGDOs include very diverse organisations involved in one or more of the following activities: technical advice (appropriate technology, livestock techniques, management and administration models); the sending of volunteer co-operants; the funding of development programmes; development education, (including publications and activities aimed at the general public, teachers, and a range of educational levels); fair-trade issues; and research and lobbying.

While there are some 4,000 NGDOs in the 20 member countries of the DAC (which handle more than 95 per cent of official development assistance), a small number account for most of the sector's activities, including public and private fund-raising. Certainly, if an NGDO wants to work without external impositions or conditions, it needs the kind of economic independence that comes from private funding. But the OECD has found that 90 per cent of the available resources are concentrated in only 20 per cent of the NGDOs registered. This is not to deny the important role played by smaller organisations, in terms of their critical input and their capacity to complement the vision of the larger NGDOs.

In terms of development education, a 1990 OECD survey of 2,542 major Northern NGOs showed that, while 75 per cent ran development education programmes, only a small proportion of these involved activities that went beyond, for example, publishing materials or organising conferences. Development education continues to be a pending item on the agenda of many NGDOs which have the means to promote it, but choose to focus instead on their overseas assistance programmes, even at the expense of making an impact in their own societies.

Julius Nyerere, the former president of Tanzania, replied to a question put to him 30 years ago by Leslie Kirkley, the Director of Oxfam, on how best this organisation might help Tanzania. His advice is still valid: 'Take each and every penny that you have planned for Tanzania and spend it in the United Kingdom explaining to your co-citizens the nature and causes of poverty' (Harris, in Harris and Poulton (eds) 1988:7). Similarly, Southern NGDOs and more progressive networks constantly request that their Northern counterparts re-direct their activities in order to give more importance to defending the interests of Southern people, and especially to influencing the business, financial, and development-aid policies of their governments, their transnational companies, and the multilateral institutions that are having such an adverse effect on people's well-being and their chances of social and political progress.

Southern NGDOs have therefore called on their Northern counterparts to intervene decisively in awareness-raising, protest, and lobbying activities. Two key declarations in this regard are the June 1989 Manila Declaration on People's Participation and Sustainable Development, prepared by 31 Southern NGDO directors; and the so-called 1990 Arusha

Declaration — the African Charter for Popular Participation in Development and Transformation — proposed by a large group of NGDOs and African grassroots organisations (though representatives of Northern NGDOs, governments, and multilateral organisations also attended).

Clearly, the leading NGDOs do have enormous value. Their three main activities are mutually reinforcing: the transfer of resources (funds, goods, and services), public awareness-raising, and political campaigning. The last two may be specific — such as lobbying around the final phase of the UN inter-governmental conferences, GATT negotiations, or Lomé Agreements); or more general and sustained — for instance, working on foreign debt, official development aid, gender policies, or follow-up on inter-governmental agreements. The synergistic nature of activities carried out 'here' in the North and 'there' in the South is possible because:

- collaboration with Southern NGDO allies provides their Northern counterparts with first-hand information and analysis of the political, economic, cultural, and social situation in those countries;
- awareness-raising activities both draw on and adapt this flow of information (opinions, concerns, struggles, readings of the international situation) and make it accessible to their various target groups; and
- lobbying activities based on seeing the repercussions of decisions taken in the North on the people who live in the South demand an attitude of solidarity, and condemnation of the stubborn defence of the privileges enjoyed by Northern interest groups. And while Northern NGDOs are putting pressure on their governments to spend their aid budgets effectively (through, for instance, the work done since 1972 to reach the UN target of aid allocations equivalent to 0.7 per cent of GNP), Southern NGDOs should be enabled to demand from their own governments that this aid be used to benefit those most in need.

Lobbying also presents NGDOs with a great opportunity to keep faith with their central objectives. The major UN conferences and inter-governmental 'Summits', especially since UNCED in 1992, have been forums in which, despite the lukewarm commitments of their governments, many NGDOs have learned how to develop lobbying strategies by establishing contacts and forming networks to promote mutual concerns. Between 4,000 and 20,000 NGO delegates have participated in the alternative forums held alongside each of these conferences, while some 2,000 to 4,000 have attended the official events.

In the 1970s and 1980s (and even before), the emergence of Northern NGDOs that specialised in lobbying campaigns (such as World Development Movement in the UK, Bread for the World in the USA, Agir Ici in France, or the Berne Declaration in Switzerland) represented a milestone. Notable achievements included the 1979 campaign started by 150 NGOs worldwide as part of the International Baby Food Action Network (IBFAN), which gained UN approval for a Code of Conduct prohibiting the immoral promotion of breastmilk-substitutes by transnational companies such as Nestlé.

At present, in the North as in the South, there is enough accumulated campaigning experience to make it possible to speak about an embryonic lobbying movement that, through concrete and well-planned actions, and thanks to the ideological synergy, complementarity, and like-mindedness of the major NGOs, is itself generating an alternative globalisation process. With or without the backing of Northern NGOs, there is for instance a remarkable Southern movement opposing the construction of 30 large dams (besides 135 of medium size and 3,000 small ones) in the sacred Narmada river valley in India, just as the felling of the Sarawak forest is opposed by the movement of the Penan indians who live there.

But despite all this, there is no call for complacency. There is a long path to tread before we reach the hypothetical alternative globalisation to which we referred above. As we have been warned: 'If [the ineffectual public bodies] make ordinary citizens giddy by sending them from one counter to another, [they also] make the NGDOs waste time by calling them to endless meetings', without making any real progress (Vázquez, 1996). Undoubtedly, the same warning is relevant to other organisations with which the NGDOs must engage within their respective spheres of influence.

Northern NGDOs on the threshold of the twenty-first century

The world (dis)order in which we are immersed is characterised by dependency relationships between the periphery (or peripheries) and the centre (or centres) at both a global and local level, peripheries that have been extended by the populations of Eastern Europe. This situation has allowed increasing wealth, resources, and political power to accumulate in the hands of the few, while the system is kept relatively stable, thanks to patronage, the use of commercial or financial pressure or, quite simply, repression or military force (as in the case of the 1991 Gulf War). Even if we all do so to an extent, those who benefit most from the system ensure that they have the necessary means to maintain this unequal division of power at the local, regional, national, and international levels.

In the context of the processes of economic globalisation, two worrying elements stand out: firstly, the absence of opposing models for social progress and participatory, equitable, and environmentally sustainable economic development (though these have been outlined on a small scale and there is a major body of accumulated historical wisdom now concealed by obsolete modernisation models); and secondly, the lack of genuinely representative international institutions in a world in which the nation state appears to play an increasingly insignificant role, especially in order to defend the most vulnerable sectors. This neglect by the public authorities is only countered and moderated by strengthening the New Social Movements mentioned earlier, and by the growing organisation and participation of poor communities in creating a more equitable economic and social order at the local level.

Within such a context, and given all their accumulated experience, what role can those NGDOs play that have reached, or largely taken on board, the Fourth Generation? What might a Fifth Generation look like?

Twelve steps towards the future

As they evolve, Northern NGDOs must become more sensitive and critical of their role in mediating between poor communities in the South and their own fellow citizens and governments. And they must also abandon their old function as mere financial intermediaries by trying to incorporate the maximum *added value* that would justify playing this role. At present some NGDOs, albeit a minority, are simply a *modus vivendi* for their staff, in an ever more precarious job market. The challenge is for Northern NGDOs to transform themselves into reliable 'transmission belts' for the perceptions, concerns, and struggles of the South, while also assuming their role as funders of 'added value' via development education, awareness-raising, and lobbying — all with the objective of democratising and transforming the structures of their own societies and, as equal partners with Southern NGDOs, global society itself.

Among the foreseeable changes and risks that are entailed in steering a course between pragmatism (the best possible option) and utopia (the most desirable option), Northern NGDOs should bear in mind the twelve following courses of action — directions that also apply to some extent to Southern NGOs, as to those of Eastern Europe as these become stronger:

1 The decrease in private funding in absolute terms, and certainly relative to public funding (especially assistance which is destined for humanitarian and emergency aid), will make it imperative that NGDOs should be doubly aware of the risk of being co-opted or manipulated by the public authorities.

2 Those NGDOs that depend largely on public finance run the risk of becoming mere government subsidiaries or substitutes, by implementing activities formerly carried out by their own governments or multilateral institutions.

3 Fundraising campaigns will have to be scrupulous in their image codes, resisting the temptation to be sensationalist, even more so when some NGDOs still have no qualms about using what has been described as 'the artery that connects the heart with the wallet' (Clark, 1991). Equally, we must not forget that 'NGOs, in contrast to profitable companies, do not work to gain a bigger slice of the "market", but to help others to grow. At the end of the day, our commitment as an NGO is to withdraw ourselves from the *business*' (Dichter, 1989).

4 There will be a restructuring of the non-governmental co-operation sector, with a drop in the number of generalist NGDOs, an increase in the number of those specialising in emergency activities, and an increase in mergers between small and medium-sized NGDOs.

5 There will be a major increase in the number of civil-action and lobbying campaigns, as well as in the number of organisations and networks involved in them. Likewise, spontaneous movements for change and social protest must be monitored, and on occasion supported — movements that will probably be on the increase in the years to come.

6 NGDOs will become more involved in poverty-eradication activities in their own societies — a step already taken by the Comité contre la Faim et pour le Développement (CCFD) in France, and Oxfam in Britain, among others, and by some Austrian, German, and Swiss NGDOs elsewhere in Europe.

7 NGDOs should not fear growth (Schumacher would have agreed that, even if 'small is beautiful', large is not necessarily ugly), but must maintain the balance between such growth and their capacity to adapt to a highly changeable economic and social environment.

8 NGDOs should dedicate a far greater proportion of their resources to activities which mobilise and raise the awareness of their fellow citizens. NGDOs involved in fair-trade activities must put more effort into making this an effective tool for development education, while offering greater economic support to producer groups and co-operatives in the South.

9 NGDOs should push, both individually and with other organisations and academic institutions, for research and analysis into all the issues related to their practical work in the context of North–South–East relations. This research is essential, if their campaigns are to achieve maximum impact.

10 NGDOs should face the challenge presented by modern telecommunications and the need to be more efficient in sharing information and ideas through meetings and other forms of exchange.

11 NGDOs should increasingly apply the principle of subsidiarity (decentralisation), so that activities that can be carried out by Southern NGDOs and grassroots organisations should not undertaken by their Northern counterparts.

12 Northern NGDOs should share their private-sector fund-raising experience with those from the South, so that the latter may reduce their dependence on external finance, including bilateral and multilateral aid (direct financing).

Finally, we should ask if it is possible, or indeed desirable, for NGO networks to become political parties; or for political parties to evolve from them, as has happened with environmental NGOs in Germany. Unlike the Greens, the parties we envisage would set themselves up in different countries, both Northern and Southern, eventually allowing for the emergence of transnational organisations which supersede present models (such as those of the International Socialist or Christian Democracy). Given that there will always be a need for some NGOs that are distanced from and critical of institutional power, and assuming that parliamentary representation will survive as a political model, will some governments even regard such a conversion of the NGO sector as necessary, given their own declining decision-making power, and the fact that they are increasingly beholden to the interests of minorities who cling to national and transnational economic power?

Northern NGOs must listen carefully to criticism and be prepared to be self-critical, since this will help them to become more effective and publicly transparent. Galand (1994) questions whether Northern NGDOs have become victims of their own success — or at least of their good public image. If so, he believes, the price would be the loss of their original protest image for one of 'consensual' organisations that are more docile in their opposition to power and more likely to conform to the lowest common denominator. Others go further, claiming that Southern NGDOs (we assume they refer especially to Quangos, quasi-NGOs, or para-statal NGDOs) that are funded by multilateral agencies and Northern

NGDOs 'have ended up playing a subordinate, if ever more important, role in putting structural adjustment into practice' (Petras and Vieux, 1995). They add that 'NGOs have had a negative impact on autonomous social movements'.

Tandon (1991) further questions the role of some African NGDOs, criticising what he considers to be their lack of transparency in decision-making and the handling of funds. He also accuses them of frequently imposing Western cultural models, of shackling the evaluation of their work by other African NGDOs, of paternalism, and of establishing dependency relationships that hark back to the colonial era. His views are shared by others who perceive Northern NGOs to be imposing an alien 'agenda' on those of the South, one that changes according to *fashions* in development — whether gender, human rights, environment, or whatever.

We believe that NGDOs are at a crossroads in their history, which calls for a serious re-think of their social function. To avoid lurching between cautious reform and violent revolution, they must strengthen those activities and objectives that will enable them to contribute to a radical reform of the system. Doing so will certainly provoke tensions and confrontations at both an inter-personal and institutional level. However, NGDOs that are committed to defending the interests of those worst affected by the present economic and political system (and to working alongside them in this) *must* denounce mechanisms and processes of oppression and social exclusion. They may also have to oppose those NGDOs that are motivated by interests which ultimately impede the eradication of poverty and the full participation of men and women in the processes of emancipation, and their efforts to create a society which arises from their own perceptions and priorities.

'Action involves conflict of interest', claims Robert Chambers, adding that 'the periods of confrontation and big reversal' are not the most frequent, but rather those 'for patient work on small things'. We should, then, blend the patience needed when we compare utopia and reality, with the impatience of radicalism, the indignation of seeing the avoidable suffering of so many men and women, and the abuse of power and arrogance of the minority.

One central idea stands out from these reflections: co-operation between Northern and Southern NGDOs should be much more than the mere transfer of appropriate knowledge, technology, and financial resources. For the ultimate goal of development is not economic growth, but the well-being of the most vulnerable, with their full participation in local and global issues that affect their lives — *empowerment*.

Secondly, development co-operation entails, among other things, the exchange — and in the long term the blending — of cultures between North and South. This still largely remains as an agenda item, but could be seen as an authentic contribution to sustainable development that Southern societies give to the North (CRIES, 1990). Such a model also implies an integrated vision of human relations, one which would facilitate the structural change and democratisation of global society on the basis of inter-cultural dialogue and solidarity-based co-operation.

We conclude with the words of Jon Sobrino SJ, a colleague and friend of the late Ignacio Ellacuria SJ (one of the six Jesuit priests assassinated by the Salvadoran Armed Forces in 1989), and a teacher at the University of Central America (UCA) in San Salvador:

> From an anthropological point of view, if solidarity were merely aid, it would be no more than a praiseworthy act of charity, in which the donor gives something of what he has, but without seeing himself as being deeply committed, or under any compulsion to maintain the aid. Seen in this way, aid would only be in one direction, from the person who gives to the one who receives. In this way, two essential elements of solidarity would be overlooked: *personal commitment*, not only material aid; *the decision to offer help in the long term*, not merely to offer immediate relief, *and the willingness to receive*, not only to give (Sobrino, 1995:293, our emphasis).

References

Arusha Declaration (1990) *Charte Africaine de la Participation Populaire au Developpement et à la Transformation.*

Chambers, R. (1983) *Rural Development: Putting the Last First*, Harlow: Longman.

Clark, J. (1991) *Democratising Development: The Role of Voluntary Organisations*, London: Earthscan.

CRIES (1990) 'Diez tesis sobre la cooperación al desarrollo: Europa y Centroamerica, *Análisis de coyuntura*, No. 2.

DAC/OECD (1996) *Development Cooperation Report 1995*, Paris: OECD.

Dichter, T. W. (1989) 'The changing world of Northern NGOs: problems, paradoxes and possibilities' in J.P. Lewis (ed.): *Strengthening the Poor: What We Have Learnt*, US Third World Policy Perspectives, No. 10, Overseas Development Council, 1989.

Galand, P. (1994) 'Fiction ou realité: Les ONG victimes de leur(s) succes ...', *Dialogue*, No. 4, July/August.

Gill, P. (1988) 'Conclusion: helping is not enough', in Poulton and Harris (eds), 1988.

Harris, M. (1988) 'On charities and NGOs', in Poulton and Harris (eds), 1988.

Korten, David C. (1990) *Getting to the 21st Century: Voluntary Action and the Global Agenda*, West Hartford: Kumarian Press.

Manila Declaration on People's Participation and Sustainable Development (1989), cited in Korten, 1990.

OECD (1990) *Directory of Non-Governmental Development Organisations in OECD Countries*, Paris: OECD.

OECD (1988) *Voluntary Aid for Development (The Role of Non-governmental Organisations)*, Paris: OECD.

Petras, J. and S. Vieux (1995) *Hagan juego!*, Barcelona: Icaria.

Poulton, R. and M. Harris (eds) (1988) *Putting People First (Voluntary Organisations and Third World Development)*, London and Basingstoke: Macmillan.

Senillosa, I. de and J. Sobrino (1992) *America: 500 anos*, Barcelona: Christianisme I Justicia.

Singer, H. W. (1988) 'Development in crisis in the North', *Development* 2/3.

Sobrino, J. (1992) 'Los pueblos crucificados' in Senillosa and Sobrino, 1992.

Sobrino, J. (1995) 'Los unos para los otros. Hacia una cultura de la solidaridad en medio de la injusticia y el desencanto', in F. Alburquerque et al (1995) *Hacer futuro en las aulas (Educación, solidaridad y desarrollo*, Barcelona: Intermón.

Tandon, Y. (1991) 'Foreign NGOs, uses and abuses: an African perspective', *ifda dossier*, No. 81, April-June.

UNDP (1993) *Informe sobre el desarrollo humano 1993*, Madrid: CIDEAL.

Vásquez, F. (1996) 'Desnonaments i marginacio', *Papers*, No. 37, Justicia i Pau, gener.

Wallerstein, I. (1984) *The Politics of World-economy*, Cambridge: Cambridge University Press.

■ **Ignacio de Senillosa** *was a medical doctor who worked for the Spanish NGDO, Intermón, from 1985 until his death in 1998, initially as Director of the Overseas Department, and then as Director of the Research Unit. This article is based on a paper delivered at the 1996 'South-North Conference: Together for the Eradication of Poverty', organised as the main event of the celebrations of the agency's fortieth anniversary. It was first published in* Development in Practice *Volume 8, number 1, in 1998*

NGOs and advocacy: how well are the poor represented?

Warren Nyamugasira

A growing number of non-government organisations (NGOs), North and South, have intensified their advocacy work in an attempt to surmount the constraints placed on their development efforts by the global powers that be — both economic and political — which they allege serve interests other than those of the poor. They have come to the sad realisation that, although they have achieved many micro-level successes, the systems and structures that determine power and resource allocations — locally, nationally, and globally — remain largely intact. Therefore, they need to find ways to 'scale up' their influence upon these determinants, so that their small-scale successes have greater and more lasting impact (Sutherns, 1996).

Until the 1980s, greater impact was thought to come about through replicating successful projects, or what Clark (1992) refers to as the 'additive' approach. However, many strategy-minded NGOs find expansion by replication too slow and resource-stretching, especially as those restricted resources are declining. They seek to move into the 'faster lane' of positive and strategic social change by influencing attitudes, policies, and practices of the decision-makers at critical levels (op. cit.). In their advocacy work, such NGOs 'have assumed the role of ambassadors for the World's poor' (op. cit., p. 195). They see part of their mission as being to represent the political concerns of the poor, injecting the voice of the traditionally voiceless into international decision-making, facilitating the two-way flow of information, and helping to make the world's political and economic institutions more broadly accountable.

However, achievements by NGOs in these areas are, at best, mixed. Some do argue that enormous successes have been won. Caldwell (1990), for example, contends that 'the growth of NGOs during the past century has changed the character of international relations, broadening their scope, multiplying the number of participants, and sometimes outflanking the formal protocols of international diplomacy'. The North–South Institute would seem to agree when it argues that the education and advocacy role of Canadian NGOs over 15 years may have been their most significant activity and contribution, having had a more lasting effect than the millions of dollars they used in programmes in the developing world in the same period (op.cit., p.7).

According to Clark (op.cit., p.197), the combined influence of NGOs and public opinion has initiated major policy changes by Northern governments on several issues, including the production of a code of conduct for the marketing of baby milk, the drafting of an international essential drugs list, concerted action on international environmental issues such as global warming and rain-forest destruction, and affording special debt-relief to the poorest countries. Edwards (1993, p.166) adds to this list, citing developments in the food régime of refugees and displaced persons, and modifications in 'structural adjustment packages' to take more account of social impact, among others. Quoting Clark, he concludes that 'if it were possible to assess the value of all such reforms, they might be worth more than the financial contributions made by NGOs'.

Edwards, however, is more circumspect, and argues that most achievements have been at the level of detailed policy and/or on issues where NGOs have not encountered strong interest-group pressures. According to him, little progress has been made at the level of ideology and global systems. Furthermore, progress on more fundamental issues, such as the conservation of the environment and the impact of structural adjustment on the poor *en bloc*, appears less impressive on closer inspection. While there have been superficial responses, the basic ideology and structures have remained largely intact. Where changes have occurred, they may have been damaging in their impact on women and children. And there is no conclusive evidence that changes have been due to NGO pressure, except in a few instances. Finally, 'NGOs have failed to build an international movement for development' (Edwards, p.167).

The new division of labour

To enhance the effectiveness of their advocacy, NGOs have evolved a new division of labour. Northern NGOs are relinquishing the more operational roles to concentrate on ideas, research, empowerment, and networking (Clark, 1992). They are increasingly focusing their efforts on development education, advocacy, and information flows, and challenging policies of their governments and of the corporations and multilateral institutions that are perceived to block, undermine, or co-opt 'genuine' development initiatives. They are leaving the 'hardware' — the time-bound, geographically fixed projects, such as building schools or health centres, or installing oil mills and so on — to their Southern counterparts. They are also assigning to these the advocacy task of addressing the forces emanating from the national or sub-national political economy. Northern NGOs prefer to concentrate on forces of an international character, such as the structure of the world trading system, financial and investment flows, energy consumption, technological innovation, and intellectual property, and the policies of multilateral and bilateral donor agencies. 'The increasing internationalization of decision-making in economic and political fields, and the limited accountability of global institutions, have increased the power of these interests' (Edwards, p.163) and made the task very urgent. Nevertheless, it should be acknowledged that most NGOs are still relatively weak on advocacy, not yet having the stature, expertise, and reputation to match their capacities to deliver material assistance.

Sutherns views the need for the new division of labour as arising from a commitment to local empowerment: '[w]hatever division of labour is considered optimal will be grounded in our fundamental values and beliefs about development ... A commitment to local empowerment will lead us to organize ourselves in such a way as to affirm that the burden of responsibility for development in the South lies with indigenous NGOs', adding the punch-line '... no matter how poorly managed or ill-experienced they may currently be. Strengthening the competencies of Southern NGOs means Northern NGOs moving away from a directly operational approach.'

The decision of Northern NGOs to relinquish the directly operational role to their Southern counterparts may be strategic, but it certainly is not altogether voluntary. Southern NGOs have for years been calling for it. They have been highly critical of Northern NGOs for being operational, and have long pushed to be given the funds and left to do the job.

Underlying this separation of roles seems to be the assumption that Southern NGOs more effectively hear and represent the authentic voices of the poor, while Northern NGOs are better able to articulate — in sufficiently sophisticated language — their concerns to Northern governments, multinational corporations, and global institutions. The law of comparative advantage is thus employed.

Southern NGOs: the authentic voice of the poor?

Southern NGOs have made many positive local-level advocacy-type contributions. As one respondent to the draft of this article wrote:

> we have ... to acknowledge the great efforts and the remarkable accomplishments of (S) NGOs, as part of civil society, over the last decade, especially when we have to consider the political and cultural constraints they had to struggle with. The role they are playing, contributing to the democratization process in Africa, the recent changes of family and customary laws (marriage, inheritance, child custody) in many countries; and their contribution to the reshaping of state vis-à-vis society relations on the continent is worth pointing out. (personal communication)

However, uncritically to equate Southern NGOs with the voice of the poor could be somewhat misleading. Another respondent — a senior staff member of an international NGO — put it thus:

> There is the danger of assuming that Southern NGOs necessarily speak for the poor and the marginal. This is a matter which is sometimes avoided out of politeness or fear of offending (S)NGO colleagues. Listening to those on the margins requires a stretch for anyone who has become part of the 'development set'. It is harder when based in the North, but even when working for an NGO in the South, there are many filters, barriers and distractions. How to genuinely listen and represent (as opposed to speaking for) different poor communities is a significant challenge for all NGOs. (personal communication)

Even for Southern NGOs, poorer people are, for a start, hard to reach. Chambers (1993, p.28) argues that:

> they are typically unorganized, inarticulate, often sick, seasonally hungry, and quite frequently dependent on local patrons. They are less educated, less in contact with communications, less likely to use government services, and less likely to visit outside their home area ... They are relatively invisible, especially the women and children ... Visitors could easily spend a week in a village without either seeing or speaking to the poorer of its inhabitants; and without ever entering one of the colonies where many of the poorest live, visitors tend to see, meet, and interact with, only the more influential and better off rural people.

We can quote the example of some villages in Kabale in south-western Uganda which the author recently visited. There, NGOs are little known. In fact, only one — World Vision, which runs the Rukiga Area Development Project — is resident and operational. NGOs are not evenly or systematically distributed in geographical terms. Rather, there are pockets of concentration and competition in some areas, but in many others NGOs are virtually absent. There are, however, a number of community-based organisations (CBOs) in Kabale as elsewhere, stretcher (*engozi*) groups, *Biika-Oguze* (savings and credit) groups, and digging groups. CBOs are working throughout Uganda (Nyamugasira, 1995) and are making substantial contributions in forging community solidarity, uplifting the human spirit, promoting togetherness, and helping to combat the feelings of helplessness that poverty can induce.

CBOs are, however, primarily a coping mechanism. They cannot encompass everybody, and often the poorest do not belong and do not voluntarily participate. CBOs are typically functional, addressing one specific need at a time. People are simply preoccupied by the struggle for survival and do not have time to think about longer-term objectives. In the area visited, there was little evidence of CBOs interacting to develop any semblance of a common advocacy strategy. Neither did the author find any systematic gathering of information for such purposes by the operational NGO. On the whole, CBOs are too small and localised to have an impact on poverty reduction, let alone on its elimination. They do not add value to what the poor already do, for example by encouraging the planting of high-value crops to maximise effort. Recent research into improved crops and better markets is simply inaccessible to them. And neither NGOs nor government bodies are effectively bringing these services to the people.

Even *in loco*, Southern NGOs can, at times, be a poor imitation of and often distort the voices of this 'silent' mass. All NGOs tend to be self-appointed, and neither consult nor give feedback to their constituencies. As Sutherns (op.cit., p.5) puts it, the people 'have no independent voice or authority over the NGOs in their midst'. In fact, NGOs rarely have constituencies which have mandated them as their advocates. Rather, NGOs have often created their own abstract constituencies; are socialised in the value systems and thought patterns of the global élite; and project their own construct of the issues purported to be those of the poor, while they consciously or unconsciously protect their own interests and those of their kind. It is not a question of Northern versus Southern NGOs, as is often portrayed: it is the poor versus both.

The bottom line

With all due respect, many Southern NGOs do not qualify as 'indigenous', in that they are not born out of the situations in which the poor live. Rather, they are modelled on the Northern NGOs who founded and/or fund them, often with strings attached. Consequently, they feel accountable more to the North than to the local poor, whose values and aspirations it is hard to prove that they represent. Indeed, they seem to be more concerned with their own survival and advancement. In situations where poor people still walk bare-foot, for example, their purported NGO representatives will insist on the latest four-wheel drive vehicles and so are necessarily biased to roads and urban areas. Many are thoroughly foreign, with all the trappings of the aid industry, and can be accused of patronising the poor. They love status and are committed to maintaining the status quo so long as it works in the their favour. They have weak management structures, as well as problems of vision and accountability in relation to their local-level partners.

This situation will not get any better simply by Northern NGOs' delegating more development responsibility to their Southern counterparts. It will be improved only through the genuine search for viable alternatives. The good news is that the NGO sector has become a growth industry. The bad news is that this growth has spawned a multitude of small, localised organisations which are often invisible and ineffectual and have little influence on local or national development processes. This truth must be faced. In our view, a relinquishing of operational roles by Northern NGOs risks being an abdication of their responsibilities to the poor.

The poor need effective organising, and need to be perhaps more aggressive in order to be competitive and more efficient. Southern NGOs have little track-record in high-level organising, constrained as they are by inherited shortcomings in this realm. The capacity to organise independently was destroyed during the long period of colonialism and neo-colonialism. The poor need access to capital, technologies, and markets. Indeed, the very term 'South' is almost synonymous with their absence, as if they were intrinsically incompatible. What the poor do not need is pity, exploitation, or patronising; they already endure more than their fair share of these. Their genuine partner is one who adds value to what they are already doing. NGOs should perhaps concentrate less on projecting their supposed altruism and work harder to develop more of the appropriately selfish interest that spurs and drives people's (including poor people's) entrepreneurship. Aid must be run on sound business principles of measurable efficiency and effectiveness, even in respect of qualitative parameters. For this, NGO philosophy has to change. A world is passing away, leaving a fine line between myth and reality in terms of what Southern NGOs can and cannot do. There is value and strength in being interdependent, if the terms of this interdependence are equitable — a view that is now beginning to emerge from the South.

Northern NGOs: chasing an advocacy agenda

Northern NGOs also need to get their priorities right in defining their agendas. Agendas for advocacy should grow out of action and practical development experience, not from the minds of thinkers in the North, however brilliant these may be (Edwards op.cit., pp.168, 173). For when government policy-makers are challenged by advocates from the North, their line of attack tends to be to question these advocates' mandate to speak for the poor. There is a need to rise to such challenges, for the real strength of NGOs lies in their simultaneous access to grassroots experience in the South, and to the decision-makers in the North.

By the same token, Northern NGOs must be held accountable for the advocacy agenda they pursue. Otherwise, information flows between field and Northern headquarters may be weakened, because field-staff do not feel part of one system with common objectives, driven by and supportive of their own work. Without a constant supply of high-quality information, advocacy cannot be successful. But if the desire is to focus attention on the opinions of the traditionally voiceless, then their voice must be clearly heard before their message can be clearly articulated. This voice is constantly changing. However, if Northern NGOs are still relatively weak in advocacy, then Southern NGOs are even more so, while the linkage between them and the local or grassroots organisations who are in direct touch with the people on whose behalf they purport to speak is weaker still. NGOs need to stop being preoccupied with their own narrowly interpreted bureaucratic mandates and get down to the business of seeking out and listening to the poor in order to secure a mandate to speak clearly and with conviction on their behalf. The poor live in the so-called culture of silence from which they must be liberated. The first step is, then, to meet them at their own level before they will speak.

Doing so must mean seeking out all the sections of society, in particular women and children. Gender-awareness campaigns have shown us that there is a marked difference in the perspectives of women and men, arising from women's lack of social, economic, and political power. What is not yet emphasised enough is the perspective of children. For example, as a result of genocide in Rwanda in 1994, a new phenomenon called 'child-headed households' has appeared, with families being headed by children as young as 10 years of age, of whom 75 per cent are girls. Prior to the genocide, the child in Rwandese society occupied a central and key position. Although children-headed households are a reality, it is one still not acknowledged by most Rwandese in their thinking and planning. The children say that they are not involved in making the important decisions affecting the nation or even their own well-being. Now, according to a qualitative needs-assessment study conducted by World Vision and supported and publicised by UNICEF, these children feel detached from the community, to which they desperately want to return. But they are becoming resigned to their situation. For example, when children are asked to draw pictures to show how they feel, they sometimes draw pictures of people with no mouths, signifying that they no longer want to speak, because they feel that no-one is listening. Yet they also argue that they have something to say that no-one can say for them. These children have latent abilities which can bring benefit to those communities who choose to listen to them.

There are other examples of children in need of a voice: those abducted by the Lord's Resistance Army in northern Uganda, those taken into prostitution in many countries of Asia and Latin America, and more recently in Europe and Africa, AIDS orphans in East and Central Africa, and many other examples. All this implies that there are different and sometimes even conflicting needs and perspectives among the poor, even when they are united in their poverty. Various groups and sub-groups have very different stakes in the status quo, as they do in engendering change. Priorities for advocacy and other appropriate forms of support can emerge only if we listen, so that we gain enough trust to enable the different groups to 'articulate' their needs. While the issues are urgent, nevertheless we must hasten slowly, ensuring that we have not left behind those very sectors for whom we purport to speak.

Redefining partnership

Rather than 'specialise' in different roles, NGOs North and South would do better to revisit the concept of true partnership. A first element must be making space for each other within their traditional domains. If advocacy must grow out of, and be informed by, grassroots experience, Northern NGOs can ill afford to abandon the operational arena. It may be their only way to retain an 'authentic' voice, and hence there continues to be plenty of room for them to co-exist in partnership with their Southern counterparts. To hear and join in with these 'authentic' voices, however, they also need to go beyond their partners and counterparts to the people to whom these voices belong. Relying on second-hand information is inadequate, especially as this is filtered and necessarily distorted. For too long, the sources of information have been the small select group of intermediaries who largely share the Northern NGOs' basic philosophy and objectives. But these do not necessarily represent the poor in any significant sense (Edwards, op.cit.). The need to go to the people themselves may call for a greater rather than a diminished presence, albeit one of a different kind. There is a call for a new generation of partnership, or 'joint ventures', to use the language of modern commerce.

Making room for Northern NGOs to have greater access to the authentic grassroots experiences must, however, be reciprocated; Northern NGOs should not seek to monopolise access to Northern-based institutions. Representatives from the South must also be afforded unrestricted access into these enclaves of power so that they can engage with the relevant actors directly. Ultimately, the people must represent themselves, and all NGOs — Northern or Southern — need to internalise this way of thinking. After all, most of the global institutions do not belong exclusively to the North. They are universal, and are only housed in New York, Washington, London, Geneva, or Paris. Conceptually, we need to view them as belonging to all of us, which is how they too must learn to see themselves. They do not represent just a Northern NGO constituency; NGOs and people from the South need no 'permission' to engage constructively with these institutions, but simply require certain barriers, such as language, to be removed.

In short, we should aspire to a joint venture of effective engagement with the political and economic powers that control and allocate the world's resources, and not get excessively concerned about interfering in each other's supposed constituencies. A free unhindered flow of, interaction with, and access to authentic opinions and experience in the South and to policy institutions in the North and the South is what one could call genuine partnership. We believe that this is the alternative to the current division of labour in which Southern NGOs literally do development 'hardware' in the South and Northern NGOs do development 'software' in the North. The ultimate objective against which success must be measured is that the people's voice increases, while that of NGOs themselves declines. The litmus test is that this withdrawal becomes voluntary on the part of the NGOs. For the goal is not to build up NGO empires but to integrate the poor into the global mainstream in a manner that maximises their benefits and minimises their exploitation.

In search of 'linguistics'

Whether from North or South, advocates must obtain the people's mandate and regularly return to have it renewed. At best they must have twin citizenship, or be what Chambers (1993) calls 'new professionals', and Bourdieu refers to as the 'new middle class'. This is not the monopoly or preserve of people from one hemisphere. An advocate from the North should not be written off just because of geographical origins. S/he could, with some effort, be as effective, even 'authentic', as someone from the South, especially if s/he spends quality time with and has the right attitude towards those who are poor. The poor are universal. (A better criterion for carrying out genuine advocacy might be that the 'advocate' goes to the poor and immerses herself or himself in their lives, value systems, and thought patterns and regularly returns, so as to be sure that s/he keeps in touch.)

We believe that the poor, in spite of the supposed proliferation of Southern NGOs, do still lack 'linguistics', a term used in West Africa which here would describe a capacity to interpret the reality of the poor, and translate it into conceptual frameworks and policies that are intelligible to the outside world but retain the original meaning. Exploiters have never been limited by language barriers, so why should do-gooders be so limited?

Interim representation

Interim representation, the duration of which is jointly defined, is another approach to genuine advocacy. Ultimately, the poor must be the ones to make their voices heard at the highest levels possible, and they have the potential to do so. 'The ability to analyze life situations, structures of society and development processes is not the preserve of intellectuals or development professionals. Individuals and communities possess these abilities in varying degrees ... A transformed people need no outside representation' (Muchina, 1995, p.4). This is the ultimate in capacity-building: a matter of emancipation, working oneself out of one's job.

Part of capacity-building is to enable advocates to acquire the ability to disempower themselves in order to empower others: self-disempowerment. Muchina suggests that beyond ten years, expatriates (who see themselves as interim representatives) cease to enhance others and start to perpetuate themselves. Muchina is brave in assigning a timeframe to a process, but she speaks for many who feel that open-ended timeframes are unacceptable.

'Linguists' in this sense need not lose their identity completely. Rather than attempt to identify with their target group by adopting a similar and literal external social style (where they are obvious misfits), external advocates need to realise that they can instead adopt the attitude of 'accompaniers', for which all they require is respect for their partners. They can act as sounding boards, asking the kinds of question that enable people to identify the real issues and in turn formulate their questions to those in power. The accompaniers can be there as people discuss these questions with the policy-makers. They can also be there to help them evaluate their achievements and set higher objectives. They can use their contacts to gain access for them and give them confidence when walking in the corridors of power, which can indeed be daunting to the uninitiated. But they must never lose sight of the fact that they themselves are not the actors. They only accompany and act as temporary brokers.

Looking to the future: alternative approaches to capacity-building

Critically analysed, capacity-building as we now know and interpret it often results in further alienating the advocates from the grassroots by coaching them to speak the 'language' of the advocacy target while ignoring that of the grassroots. Genuine capacity-building must incorporate an aspect of 'reversal' if, as Edwards (op.cit., p.174) argues, we need better ways of linking local-level action and analysis with international advocacy. To achieve this, we need the 'linguists' and accompaniers who can enter into the reality of the poor and interpret or translate it into the sophisticated conceptual frameworks and detailed policies intelligible to the relevant policy-makers, without compromising the authenticity of the original views.

'Linguistics' must acquire the capacity to cross social class boundaries for the '[v]alue systems of those with access to power and those far removed from such access cannot be the same. The viewpoint of the privileged is unlike that of the underprivileged. In the matter of power and privilege, the difference between the "haves" and "have-nots" is not merely quantitative, for it has far-reaching psychological and ideological implications' (*Development in Practice* Editorial, 6/4, p.291). As we have already argued, the problem goes deeper than North versus South: '[C]ultural differences play an important part … However, in the process of communication, intracultural differences are more difficult to bridge than intercultural differences … it would be rather naive to assume that because they [local elite], work in their own country, (they) will communicate as equals with "target groups"' (Vink, 1993, p.25). We need 'linguistics' from both the North and South, learning together to listen and correctly interpret the voices at both ends. Presently, good 'linguistics' are few and far between.

Clement, commenting on a draft of this article, argued that churches may be well placed to play a 'linguistics'-grooming role, since they are, through their missionaries and priests, close to the poor and to some extent living almost like them. This is exemplified by the fact that there are numerous examples of leaders in Africa and elsewhere who were identified as potential leaders by the church and groomed accordingly. An 'incarnational' development approach is highly commended, especially if ultimately people can then rise beyond their current limitations. Unfortunately, in the case of Rwanda, for example, the church divided itself along ethnic lines and, instead of advocating for the poor, identified with those in power and now finds itself too divided and compromised to play a meaningful role in social reintegration, mutuality, and cohesion. Even now, when children speak of support they receive from family members, neighbours, churches, local associations, and local authorities as well as international NGOs, the churches fare poorly, rated only a shade better than local associations. (According to the children, the greatest assistance is received from international NGOs and neighbours, while the least comes from family members.) This type of behaviour is consistent with the kind of misrepresentation of the South by the South, of the serious gap between rhetoric and reality that is rarely exposed. It is reminiscent of tribal and religious wars elsewhere, where elephants fight and the grass gets trampled. The churches' grooming of future African leaders has, nevertheless, much to recommend it.

There is room for NGOs today to carry out a similar role, and equip and facilitate good 'pro-people' candidates to enter strategic representative forums, such as parliament. Although they may risk being accused of exceeding their mandates, unless good people are encouraged and supported to enter politics, 'other interests' will continue to dominate and misrepresent those of ordinary people.

World Vision Uganda developed a programme which is currently being successfully replicated in Tanzania, and serves as a good example of what can be achieved. Well-qualified university graduates are offered an opportunity to live in remote villages, and to research and initiate simple activities as a way to get to know the community well. After a short orientation, they are abandoned there with no 'basic' facilities as they knew them. World Vision enters a contract with the community to 'facilitate' these volunteers. In some cases, the houses provided are open shells with no doors and windows. Often there is no latrine in the compound. Beyond a little pocket money, these Technical Associates (TAs) have no regular salary. For the first few days, they are scared and want to run away, back to urban 'civilisation'. A few actually do so, but many stay and become part of the community.

The TA Programme has proven to be an effective process of dialogue, of mutual discovery. Volunteers acquire 'community degrees' in addition to their formal university degrees. Many are surprised at how their cherished university degrees pale into insignificance next to the experience gained by living in the villages. TAs also add value to communities which, through admiration for their new 'son' or 'daughter', are inspired to set higher horizons for their own children.

The TA Programme also builds capacity for future leadership. The process needs to be made more clearly focused as a way of grooming leadership and engaging in authentic advocacy. If there is a critical mass of such people, the voice of the poor will begin to be heard. If a good proportion keep the contract, in ten years they will be the policy-makers in their respective countries. NGOs which invest in this kind of process are building invaluable policy capital.

Conclusion: learning from liberalisation and globalisation

Generally speaking, Africa as a whole is not part of the global agenda-setting mechanism. It does not in any significant way bring values or systems to the global table. It takes what is given: it has no authentic advocates. Africa is disenfranchised. In fact, one respondent during the research for this article commented that 'sadly, Africa's voice is absent in most global discussions. I would imagine that little interest was given to African perspectives at the recent meeting of the World Trade Organisation. Similarly, when I was at the Annual Meeting of the World Bank and IMF, although there were many African representatives present, there were no real alternative voices from Africa' (Commins, personal communication). There is no distinct African voice in global forums. 'Representatives' for Africa either sing the tune of the global élite or simply occupy space at the table. There is an urgent need for NGOs, governments, and global institutions to change the way in which they present and represent Africa. This is a real challenge in a world that is seemingly indifferent to the continent's future.

This is not a time for 'business as usual'. The lack of distinct African voices is neither the creation nor the fault of NGOs; but one wonders whether NGOs have fared any better than governments. Have they sufficiently challenged the status quo? As the burden may fall on NGOs to push for this, change must necessarily begin at home. It is ironic that NGOs — the proponents of 'speaking truth to power' — are often unable to speak the truth to themselves. By obstructing such essential feedback, NGOs prove how big is the gap between rhetoric and reality. It is difficult to strengthen the competencies of NGOs if they take offence at the truth. Related to this, another respondent raised the issue of NGO ownership:

[O]ne of the major issues in this discussion is who owns the NGOs. Who makes the final decision as to the leadership of the NGOs, especially in Africa. Also who pays for the NGO's existence. Often staff who hold radical views or 'revolutionary' ideas never reach the top. They are perceived to be difficult to work with, a threat. They are an embarrassment to the donors. Obviously the voice of such an NGO is muffled. It is a poor imitation of the people's voice. Gagging the voice of upcoming leaders, often the brightest and the best, failure to tolerate dissent, can certainly have far-reaching adverse effects. (Pappetta, personal communication)

Unfortunately, such influence, whether by remote or direct control, is disempowering. With their own houses in order, however, NGOs that survive can take leadership in giving Africa a voice.

Secondly, NGOs should take a cue from the paradigm of global economic liberalisation which challenges us to adopt new ways of thinking, new ways of doing business. It represents aggressiveness, competition, dynamism, and other survival strategies. Southern NGOs cannot be immune from this, and cannot develop a capacity to represent the poor through holding on to the 'protectionism' of the past; old forms of propping up NGOs in the South need to be re-examined and transformed. They should not settle for being handed responsibility for development in the South merely because they are Southern. They must be open to competition and be aggressive but business-like, proving that they can deliver. They must find out from the people they claim to represent how well they are doing. They must seek and accept feedback, including constructive criticism, if they are to continue to be relevant. Maybe some must also accept death or at least retrenchment in order to rise again in a better and more effective form.

Finally, we must seek to empower the poor to act as their own advocates, so that when speaking for them we avoid giving the impression that someone somewhere owes them a living, and that this someone is most probably the government, primarily their own, but also governments of rich industrialised countries. It is this tendency that seeks answers from out there, not from within the people themselves. We in the NGO sector have not promoted, by our own example, the entrepreneurial spirit, creativity, and initiative inherent in people who are poor. (The children in Rwanda accuse us similarly.) We have demanded more and more aid, which in general has been badly administered and is now dwindling or being withheld. The new paradigm insists that the poor are primarily responsible for finding ways out of their immediate problems, though we are well aware that the perpetual struggle to survive is immensely tiring. But it is dead fish that swim downstream. Needs are not necessarily rights, in the sense that someone else has the obligation to provide for them. The poor need to demand accountability from their leaders who take loans on their behalf. They must be vigilant against corruption, a form of mis-allocation of national resources. But they must also create wealth and safeguard it. Ideally, inter-dependency in advocacy will mean that poor communities who 'pull themselves up by their own bootstraps' do not get repressed for doing so. Instead, there should be sufficient solidarity to fight even powerful adversaries.

To enable the poor to engage in their own advocacy, we should encourage global institutions to release resources to be used to finance wealth-creation by the poor themselves. We must form partnerships with, among others, the business community, and, where feasible, commit resources to attract its investment to areas where poor people live. We must engage the business community to pay decent prices for labour and primary products, but also facilitate the poor to produce high-quality products. The poor must find a niche in global trade, but must also appreciate the need to save in order to invest, to forgo consumption today in order to accumulate, grow, and so afford more tomorrow. In short, the challenge is to make trade liberalisation work for the poor (even though it is now seen to be 'anti-poor', notwithstanding some small gains made by a temporary opening up of more job prospects for women — albeit often in insecure, part-time, low-paid, and low-status work. We need to exploit the revolution in communication, opening up the world of the poor. For example, through radio programmes in their own languages, poor people can know the world market prices for their products. They can then organise to get the highest prices. It is in such activities that NGOs should be investing to make the poor more dynamic, aggressive, and competitive; so that they bring themselves into the economic and political mainstream and so widen their overall opportunities. This is what will make it possible to break the vicious cycle of poverty. We must believe it and make the poor believe in themselves. In supporting them, economic advocacy perhaps has to take precedence over political advocacy on the NGO agenda. Otherwise the poor, and perhaps NGOs along with them, will continue to be marginalised in the emerging dynamic of the global economy.

References

Caldwell, L.K. (1990) *International Environment Policy*, Duke University Press.

Chambers, R. (1993) *Challenging the Professions: Frontiers for Rural Development*, London: Intermediate Technology.

Clark, J. (1992) 'Policy influence, lobbying and advocacy' in M. Edwards and D. Hulme (eds) *Making a Difference: NGOs and Development in a Changing World*, London: Earthscan.

Eade, D. (1996) Editorial, *Development in Practice*, 6/4, pp. 291-2.

Edwards, M. (1993) 'Does the doormat influence the boot? Critical thoughts on UK NGOs and international advocacy', *Development in Practice*, 3/3: 163-75.

Muchina, O. (1995) 'Qualitative indicators of transformational development', *Together*, October-December 1995: 3-5

Nyamugasira, W. (1995) 'Vulnerable Groups and their Coping Strategies', unpublished paper.

Sutherns, R. (1996) 'Advocacy: A Call for Renewed NGO Commitment', unpublished paper.

Vink, N. (1993) 'Communication between inequals: development workers and the poor', *Bulletins of the Royal Tropical Institute: Culture and Communication*: Number 329.

World Vision (1998) 'Qualitative Needs Assessment of Child-Headed Households in Rwanda', internal report.

■ **Warren Nyamugasira** *is a Ugandan economist with almost 20 years' experience of NGO work. He holds an MSc in Development Policy and Planning from Swansea University, and is currently Director of World Vision International's Rwanda Programme. This paper was first published in* Development in Practice *Volume 8, number 3, in 1998.*

Disaster without memory: Oxfam's drought programme in Zambia

K. Pushpanath

Introduction

Disaster response has been described as the last resort of the amateur, an unkind assessment but not without a grain of truth. Disaster generates an emotional response and, with each new disaster, new disaster organisations are born. And past lessons on disaster management have to be learnt anew. (*World Disasters Report 1993*, International Federation of Red Cross and Red Crescent Societies, Geneva)

Disaster in Southern Africa is not a new phenomenon. Indeed, the region has suffered and continues to endure more than its share of disasters — political and so-called natural. In Angola alone, the UN currently estimates that at least 1,000 people die every day as a result of war and its devastating consequences.

Even against this backdrop, the drought of February 1992 to September 1993 was significant, because of the extent and scale of its impact on an already vulnerable population, in the context of the limited capacities of governments in the region. Indeed, most independent observers and development workers feared that relief measures would be neither effective nor sufficient to stave off a major tragedy.

In retrospect, however, the collective response to this impending disaster demonstrates that, if there is political will and a commitment to work with the people affected, real achievements are possible, in terms of development as well as relief. For many Zambian NGOs, the experience was one of remarkable co-operation and co-ordination, including innovative relations with the government. Most commentators and politicians agree that the experience of collaboration between the Zambian government and the NGO community in Zambia was very positive indeed, and quite unprecedented.

Background: Oxfam in Zambia

Zambia's economy is overwhelmingly dependent on copper as its major export commodity — a legacy which it inherited from its colonial past. Its economic and social development has thus been intricately linked to the ups and downs of the international market for copper. During the boom years of the 1960s-70s, Zambia was able to adopt a benign, social-welfare model of development, pumping substantial resources into health, education, and urban infrastructure, and generous food subsidies to an already predominantly urban population.

Zambia showed spectacular achievements in education and health during this early period of post-independence. Some areas of the economy were nationalised, and a highly centralised state apparatus emerged. A new Zambian middle class developed, along with a tiny elite which controlled the economic and political reins of the country. Political changes, in the form of a one-party state, reflected an ideological alignment with the then Soviet bloc countries. However, fluctuations in the world copper market led President Kaunda's government to borrow heavily from the IMF and commercial banks to fuel the state-subsidised economy. Accumulated debt started weighing down on the economy, and the quality of life of most Zambians began to suffer. In the largely neglected rural areas, women-maintained households had already become the norm, because of extensive male migration to the urban centres.

Access to land is not necessarily a problem for these rural households, but the lack of appropriate and effective commitment, in terms of either policy or resources, has been a severe constraint on their capacity to break out of the poverty to which their subsistence economy confines them. Food insecurity has become severe in the rural sector, as confirmed through indices of malnutrition and mortality. Economic liberalisation has made these problems even worse.

Oxfam's pre-drought programme in the rural sector kept these factors in view, aiming to enhance and strengthen people's productive capacity through the sustainable use of available natural resources. Oxfam's programme in Zambia is thus characterised by support for local-level groups — such as women's associations, youth groups, organisations of disabled people, cooperatives, and so on — who are engaged in a range of productive and economic activities, as well as support for skills development and small enterprises. Training is also encouraged, through workshops and meetings. A small proportion of Oxfam's support is channelled through intermediary NGOs.

It was the combination of this micro-level experience in Zambia, together with the opportunity to draw on the previous experience of the Country Representative in development and relief programmes in India, which enabled Oxfam to embark on a large-scale drought-relief and rehabilitation programme in the Eastern Province of Zambia. The programme enhanced existing capacity and confidence within Oxfam's team in Zambia, while also laying the foundations for a recovery programme which aimed to secure rural livelihoods. Oxfam's experience in Zambia has also attracted the attention of other international NGOs and official aid agencies for its innovative approach to disaster relief.

Oxfam's approach was based on two assumptions:

- it is possible to approach relief within the framework of development;
- it is feasible to facilitate, motivate, mobilise, and train local people to take charge of the relief effort.

In other words, Oxfam wanted to resist the temptation to administer relief through high-profile operational programmes, which are so beloved of the international media and (consequently) of the people who donate money to aid agencies. For instance, the international media constantly criticised the Indian government for being 'too rigid' to invite foreign aid-workers to assist after the 1993 earthquake — even though well-informed observers were pointing out that the government could rely on the enormous reserves of in-country ability to deal with such disasters. Without denying that there were problems, gaps, and considerable political posturing in the provision of post-earthquake aid, this serves as a good example of the collective mind-set of agencies and media alike in relation to disaster response.

This article suggests that operational aid programmes are not the best way to approach relief work, and that often these are not only expensive, but unsustainable and disempowering. The approach adopted by Oxfam in Zambia aimed not only to empower the immediate constituency — the people affected by the drought — but also those who worked alongside them, and ultimately the donors themselves, who became involved in the struggles of ordinary people in an active and dynamic way.

Oxfam's drought programme

The mandate of field staff employed by Oxfam (UK and Ireland) stipulates that 'it is a priority ... to investigate a disaster and to assist with appropriate relief'. In the context of Zambia, this was interpreted as aiming to:

- support the capacity of Zambian groups and NGOs to prepare for and respond to emergencies, thus reducing the temptation for Oxfam to go operational during disaster situations;
- make its own independent assessment, while training its counterpart organisations to become involved in the assessment process;
- ensure that responses are informed by an analysis of the respective roles of men and women, and by attention to issues of sustainability;
- design relief interventions to address causes as well as effects, so that relief and recovery are seen as the two sides of the same coin;
- communicate the underlying causes and future implications of the disaster for vulnerable people to policy-makers, donors, and others, through all possible channels;
- share and build on Oxfam's in-country and international experience;
- promote co-ordinated and integrated approaches among and within NGOs;
- encourage and give voice to local perceptions of problems, and to community-based participation, especially of the most vulnerable categories of people.

The first assessment was undertaken by Oxfam staff, through which a number of civil servants who had had some previous contact with Oxfam were encouraged to act as link people, informing and mobilising other volunteers. Over the following two months, 'information gatherers' were asked to use a standard questionnaire to identify two geographical areas in each of the seven districts in the province to show (a) households that were completely without food; (b) households that might soon run out of food; and (c) households that might run out of food before the next crop. They were also advised to look for other significant factors, such as water shortages, which would intensify the impact of drought. These 'information gatherers' received some token assistance for travel, but otherwise worked mainly as volunteers.

Running parallel to this, a more comprehensive drought profile was being built up by Oxfam across the country, using organisations and individuals who had been trained in the 1991 Development Communication Workshop in Lusaka.[1] This documentation was greatly valued by policy-makers and official aid agencies, and has continued to be used extensively.

It is important to note that most of the 'information gatherers' had no specialist or formal training, but were backed up by Oxfam's staff through means such as telexes and telegrams to remote areas of Zambia. The fact that their feedback came back in time to compile the drought file is a testimony to the commitment and motivation of these individuals, as well as a demonstration of their good grasp of the issues.

Community mobilisation

From May 1992, over a period of 40 days, Oxfam staff held 14 community workshops in all the seven districts of Eastern Province in Zambia — mass meetings under the sky. These open meetings (using public-address systems) were attended by between 1,000 and 5,000 people each, women and men, old and young — an unprecedented event in the history of NGOs in Zambia. Critical to their success was the participation of women in not only sharing their particular problems, but taking leadership of the various committees that were elected during the meetings.[2]

These mass meetings achieved the following:

- A clear perception and recognition of problems faced by the people, as articulated by them.
- Ways and means to address these problems by enlisting support from within the community, and thus strengthening its capacity.
- Identification and election of new community leaders.
- The development of a new relationship between government district officials and local communities.
- An enabling climate for the open and confident participation in relief interventions of those people directly affected by the drought.
- The transformation of despair and dejection into an opportunity for people to take control and embark on many new collective activities.

The process also led to setting up village-level and chieftain-level committees to oversee working parties charged with receiving, distributing, monitoring, and accounting for food aid. At district level, it became possible to create disaster and development support groups, consisting mainly of civil servants who came forward as volunteers.

This process mobilised communities and motivated civil servants to work in a radically different way from what they were used to. In all, over 150 civil servants from different ministries came forward. More striking still was the democratisation process that got started at the village level. There were, of course, many problems in terms of party politics, as well as from within traditional areas of authority. The district groups did not always find it easy to work together in a people-focused and sensitive manner. But the fact remains that, in spite of the many hurdles, the programme gradually developed and started bearing results.

Programme implementation: June 1992— September 1993

The Eastern Province became a bee-hive of activities, which included a government-run Programme for Prevention of Malnutrition in which Oxfam played a major role. The sheer dimensions of the programme attest to the capabilities and capacities of the structures that were established. Over 35,000 tonnes of white and yellow maize had been delivered within 14 months of the programme's launch. An estimated 70,000 households (that is some 350,000 people, representing 33 per cent of the population of the province) were involved, of which about 70 per cent were maintained by women.

A number of Food For Work (FFW) programmes were also planned, monitored, and implemented by the community structures and the district groups. The figures for the year show a remarkable achievement: in a total of seven districts, 2,673 km of roads were constructed and 807 wells built or repaired, in addition to the construction of 82 bridges, 150 houses, 77 clinics and classrooms, 12 storage sheds, 947 pit latrines, and 22 earth dams.

In some areas, the choice of a particular activity was clearly made by the community, while in others it was strongly influenced by the district volunteers. Consequently, the sense of ownership over each FFW programme varied from one area to another, though in general a fair level of success rate was recorded.

There is no doubt that some activities took place because the community had only one option: to participate in the FFW programme in order to get food. But equally, there were cases where the activity started before the food arrived, and others where the activity was completed even when there was no assurance of food. This is an impressive reflection of the efficacy of a people-oriented approach, especially considering that most of the people involved (including Oxfam staff) did not have a great deal of previous experience. More impressive still is that communities were able to achieve all this.

Of course, there was a lot of learning on the job. We improvised and adjusted directions as the programme unfolded. For instance, a technical team, assembled within one month of starting the relief work, went around the province assisting other groups. Oxfam staff made repeated visits to monitor, advise, and resolve outstanding conflicts through the structures that were established. The process gave people an experience of grassroots democracy at work.

Recovery: agricultural production

A crucial part of the relief response was to integrate Food For Work programmes within an agricultural production programme. Oxfam's experience in the Eastern Province before the drought enabled the staff to identify the main factors behind food insecurity at household level, particularly among the women-maintained households that comprised over two in three households in the area. It was established that these suffered mainly for want of adequate labour, proper and sufficient tools, and reliable fast-maturing seeds.

An outstanding feature of the agricultural production programme was the revival of a cultural practice of working together in groups, but within individual families. This helped labour-deficit women-maintained households to meet planting schedules, and slightly to expand the amount of land under food cultivation.

The same structures which were established for other FFW programmes undertook the distribution of 350 tonnes of maize seed, 10,000x30kg bags of groundnuts, and 34 tonnes of newly-introduced sorghum seeds. The anticipated yield was 450,000x90kg bags of maize, 6,290 tonnes of groundnuts, and 7,150 tonnes of sorghum. In other words, almost 20 per cent of the maize output of the entire province was to be contributed by just 70,000 households!

Distribution and production were not uniformly successful, with occasional practical problems, such as the late delivery of seeds, unmet demand for seed in some areas, and excess supply in others. Overall, however, the intervention justified the assumptions that had been made, and proved that the programme has potential for replication. Perhaps for the first time in decades, many subsistence households produced considerably more than enough to cover their own food needs. A foundation was laid for development work to increase food security and establish sustainable livelihoods in the district, as a part of Oxfam's longer-term strategy in Zambia. Furthermore, the programme proved that relief work can take special account of women's needs — opening up new ways of thinking about the issue among women and men at village level as well as district level.

Communications: advocacy and lobbying

As the relief measures were being implemented on the ground, we as Oxfam staff saw the critical need to communicate what we were witnessing and hearing, and what was being done about it. Every possible opportunity and channel was explored and used to communicate our findings, and people's responses to the drought-intervention programmes — from village level through to government officials, politicians, and international agency representatives.

For over a decade, Oxfam's programme in Zambia had tried to communicate its micro-level experience within the framework of macro-level policies. The pre-drought work on issues such as debt, poverty, and economic structural adjustment had a comparatively low profile, but nevertheless Oxfam initiated and led many small-scale research projects.[3] Interestingly, some of these campaigns had very good support from the government of Zambia.

In October 1991, after the multi-party elections, Zambia saw the emergence of independent mass media, lobby groups, and a more dynamic judiciary. Civil society started to become more vigorous, and non-partisan organisations were slowly showing more courage and determination. In other words, new political spaces were created, discovered, and revived.

The change in political climate meant that Oxfam was able to take a more public stand than before. Other factors also played a part, including:

• its reputation as a genuine grassroots support organisation;
• its effective and substantial response to the drought;
• the Zambian government's invitation to Oxfam, through the Minister of Agriculture, to activate the relief process, because of its own limited experience of drought-response work;
• the government of Zambia's openness and commitment to NGO-led relief activity and the de-politicisation of aid;
• Oxfam's direct and indirect support for communications work in the past;
• a positive climate from official donors towards NGOs;
• Oxfam's capacity to respond rapidly, through providing information and supporting local organisations to undertake campaigning and advocacy work, including through media channels;

- Oxfam's ability to seize the opportunity and mobilise the people affected by drought in such a way that they felt confident to articulate their concerns and aspirations.

The combination of these factors enabled Oxfam to take a more solid public stand in the context of the drought programme. The most strategic aspect of the communication work was through the mass media — radio, television, and newspapers. Many national journalists found that the Oxfam office was an important source of up-to-date and accurate information.

The staff were also able to co-ordinate with the broader campaigning efforts of Oxfam (UK/Ireland) and other European initiatives. Three successful media visits were made at the beginning, middle, and end of the drought programme: reporters from the BBC and *The Observer*, and other European and North American journalists, were helped to understand the drought, its impact, and various responses to it. In every case, a great effort was made to communicate the *context* of the drought, including the transitional nature of the Zambian economy and the country's new-found democratic process.

In conclusion, it was felt that communication is a vital component of relief work, and that our investment repaid positive dividends, not just to Oxfam as an institution, but also in helping people to gain greater control over the relief efforts. The voices of ordinary people were heard, loud and clear, placing those in power under pressure to respond quickly and sensitively to their demands.

Villagers and civil servants for the first time experienced the potential for using the media and other communication channels to influence events and bring about positive change for the benefit of disadvantaged and voiceless people. It was a significant departure for Zambian NGOs to see, appreciate, and make use of these opportunities. Similarly, Oxfam's constituency in the UK and Ireland was actively engaged. The team in Zambia facilitated a visit by a young journalist from a popular music programme on BBC Radio 2, and visits by Oxfam communications staff; their findings helped to inform Oxfam's fiftieth anniversary campaign messages. An outstanding piece of North–South collaboration was a letter-writing campaign, in which the team in Zambia encouraged 15,000 ordinary people, young and old, male and female, to write letters challenging the Structural Adjustment Programme, and describing the impact of debt repayments and government cut-backs on their lives. Oxfam staff in the UK organised the presentation of these letters to world finance ministers at an IMF/World Bank meeting in Washington in 1993 — an initiative which generated much interest in the press.

Lessons from the drought

Oxfam's drought programme in Zambia represents a departure from the usual operational approach to emergency relief. The process was very much an intensive, people-oriented one. The operation faced innumerable hurdles: logistical problems, difficulties in social organisation, and problems of intrusive party politics. Some of the elected committee members distorted information, and abused the trust and confidence of the people. There were sporadic cases of the misuse of maize supplies and improper accounting for relief goods. However, all these problems pale into insignificance when they are put into context — a context in which there were very few people in Zambia with experience in drought-relief operations, particularly at the ground level; where (at the outset) there was no commitment to the level of funding required to respond to people's needs and expectations; where most of the civil servants opted to work as volunteers (though the government did offer some form of subsistence later); where there were extreme difficulties in transport, and communications systems were unreliable. It must also be noted that Oxfam staff were new to this type of work, and the scale of operation in financial terms was at least four times more than anything the office had handled before — indeed, for six months there were only three staff handling the whole operation, besides managing an on-going development programme in the rest of the country.

Irrespective of the programme's serious and admitted shortcomings, one of its major achievements was to incorporate its drought-relief work into a longer-term strategy for ensuring livelihood security — not only where Oxfam continues to be actively involved, but also in those districts where there are no plans for further follow-up.

The programme's five principal achievements can be summarised as follows:

- It has been shown in Zambia for the first time that ordinary people, given an enabling climate, can make enormous positive breakthroughs.

- A body of experience has been developed which will remain in Zambia as a basis for future work. This applies not just to Oxfam staff in Zambia, but to the civil servants and, most importantly, at the grassroots.

- The approach has laid solid foundations at the community level for other initiatives to find long-term solutions to problems such as insecure livelihoods and food insecurity; it opened up new approaches to drought mitigation and preparedness, and to communication, campaigning, and advocacy work.

- It has exposed many civil servants to a more people-sensitive approach to the issues and challenges of development, and reinforced this through practical experience.

- It released the creative energy of villagers and gave them a means of challenging authority, taking charge, and implementing programmes that were relevant and accessible to them.

The programme represents an experiment with new ways of thinking, and daring to travel on uncharted roads. It is an experience with real potential for replication. It challenges the conventional approach of disaster-relief agencies which prefer to embark on their own operational programmes because these seem to offer easier, more predictable, and more superficially attractive programmes — but which, in so doing, miss the opportunity to develop more sustainable, people-based approaches.

Often when development projects are assessed, there is a tendency to view sustainability only in terms of the material and physical inputs that are needed to run the programme. But the human and social dimensions are even more crucial. The drought crisis was confronted in many different ways, by different people. This is one form of empowerment: people developing the confidence to confront a situation, and daring to do something about it.

In the Zambian context, people's public behaviour had been largely conditioned by their experience of a one-party state. Anything not initiated by the Party was to be viewed with suspicion. It was important for Oxfam staff to demonstrate the importance of accountability in the context of the drought, and the relief goods that were arriving. It was a novel experience for many people to realise that they had a right to have a say in the process of implementing relief programmes. Similarly, it was new and exciting for people to learn that mistakes made by the elected leadership could — and, where possible, should — be rectified.

The way in which the district volunteers were dealt with by the village participants in a recent workshop, especially by women who stood their ground in wanting direct dealing with Oxfam, is a case in point. Their new-found self-confidence had come from actual experience of doing things, having access to information, confronting those in positions of superiority, removing those who obstructed the smooth running of the programme. All this does not mean that villagers have for ever overcome their powerlessness and silence, and will never revert to the obedience and meekness of the past. Rather, the experience has shown that there are alternatives, and has given them confidence to believe that these are possible. That is perhaps the most important lesson to learn from this experience.

This article opened with a quotation from the IFRC *World Disasters Report*, which suggests that every disaster means that we have to learn lessons anew. Must we really invent the wheel every time a disaster strikes, or can we usefully learn from what we have done so far?

Notwithstanding all the efforts of governments, donors, NGOs, missions, and charities, it was mainly the courage and remarkable determination of ordinary people that contained the disaster in Zambia. This is not to deny the value of all the aid programmes that were so effectively carried out, but rather to pay tribute to the people who were at the receiving end, and in particular to the peasant women of Zambia.

Notes

1 The proceedings of this workshop are recorded in the 'Report of the Development Communication Workshop Jointly Organised by Oxfam and The Weekly Post and UNZA Great East Road Campus, 25th – 29th November 1991', compiled by Moses John Kwali. The workshop was organised in order to take advantage of the emergence of a more confident, independent national press in Zambia. It was attended by 25 people from both rural and urban areas of the country, to learn about information-gathering techniques.

2 The mass meetings were possible in part because of disaster-relief training run by Oxfam in 1989, which had been attended by senior civil servants and village activists. These contacts were critical in mobilising others to gather and communicate more information, and to identify areas of action. Oxfam's existing counterparts, especially the women's production groups and youth programmes, played a pivotal role in gathering and

disseminating information, and mobilising others. The whole process took 40 days, and the running of the mass meetings improved with practice. The original idea was adapted from previous experiences of the Representative in disaster work in India.

Each mass meeting was run like a training workshop, with Oxfam staff acting as facilitators. The logistics (food, material, money, public-address systems) were set up before each visit. The whole discussion was recorded for further use. Each district report was fully compiled within five days of returning from the tour. Oxfam staff mediated where conflicting opinions were emerging.

The participants were given general information about the drought, about Oxfam, and about existing government policies. Brain-storming sessions (each of about 2-4 hours) enabled people to come forward. Open elections were held to select representatives, of whom Oxfam stipulated that 50 per cent should be women. While this was a condition imposed by Oxfam, there was discussion in the meetings about why this policy had been adopted. The volunteers from the districts who accompanied Oxfam staff at the village level were then asked to facilitate district meetings, in order to set up the district-level organisation.

3 For example, *Adjusting to Adjustment in Zambia: Women's and Young People's Responses to a Changing Economy*, a report commissioned by Oxfam from Gabriel Banda, and published in 1991 in the Oxfam Research Papers series.

■ **K. Pushpanath** *has worked as an agricultural extension officer for a development trust in Karnataka, and as an agricultural development officer at the Syndicate Bank in south India. He gained an MA in Development Studies at the University of East Anglia in 1984, the year in which he joined Oxfam, initially in the South India Office, and then as Oxfam's Representative in Hyderabad. He worked in Zambia, as the Regional Representative for Zambia and Malawi, from 1988 to 1993. This paper was first published in* Development in Practice *Volume 4, number 2, in 1994.*

Development theatre and the process of re-empowerment: the Gibeon story

Alex Mavrocordatos

Empowerment, the ultimate goal

Without empowerment there can be no development. Ownership of knowledge and action by a community must underpin any project undertaken in partnership with them. The case for empowerment has been argued frequently and eloquently elsewhere. The question is where to begin in the process, identifying the point of entry or initial engagement between partners, and the guiding principle or methodology that may be involved.

In the context of the sometimes systematic disenfranchisement of communities by government or colonising powers, it may be preferable to address the notion of 're-empowerment'. Thierry Verhelst has argued that it is those 'internalised features' of a community's indigenous cultural roots in religion, morals, and myths that underpin the traditional way of life and earlier (em)power(ment) of its people. When this cultural base is disturbed, Verhelst fears that 'there is then a 'withering away', an atrophying of consciousness itself and, unless the latter can recover, the process may well become irreversible'. He goes on to stress that '[w]hen a people is stripped of its identity, it is no longer capable of self-determination. ... Such is the nature of under-development' (Verhelst, 1990).

Carl Gaspar, working among his own people in the Philippines, considers that 'the whole concept of community theatre is not complete if there is no corresponding conscious effort at organising the people around issues that affect their lives, thereby developing communal action tailored to their needs' (Gaspar, 1991).

The Gibeon story charts one path from 'withered away' to re-empowered. It describes a culture already suffering from the malaise described by Verhelst, stripped as it is by 200 years of foreign presence. It shows how a small community group explored its own 'self-oppression' before going on to organise itself around specific issues, taking action towards its own re-empowerment.

RISE and the Community Listening Theatre (CLT)

The Rural-People's Institute for Social Empowerment (RISE) is a Namibian non-government organisation (NGO) working with the mostly Nama communities who live between the Rehoboth plains and the mountains of the Karas region which give way to the Orange river and the border with South Africa, some 700 kilometres to the south. The best land is still privately owned by 'commercial' farmers, while the rest is designated as 'communal' land available to the landless farmers, who must try to raise a living from the desert soil. In the distant past, large herds grazed and 'rivers of cattle' flowed to the Cape colony, having been bought by the traders in exchange for trinkets, household goods, guns, and some money. Now there is too little grass for too many goats, it is difficult to sustain the caracul sheep farming for which these parts were renowned, and there are no more cattle.

As its title suggests, RISE's overall aim is the empowerment of communal farmers and their families. Its field-staff work with community members on a variety of project activities, based on savings and loans schemes and ranging from pig-farming groups to village bakery and sewing cooperatives. Programmes also cover sanitation and the digging of pit latrines, with workshops and seminars at local and regional levels.

With empowerment as the ultimate goal, RISE is committed to facilitating a process whereby communities can define and address the constraints that impede their development. The aim is to avoid being project-driven, and its work is underpinned by establishing unifying Community Based Organisations (CBOs) such as the South Namibian Farmers' Union (SNAFU), the Good Hope Women's Development Forum, and, more recently, the Youth Enterprise Support Scheme (YES), which brings together unemployed youths whose families are suffering the vagaries of drought — since farming has come almost to a standstill — and whose sole source of income may be their grandparents' pensions.

The Community Listening Theatre (CLT) programme, with support from Oxfam (UK/I), was to introduce Theatre for Development (TFD), concentrating on staff training. I was with RISE for some 18 months, spread across three years (1992-5). We held monthly TFD training workshops for staff, and I worked on a one-to-one basis with the field-workers in one pilot community each: together we would set up and run a CLT programme, with existing or new RISE partner groups, along with their project activities. The field-workers learned to absorb theatre facilitation skills into their work, establishing community groups who now include performances alongside and within their other activities. CLT/TFD helps to bind these groups, while addressing social constraints directly and at an early stage.

The Gibeon Youth Programme

Gibeon is a town of some 4,000 people. It has a densely populated shanty-town area, served by communal water stand-pipes whose source is a dam over 30km away. Toilets are of the old, unpopular, 'bucket-in-a-tin-shed' type: the bucket is collected in the small hours of the morning by council workers in an old truck which often drips its unsavoury contents along the dusty streets. Unemployment is the norm, alcohol is over-used, pregnancy comes early, and there is little energy for change.

RISE had been active in Gibeon for some years. The centre-point was the well-established community bakery; there were also sewing and brick-making projects, and a Ventilation Improved Pit-latrine (VIP) programme that became the focus of discrimination and clan conflicts which will be described below.

Just as the CLT started early in 1992, RISE was establishing the Gibeon Youth Programme (GYP). Members of the GYP were receptive to the idea of a drama activity, so it was in Gibeon that I began with my colleague and trainee Johannes Jansen a programme of fortnightly theatre workshops. After a six-month period, Jansen would be fully trained as a CLT/TFD facilitator, repeating the process with other communities, while the Gibeon group would be continuing with their own project activities — able to explore their own social reality through improvised plays and scenarios.

At first, the youth members saw the drama work as a potential money-earner, hoping to put up a series of *Konsert-aande*. These are concert evenings consisting mostly of choral singing of familiar Christian and secular songs, some of which would be accompanied by the traditional Namastap dance. They have a prodigious talent for song, and in a typical *Konsert-aande* the audience may 'buy' a repeat performance of an item they have particularly enjoyed, over and above any entrance fee they had paid.

It was not difficult to add short scenarios to such a programme, and this could have presented a way for the TFD initiative to be built upon a local cultural tradition that even offered the potential of interaction with the audience. However, while the multiplicity of programme items, and thus themes, in this review-like format was a constraint that could perhaps have been turned to good advantage, the focus on money proved to be a more serious limitation. An early and perhaps impetuous attempt by the group to perform one of these shows in the local big town of Mariental was great fun and did contain brief scenarios on the obvious themes of AIDS, drunkenness, and teenage pregnancy; but the brevity of these insertions into a longer programme militated against their depth or efficacy. The group realised that they were not ready for the 'big-town big time', and that anyway they were not likely to earn money enough to split usefully among up to 20 performers.

Meanwhile, some engaging local issues had emerged from the workshops, and most members were keen to follow through these explorations of their own community life and its development. It was the group itself that determined to concentrate on such matters in the subsequent drama workshops.

Bringing in Boal

If Nama cultural tradition had ever included any indigenous form of performance, this has long been overshadowed by the influence of the Church, so powerful in this highly Christianised country. Preconceptions of drama centred on Sunday-school plays and Easter pageants. Unable to build on older cultural foundations, we were obliged to work from the Western model that the community had already accepted.

In this context, the work of Augusto Boal became appropriate, based as it is upon Freirian ideals of dialogical education and conscientisation. In Boal's Forum Theatre, the protagonist of a prepared scenario would be a victim of human circumstances, seen to make an error of judgement and behaviour that implicitly endorsed an oppressive status quo, and led to suffering and the protagonist's demise. The audience, in this interactive theatrical form, would then be invited to step into the action and replay key moments where the character might have been able to act differently and so reverse the oppressive conditions. The audience would then concur — or not — about whether this was a viable representation of reality — a rehearsal for change that has to come. We never sought to import (or impose) the strict formula of Forum theatre, but did embark on explorations around it and the more general notion of an interactive theatre that by its nature would foster the expression not only of the views of a performing group but also those of its audience, and give air to the ensuing debate. Initial work, however, was within the workshops of the activity group. Public performances would come later.

Their dramatic explorations in the workshops were pointing towards the reality of discrimination within their community. Although Namibia was by that time technically free from the chains of south Africa's illegal occupation, it still suffered from the apartheid system, and improvisations on the theme of oppression produced scenes about the general iniquities of racist oppression. Further exploration — closer to home — led us to a scenario that dealt with local clan conflicts inside Gibeon. This was the Sewing-Play, in which the group portrayed a (so-called) co-operative sewing project with alleged irregularities and differentials in payments, as well as nepotistic restrictions on the use of the machines, which had been provided by foreign donors for the use of the whole community. The project in question was managed by members of Gibeon's ruling family.

A tale of empowerment

Gibeon is no exception to the social rifts that so impede local development initiatives. Usually these are ancient quarrels that run deep, perhaps exacerbated by recent political history, and marked by distinctions relating to families and clans. Many people still insist that they could never join forces in a co-operative effort.

Although the Sewing-Play was created in the privacy of our own workshop, it was still a bold statement in the context of the 'culture of silence' and obedience to the whims of the traditional leader, or *Kaptein*. In Gibeon this was Pastor Witbooi, then Minister of Labour and Manpower and very highly placed in the party hierarchy of the SWAPO government. His refusal to countenance the RISE pit-latrine programme in the shanty-town quarter of Gibeon is described below.

During one workshop, we found the group to be divided on whether they could start up a market garden without donated resources. The sides of the argument were then represented in two separate scenarios, and a final synthesis was evolved with the whole group. In this play, the characters decide to use a set of garden tools which had previously been donated and left with the town council for the use of community members. They need seeds and are debating whether they can be acquired through donation, or whether they are going to have to provide for themselves.

Meanwhile, they determine to get on with preparing the seedbeds, and send a delegate over to the relevant authorities to request the use of the tools. They are disappointed to be refused access, even though the tools were supposed to be at the disposal of the community. Angrily, one member insists that they should all go down to demand the tools, but another retorts: 'Nobody hears our voice — there's no point. They do not see us, we are invisible.' Others add, 'In Gibeon it's *who* you are that counts. They don't count us.' 'They' referred to the town authorities from the Witbooi camp. Again Verhelst spotted the danger of this syndrome when he described 'the real tragedy of "underdevelopment" [as] the resulting disintegration or destructuration of society [which] may go so far as an internalised negation of one's self and thus of one's real vitality' (Verhelst, 1990).

During subsequent workshops, the play was refined and re-focused to express and explore these feelings of invisibility or inferiority that remained implicit and merely alluded to in the original version. The issue of self-oppression became the overt subject, and the Self-Oppression Play which developed out of it was later given in public performance at the South Namibian Youth Seminar in Berseba. The seminar brought together youth from all over the south of the country and was aimed at establishing the Youth Enterprise Support Scheme (YES). There was a vociferous response from the assembly, whose audience interventions tried out both resistance and reason against the obdurate council official in the play who had refused access to the tools. They discussed in depth the 'self-oppression' implicit in the suggestion that there is no point in doing anything, since nobody hears your voice. The session agreed that if you see yourself as inferior you will remain so, and remain undeveloped. Like empowerment, it is a question of attitude — and attitudes can be changed.

Theatre, as a social process, is ideally suited to lubricating such change — by addressing the very social issues that so often constrain the acceptance of the often unfamiliar activities that we call development.

Tackling issues of concern

A few weeks later, a Farm Labourers Play was developed for performance at a meeting of the Farmers' Union (SNAFU) which was to be held in Gibeon. Some of the actors and many of the farmers had first-hand knowledge of the plight of such labourers, many of whom still live an enslaved existence on Namibia's wealthy commercial farms. There was a lively discussion about how their exploitation could be alleviated. The audience's vociferous and active interventionsm which amplified the gravity of the situation and explored ways of finding strength to withstand the oppression had to be forcibly terminated by the catering staff, who needed the chairs for the evening's programme. Not even the smells of barbecued goat that had wafted in from outside, nor the growing festive sounds, had been enough to halt the discourse. RISE has projects in the pipe-line which relate to the farm labourers' issue.

At that time, RISE had access to a Food for Work (FFW) programme, about which the staff were circumspect, but which had allowed our group to work together while they cleared Gibeon of all the broken bottles, beer cans, and general rubbish that gets thrown out into the wind-blown streets and empty lots. Once the clean-up was over, the group turned to the overdue pit latrines, digging pits both for their own homes and those of elderly or incapacitated neighbours. In the context of Gibeon, this was an act of defiance.

Some two years previously, RISE staff had already been turned out of Gibeon for implementing a pit-latrine programme against the wishes of the ruling Witbooi town council. Pastor Witbooi still maintained that these long-drop toilets would pollute the ground-water, despite the fact that almost all of Gibeon is built on a hill, and its water is pumped from a dam more than 30km away. A recent study shows the latrine programme to be the best way forward. Although they are reluctant to come out in public for fear of offending those in power, many in the community have privately expressed interest in the pit latrines. Few people can afford the water bills (from which they are currently exempt) and price of porcelain fittings that would attend the installation of Witbooi's preferred flush-toilet system. Besides, there were fears that many of their shacks would have to be torn down to allow relatively straight pipelines to be laid where none currently existed. The Ministry of Local Government and Housing had later requested that the programme continue, and there was European money earmarked for the project. But in 1994 it was still firmly blocked by *Kaptein* or Pastor Witbooi.

So when the group, through their 'Clean Up Gibeon' campaign, now turned to the digging of latrine pits for the many community members who wanted to get away from the foul and insanitary bucket latrines, it carried a distinctly political message — defiant and empowered. Unfortunately their pick-axes soon hit rocky ground, and their labours were halted; they needed a jack-hammer to make the holes deep enough. As luck would have it, the Minister of Local Government came to Gibeon for a public meeting on another issue, on the invitation of a women's group. Again displaying their new-found pluck, the members of GYP — male and female — availed themselves of the opportunity and attended the meeting, ready for the moment when she might ask, and she did, about the delays in the pit-latrine programme that her Ministry had recommended. Members of the Youth group were quick to reply, explaining their digging difficulties. Then and there she commanded that a jack-hammer be brought to Gibeon from the government works department, in order to complete the holes. This of course raised the profile of the campaign, and the group were further emboldened by their courage in raising the issue.

Speaking out in public meetings

To announce the arrival of the jack-hammer in Gibeon and its availability for all the community, RISE and the GYP prepared a two-day celebration, which was called The Plunge. There was to be a march through the town with songs and banners calling for the right to good health, and a play in two parts, *Potte en Pitte* ('Buckets and Pits'), to be performed over the two consecutive days around the town. The group prepared the play, and we came to Gibeon the day before to rehearse it, and to help coordinate the big event.

'Buckets' portrays the insanitary bucket toilets; the play is scatological in reference and hilarious in parts, but the laughter stops when the play ends with the death from diarrhoea of the child whom we have seen going to the toilet with her mother, lump of bread in hand.

The lively audience discussion looked forward to the performance of 'Pits' the next day, which takes up from the mother's distress as she searches for a way to avoid the same fate for her other children. She considers flush toilets and is finally advised that she could make use of the jack-hammer to dig a pit for a VIP latrine. She sets her elder son to work preparing the hole and calls for the Youth Group to bring the jack-hammer.

However ... at this point the youth group, as actors, were to enter the scene, with the jack-hammer, to dig the woman's pit. But we had received bad news. Some of the Witbooi leaders had seen the enthusiastic crowd marching and singing through the town the previous day and had made a private visit to Minister Amadhila herself, persuading her to withdraw the jack-hammer immediately. She had done so, and the scenario was altered accordingly.

Instead of the youth group and RISE coming to the woman at her toilet site, she is visited by the (actual) woman from the town clerk's office, who gives her (as she had given us) the news that the jack-hammer is not to be available to the people of Gibeon. Shocked silence gave way to heated discussion, which led to a petition with 100 names, drawn up on the spot for presentation to the Minister. The youth members still continue to dig holes where they can, while awaiting response from the authorities. At the time of writing, there have been some signs of conciliation — but not before the GYP's next move.

The Youth Project annexes Vrystaat farm

The progress made by the Gibeon group demonstrated a new strength among its members: empowered — by themselves, as they had been oppressed by themselves — they had been able to take on the formidable powers that controlled Gibeon. That confidence was endorsed by their next move, which was made possible through the resources and facilitation of RISE.

The youth group, all of them unemployed or dispossessed farmers, had often spoken about starting a chicken farm. Now they determined to annexe, or squat, a small piece of land some five kilometres outside Gibeon known, ironically, as *Vrystaat* ('Free State'). Although it stands on the mostly dry banks of the Fish river, it is barren but for a leaking concrete reservoir and wind-pump. Here Sentimub, the leader of the group, had grown up.

Uninhabited for some years, Sentimub's house had lost its doors and walls to thieves and vandals; corrugated iron from the roof now formed the walls and roof of Sentimub's current home in the Gibeon shanty-town. Other houses of the old settlement were evidenced only by the concrete slabs that were once their floors, the tin walls long since relocated. Using the pretext of Sentimub's return to his family homestead, some of the GYP began to move into the area with him, intending to start a co-operative chicken farm and eventually a goat-farming co-operative. They constructed shanty dwellings out of flattened tin drums and corrugated iron. Simple chicken runs were built with the support of RISE, who also provided loans for buying chickens. There were also some rabbits, and the project was looking increasingly solid.

The move was met with official silence by Witboois and his camp, although private displeasure had been clearly indicated. A year later, in 1995, the inauguration of YES was held at *Vrystaat*. It was attended by some 50 youth members from both Hardap and Karas Regions, as well as by various local government dignitaries, and reporters from the press and national television. One of the Witbooi leaders appeared some hours before the ceremony was due to begin and, before the press and the public arrived, delivered a conciliatory and even supportive speech to the assembled YES delegates. Perhaps this marks a turning point in relations between the GYP and their hereditary leaders.

Meanwhile the plays continue

The Gibeon group by now had an identity of their own and a confidence that allowed them to create and perform plays elsewhere, in the service of the development goals of the RISE partner communities. On one occasion, they were invited by the National Youth Council to create a play for performance at a Regional Youth Seminar on Unemployment, which was to show how to move from inertia to action in building up a project activity. RISE was then on Christmas recess and the play was done without any staff involvement.

Around the same time, RISE was to hold a Health and Sanitation seminar in Hoachanas, where there had not yet been any TFD activity. An afternoon spent with the GYP yielded a new Sanitation Play: the original 'Buckets' was played out by then and wholly inappropriate, since Hoachanas had a quite different set of constraints. They had made repeated attempts at VIP latrine programmes which would start up with great gusto and very soon run out of steam, leaving people back where they started. We devised a play with a seemingly circular structure.

The play opens with two families at home. Their toilet is the dry riverbank on the edge of their settlement. An elderly man goes out into the bush to relieve himself. He is hindered by thorns, worried about the driving wind that kicks dust into his face, and the lack of leaves or paper to clean himself. His neighbour, an old woman, disturbs him, and he cleans himself hastily with a stone. She in turn is interrupted by the taunts of peeping children. Forced to chase the kids, she throws stones at them, steps in her own dirt, and finally arrives at home where the family is eating. She immediately sits down to eat, defying the complaints of the others that her clothes and perhaps her hands are soiled.

Later, after she falls ill, the two families get together and determine to join the RISE sanitation programme and build themselves a pit latrine. While they are digging the hole, someone points out that RISE will be paying for the materials but not for their labour. They fall to arguing and finally abandon their efforts.

Then follow more scenes of scatological interest during which one girl, with the urgency of diarrhoea, defaecates right next to the house, under cover of night, while another is bitten by a scorpion. The families decide to resume work on the pit latrine, but general laziness and inability to co-operate with one another again cause the project to be abandoned.

The play ends with the old man trudging off once more towards the riverbed. The audience were quick to take part in the play, indicating their own reasons for discomfort with the distant riverbank toilet system, as well as illustrating their own misunderstanding of the original arrangements with RISE for support and subsidy in the subsequent building of the toilet hut. This grievance was unlocked and aired by the performance, making it easier to share the problems and discuss action. Although the characters moved along a circular narrative path, the audience made a spiral journey, no longer fetching up at square one, as they had done in the original events as depicted by the actors. Participation in the theatre event had opened up the issue, and the conflicts depicted had moved towards resolution.

Thus, the Gibeon group and their TFD skills began to serve as a utility for RISE beyond the immediate development of the Gibeon community itself. While it would be preferable, and is indeed intended, to establish theatre activity within each and every partner group, reality recommends having key performance-skilled groups that can be called upon to create problem-posing forum plays for outside seminars and workshops. Both forms are functions of cultural action, and the touring performances also prompted some communities to request RISE to initiate performance work with them. Of course the ideal situation would be if the community sought this help from the Gibeon (or any of the other CLT active partner groups), or even embarked upon it unaided. This dependency has not yet been dispelled.

A YES troupe is formed

Prompted by an invitation from the National Youth Council to enter our 'drama group' for a national drama competition, the Gibeon group later joined forces with members of the activity groups from other communities to form a single performing company representing the newly formed YES. First prizes for best play, actor, and actress went to the group, amid great cheers of excitement and song. Using a rotating membership from the community groups, the YES troupe went on to perform in various regional and national seminars and forums, such as the National People's Land Conference, a nationwide event organised by the association of Namibian NGOs (NANGOF) to investigate the still unresolved question of post-independence land redistribution.

Needless to say, this turn of events had a knock-on empowering effect on the nascent YES organisation (as yet almost without public profile), the YES troupe itself, the contributing community activity groups and, of course, the individual performers. The group became adept at shaping plays and (re)writing lyrics for traditional songs within the context of their plays. Performances often included the Namastap dance, as well as the forum interventions of the audiences that form the second part of any of their performances. Their reputation as a cultural troupe grew; they won further prizes in regional and national competitions, and performed one of their plays at a 1995 international community theatre festival in Zimbabwe.[1]

The process

Cultural action for re-empowerment, or field-workers' tool? As Paulo Freire (1974) remarks:

> [a]ll these aspects ... (peasants' knowledge of erosion, reforestation, farming, religion, death, etc.) ... are contained within a cultural totality. As a structure this cultural totality reacts as a whole. If one of its parts is affected, an automatic reflex occurs on the others.

The theatre work of these young Namibian farmers, with the understanding of issues stemming from their dramatic explorations of current topics, has brought conventional development work and conscientisation into the cultural arena. A simple arts-based community theatre programme, within an arts-based institution or a youth centre, may do the same: it may have as its aim the (re)activation and propagation of cultural activities, with social content, so as to enrich and develop the life of the community. In both processes, community performers and, by implication, the broader community, gain a voice and some measure of empowerment for having spoken out. If it succeeds, a sustainable channel for expression will have been opened.

However, the arts-based institution may not have resources to respond directly to these expressions; the development organisations, be they NGOs or community-based organisations may be better placed, having the material resources of their actual project activities or the networks to act as go-between with more appropriate agencies. 'Theatre work needs to be keyed into organisations which are concerned with raising consciousness and strengthening people's culture ...' (Etherton, 1982). That link with a development agency — and it could be any agency concerned with a people-centred development process — turns the community's creative expressions into dialogue, by responding. It is this capacity for dialogical communication which separates Theatre for Development from Community Theatre.

At first, the RISE staff had expected TFD to be a simple communications tool in their field-work, to be evaluated in terms of its supposed impact on the implementation of project activities. Emphasis on the cultural component of TFD was thus reduced. As already stated, preconceptions of 'drama' have long been influenced by church nativity and passion plays within these deeply religious Christian communities, and it was not considered out of place to introduce these (also foreign) ideas of inter-active improvised performance. Staff and communities took to it.

Elsewhere it has not been so simple. Where local cultural activity still retains its traditional identity, field-workers may gain respect from community leaders for having respected the culture of the community. It is important that the performers work from their own traditions and forms, evolving new forms of theatre or performance appropriate to their own culture. Unless the activity has been created by the community, people may take part readily while the project is present, but sustainability may be jeopardised.

In the past, TFD was usually perceived as a tool for the field-worker. It would involve simple role-plays in meetings, or didactic playlets presented by community performers, or even outside groups contracted to research and present these plays in a variety of locations. Either makes many fewer demands of the field-worker, who often has little time to spend planning and running drama sessions. There are signs of change, however, and TFD planners are facing the choice between placing more emphasis on the complex cultural component of development activity, or retaining TFD as a simple teaching tool. As Ross Kidd and Martin Bryam were already saying in 1981: 'the prominence of Theatre for Development as non-formal education must be de-emphasised, and more attention paid to a sustained programme of group organisation' (Kydd and Bryam, 1981).

The CLT programme was never restricted to role-plays in meetings. Most importantly, we retained the emphasis on training community activity groups in TFD skills. Drama exercises focused on the group, turning its attention on itself, so that the scenarios and plays evolved by the volunteers explored their own blocks against motivation and activity. These issues may have been known to field-workers, but were difficult to address during the normal course of meetings and technical workshops.

During the course of the RISE programme, we worked through many of the ideas and activities at both ends of the continuum between commitment to the cultural component, and the promotion of TFD as a tool with immediate and palpable applications. While the staff were primarily concerned that CLT should explore specific issues, we hoped to retain significant acknowledgement of the cultural aspect of the performance work. Indeed, this was well represented by the gradual integration of song and dance into the later performances.

A local methodology evolves

Over its substantial incubation period, a RISE CLT formula gradually emerged. Typically a field-worker would take a new activity group through a sequence of exercises aimed at introducing the idea of the 'tableau' or group sculpture. These 'snapshots' or 'images' were popularised by Augusto Boal, who would use them to depict a given thematic circumstance — typically some oppressive condition. Reformulation of the images by the rest of the group constitutes further exploration of the issue and may indicate the path towards change. Such image work is also used in the field of drama therapy.

In the CLT, image work marked the beginning of exploration through abstract concepts — such as greed, oppression, power, clan conflict, education — leading into improvised scenarios and plays. These concepts would not be proposed by the facilitator unless they had emerged from other images and scenarios or in direct conversation. During this period, the community group would be learning to look in on their own social reality, exploring and expressing the constraints within themselves which may have prevented them from taking an active role in development projects and community life.

The CLT groups were soon able to create *instant plays*, where a quick workshop prepares a play for presentation at a forthcoming meeting as a participatory way of opening debate. In addition, several other formats evolved, such as the *circular play* described above, which worked well in inter-active performance: the structure remains the same, but the content can be adjusted by the audience to portray, explore, and resolve the problem that persistently pushed people back down the ladder to square one. There was also the *five-minute play*, suitable for performance several times within the same afternoon. This could be particularly useful among sprawling communities, reaching people who do not, or cannot, come to meetings, or rallying attendance at a seminar or workshop.

All of the performances are improvised and interactive: that is to say they involve the audience in discussion, at the very least, and often actual participation in a repeat of the critical scenes, replacing the protagonist so as to present strategies of their own devising which would solve the problem portrayed in the initial presentation.

These formats would be unlikely to evolve so clearly in a shorter project period, where one works on the principle of handing over the skills and allowing the trainees to make of them what they will. We had the luxury of allowing these variations to develop out of the basic approach, once that was in place: both the circular and the five-minute plays appeared in the last months of the project. If the CLT continues to be applied in direct response to varying circumstances, then new formats will continue to evolve. That is the fluid nature of sustainability.

Furthermore, if we are looking for a readily replicable TFD formula, we should be careful. I have embarked on every project confident that the previous work had provided a formula which would be applicable in this new and as yet unfamiliar context. And I always get a rude shock.

In West Africa, I had had some success in using story games as a way in to scene-creation. The first workshop with a group of Bobo youths, however, fell flat when it turned out that for them a story exists, it is a fixed entity handed down through generations and adapted only by the story-tellers. Recently, in Johannesburg, our rather cerebral (CLT) issue-and-analysis formula, described above, proved inappropriate to the group of young trainees. It seems they were aspirant actors and actresses — some from the newly-emerging middle classes — and were not from a single community with burning issues all of their own. Image Theatre was not the best way in, for it relies either on actual involvement with the issues or a commitment to community theatre work which sets out, as CLT does, to 'uncover the covered', as RISE's Director Pintile Davids puts it. What did spark the group were open improvisation exercises similar to those which had worked so well with the non-literate Bobo farmers.

The guiding principle: co-intentionality

According to David Pammenter:

> Co-intentionality depends upon agreement, on the congruence of our ambition. It is an agreement to co-annunciate those ambitions. If the agreement takes the form of a desire to 'name' or change the world, then it is, in practice, concerned with the business of development. It is constitutive of community and therefore also exclusive. It depends upon dialogue in the form of a will to know. This dialogue, once articulated in practice, reveals and develops more about the reality

and human-ness of that community than any monological task-based agenda however that agenda is constructed. A co-intentional, practical pedagogy is necessarily self-reflexive and must remain so if it is not to be turned into its opposite (Pammenter, 1996).

There is no formula, no universally applicable methodology. There are only starting points. If anything, my assumption that the RISE formula, or the Bambara stories, could work elsewhere was *disempowering*. But it is not the offering of a game or exercise that disempowers, it is the assumption that an outside formula can work. And indeed, as Zakes Mda has argued, it is the 'Anomaly of Community Participation' that it tends to be 'imposed in a benevolent style from outside the community'.

> This means that Theatre for Development ... is incompatible with the ideas of Freire, since the educator, according to him, must be a co-worker and not an applier of formulas. Theatre workers are now seeking to join the rural communities as co-workers in the process of creating a theatre that will be more relevant. (Mda, 1993).

Until I shared what I had, it could not work, and empowerment would be off everyone's agenda except my own. Only when I let go of my own vision — or is it preconception? — of what form the theatre would take could we evolve a process together. Only then could the partner group own the process; only then could there be a path towards empowerment. From that point, any action that the group is to make — be it the introspective explorations that led in Gibeon to conscientisation through their explorations of self-oppression, or to the subsequent and defiant digging of the pit latrines, or to the performance of plays about them — is their own. That ownership in itself is part of the empowerment process. And it is the (participatory) process itself that is empowering, it is both means and end, opening doors for further new beginnings.

Carl Gaspar is correct when he asserts that all empowering theatre needs to be structured around living issues, but he is describing work in his own cultural context. It may be far more difficult as an intervening outsider to arrive at the point of trust and sharing where sensitive issues can be shared publicly. The Gibeon group addressed general topics to begin with, later moving on to more or less daring allusions to local problems whose deeper subject matter was their own self-exploration and engagement with the question of empowerment. Once that process was in motion, the partners began to look at and express the broader issues that constrain. They found that empowerment came from within: it meant a change of attitude, both individual and collective, from a declared helplessness to empowerment. Spontaneous theatrical exploration may ideally be suited to that end. But there are no formulas, only starting points and the guiding principles of co-intentional, people-centred, shared exploration and analysis.

Note

1 The story of the YES group is treated in greater detail in Mavrocordatos (1997).

References

Boal, A. (1979) *Theatre of the Oppressed*, London: Pluto Press.

Boal, A. (1992) *Games for Actors and Non-actors*, London: Routledge.

Etherton, M. (1982) *The Development of African Drama*, London: Hutchinson.

Freire, P. (1974) *Education: The Practice of Freedom*, London: Readers and Writers Publishing Co-operative.

Gaspar, K. 'The history of the growth and development of creative dramatics in Mindanao-Sulu, Philippines', *International Popular Theatre Alliance Newsletter* Vol 3 (quoted by Penina Mlama (1991) in *Culture and Development*, Uppsala: Scandinavian Institute of African Studies).

Kidd, R. and M. Bryam (1981) *Demystifying Pseudo-Freirian Non-Formal Education: A Case Description and Analysis of Laedza Batanani*, Toronto: ICAE.

Mavro, A. (1988) 'Rural Theatre for Integrated Development' Oxford: Oxfam/World Neighbors, Mali (project report for Oxfam).

Mavro, A. (1992), *Development Theatre: A Way to Listen* (video), London: SOS Sahel.

Mavrocordatos, A. (1995) 'Uncover the Covered: RISE Namibia Community Listening Theatre Programme. Final Report', Oxfam (UK and Ireland)-RISE, Namibia.

Mavrocordatos, A. (1997) 'Tied up in a Rope of Sand' in *Contemporary Theatre Review*, Harwood Academic Publishers, Spring 1997.

Mda, Z. (1993) *When People Play People*, London: Zed Books.

Mlama, P. (1991) *Culture and Development*, Uppsala: Scandinavian Institute of African Studies.

Pammenter, D. (1996) Paper presented at 'Development Communications: Theatre and Community Action for Change', International Centre for Development Communications conference, King Alfred's College, Winchester.

Verhelst, T. (1990) *No Life Without Roots*, London: Zed Books.

■ **Alex Mavrocordatos** *is based at King Alfred's University College, Winchester, where he is Senior Lecturer on the MA/Postgraduate Diploma in Theatre for Development. He has extensive experience in West and Southern Africa and is currently researching the area where PRA and TFD meet. This article was first published in* Development in Practice, *Volume 8, number 1, in 1998.*

Transparency for accountability: civil-society monitoring of Multilateral Development Bank anti-poverty projects

Jonathan Fox

Background

The multilateral development banks (MDBs) have significantly increased their lending for 'targeted' anti-poverty projects since the early 1990s, but few systematic, independent, field-based assessments of their effectiveness are available. In spite of much-improved civil-society monitoring of MDB environmental and macro-economic impact, field-based analysis of their anti-poverty lending has lagged behind.

Monitoring and evaluation (M&E) is necessary to provide feedback to decision-makers and stakeholders regarding what kinds of anti-poverty programme are successful and why. M&E is also necessary to hold policy-makers accountable for policies and programmes that do not work, and it is therefore an essential component of good governance. Yet billions of dollars of international development aid continue to flow without systematic M&E. While donor-agency policy-makers may believe that they know the destination and impact of their funds, without independent confirmation they are essentially relying on information that comes from interested parties, such as borrowing-government agencies, and donor-agency staff associated with the same programmes.

Institutions based in civil society could contribute to increased effectiveness of anti-poverty investments by generating reliable analysis of the distribution and impact of anti-poverty aid flows. Independent information and analysis is necessary but not sufficient, however. In order to have 'pro-accountability impact', this information must become public and reach key stakeholders — including both the ostensible beneficiaries and the donors.

A recent World Bank evaluation of its own portfolio underscores the serious issues at stake. As of late 1995:

> ... a reduction in the failure rate of completed Bank operations has proven elusive. Today, about a third of Bank-financed projects are rated as 'unsatisfactory' by OED [Operations Evaluation Department] upon completion. And the failure rate has been stuck at about this level for five years.[1]

Since this assessment is based on the Bank's own data, which other OED studies of M&E have found to be open to serious question, it is probably an underestimate of the problem of effectiveness. Within the World Bank, the limited reliability of M&E information from operational staff has been clearly documented by the Bank's own evaluation department. The most comprehensive study of M&E within World Bank projects was carried out by OED in 1994; it found as follows:

> It has been Bank policy since the mid 1970s to promote monitoring and evaluation (M&E) of project implementation ... the overall results of the 20-year M&E initiative have been disappointing ... the history of M&E in the Bank is characterised by non-compliance.[2]

The study found that projects planned little M&E: 'The 1989 [policy] called for effective M&E in all projects, but this mandate has been respected in less than half the projects where strong M&E should have been installed' (p. v). More M&E was planned in projects in the sectors of agriculture, education, health, population, and water supply than in other sectors, and these are mainly poverty-targeted sectors. But even where M&E was planned, performance was poor. These findings should not be surprising, since neither Bank operational staff nor borrowing-government agencies have any incentive to be monitored and evaluated — especially by others. This underscores the importance of encouraging other channels for M&E, 'independent of the mainstream bureaucracy but with access to it', according to OED.[3] Yet the rest of the World Bank has not, so far, been able to create its own demand for evaluation, since management still does not encourage staff to build effective M&E components into projects. Therefore support and demand must come from outside MDBs and borrowing governments. Here, pro-accountability actors in civil society, in both donor countries and developing countries, share a common interest in greater transparency as a path towards greater accountability and more effective MDB anti-poverty investments.

Bringing in civil society

Independent and sustained M&E is part of the broader process of strengthening civil society's capacity to hold both governments and MDBs accountable for development-policy decisions. Strengthening accountability is easier said than done, however. Because of the vast diversity between and within regions, countries, and sectors, it is inappropriate to propose any single pre-designed M&E strategy. Effective approaches will need to be tailor-made for each policy area and socio-political environment. Nevertheless, civil-society M&E efforts do face some common challenges, including the following.

Learning from below

One of the main advantages of independent M&E initiatives is their capacity to cross-check official data with field evidence, and by speaking directly to ostensible beneficiaries.[4] This is crucial for assessing the difference between the delivery of services on paper and in practice. For example, water pipes may have been installed, but that does not mean that safe water actually flows. Schools may be built, but lack teachers or books. Clinics may be open, but staff may be abusive or absent. This process involves surveying non-beneficiaries too, to find out which groups may have been excluded and why. Compared with other kinds of MDB-funded project, such as large infrastructure investments, anti-poverty projects are highly dispersed and therefore assessment is highly labour-intensive.

Building networks

Civil-society M&E efforts also face the challenge of building channels of communication with government and MDB officials. Without some degree of access to officials who design and implement policy, it is very difficult to compare the official claims of resource allocation with actual patterns and impact. In many countries, access to such information is largely discretionary. MDB information-disclosure policies, while much improved since 1994, do not cover the level of disaggregated data needed to monitor flows and impact on the ground. Access to policy-makers is also critical for developing effective strategies to feed M&E findings back into the policy process. Local and international supporters of independent M&E capacity-building face the challenge of creating the necessary political space and respect for autonomy *vis à vis* both governments and donor agencies. This process usually involves building *de facto* coalitions both with pro-reform policy-makers (if any) and with pro-accountability stakeholders in civil society.

Producing reliable generalisations

Civil-society M&E efforts need to steer clear of sterile academic debates about M&E methodologies. For example, World Bank economists insist on the importance of comparing outcomes to a hypothetical counter-factual (what might have happened in the absence of the intervention).[5] Sophisticated social-science debates focus on how to determine causes of impacts, but most are based on two flawed assumptions. First, they assume that the factual information about outcomes is reliable, which OED's studies of the World Bank M&E suggest is inappropriate. Second, they assume that sophisticated statistical techniques can add rigour to arguments which are based on hypothetical assumptions. The key challenge is to find out who is getting what, as quickly as possible. Reliable generalisations involve the following procedures:

■ *Specifying indicators clearly and over the whole policy-implementation process.* This includes indicators of policy 'inputs', such as the distribution of programme spending across localities or regions; indicators of policy decision-making processes (why resources were allocated where they were); indicators of 'outputs' (services actually delivered or investment actually made); and indicators of outcomes (such as whether incomes rose, health improved or local producers' organisations were strengthened).

■ *Monitoring representative samples of areas, communities, groups, or individuals ostensibly targeted by the project or programme.* Listening to beneficiaries is often dismissed as a qualitative exercise and therefore anecdotal, but listening to large numbers of representative beneficiaries produces data that can be aggregated, thus giving a wider perspective. Combining the advantages of both qualitative and quantitative methods is critical.

■ *Monitoring unplanned programme impacts.* Many development interventions have significant effects which were not considered among the original official goals. Indeed, the whole point of independent M&E is to discover what actually happened, whether or not it was 'supposed' to have happened. This includes both positive spill-over or multiplier effects, such as reinforcing poor people's organisations and voice, as well as negative 'externalities', or perverse institutional effects, such as the strengthening of local authoritarian bosses in the name of 'participatory decentralisation'.

Building credibility both above and below

Producing reliable data and analysis is not enough: results must also *appear* to be reliable. Independent M&E units face the challenge of constructing an image of credibility among a wide range of stakeholders, ranging from project 'target groups' to the media, other researchers, government policy-makers, and international donors. By contributing to a climate of constructive, informed public debate over development policy, and by promoting the principle of public accountability, civil-society M&E efforts can help to strengthen an enabling environment, within which representative organisations of low-income people can gain greater voice and leverage over the public sector.

Making findings public

Development agency files are filled with critical evaluations which made no impact because they remained confidential. M&E is likely to make a difference only if it can be used as a tool by actors who favour change, whether they be poor people's organisations, or officials in government, or international agencies willing to challenge the vested interests that benefit from the *status quo*.

Civil-society M&E units face the challenge of promoting *two-way* information flows. From the bottom up, they need to channel their findings about the results on the ground to policy-makers and opinion-makers. From the top down, they need to disseminate information about what projects were supposed to do among their ostensible beneficiaries. By making public a project's goals and targets, questions and claims from low-income citizens' organisations can be legitimised. Moreover, if low-income groups learn that they were denied access to loans contracted in their name, they have more reason to support future independent monitoring efforts, and to use that information to influence the policy process to promote more effective investments and service delivery. In this context, promoting these two-way information flows in real time is crucial, so that the pro-accountability actions can be taken *before* project investments have been fully disbursed.

Institution-building

In some countries, or regions within countries, researchers may need additional training to develop the capacity for policy monitoring and analysis that both fits with local realities and meets international standards. To have maximum pro-accountability impact, independent M&E needs to be systematic, timely, and rigorous. This involves significant capacities for field outreach and for analysis and dissemination. Independent M&E thus requires institutional capacity, though not necessarily large investments in infrastructure or overheads. The key resources are human: institution-building depends primarily on experienced field researchers, committed to the principle of public accountability, and willing to take the risks inherent in asking sensitive questions about how public funds are used.

Cost-effectiveness

Some sceptical MDB economists question the cost-effectiveness of investing in M&E, and the usual MDB practice of bringing in expensive international consultants to produce confidential reports is open to question. If a bottom-up, independent M&E effort is linked to pro-accountability strategies, however, then allocating a small proportion of an anti-poverty loan is likely to pay off. For example, assume that one per cent of a $100 million rural health project is invested in independent M&E. Without informed debate in civil society, a significant fraction of the $100 million is likely to be used inefficiently, or some large fraction of the services is likely to be of low quality. With the small investment in transparent M&E, those significant fractions can be reduced to small fractions, through civil-society debate which focuses on the bottlenecks and problem areas. In this kind of proactive, real-time investment-monitoring scenario, independent M&E pays for itself within the terms of the project — because fewer project funds are wasted. This is hardly a new concept, yet billions continue to be lent without the benefit of such a strategy of 'effectiveness through accountability'.

In this scenario, questions about the cost-effectiveness of investing in independent M&E should address the famous 'counter-factual': what are the costs, in wasted resources, of *not* investing in independent M&E?

Concluding notes

Two different kinds of civil-society initiative stand out as important experiments.

In India, the NGO Public Affairs Center has pioneered the use of opinion surveys to find out which public services are more versus less effective. With a sophisticated combination of quantitative and qualitative research, the Center develops a clear ranking of public agencies, from most to least effective and most to least responsive to their citizen-clients. The results are disseminated through the local and national media. While not focused specifically on MDB-funded projects, this strategy is highly relevant for the many public-service provision projects funded by MDBs, especially in urban areas.[6]

In Mexico, the NGO Trasparencia focuses specifically on MDBs involved in rural poverty-related projects. It is developing the capacity to promote the kind of two-way information flows described above, providing timely and translated information about on-going and planned anti-poverty investments to representative grassroots organisations, while analysing and disseminating findings about the actual performance of anti-poverty projects.[7]

The Public Affairs Center focuses on civil society in terms of individual 'clients' of public services, and relies on the mass media to provoke the public debate necessary to turn information into pro-accountability public action. Trasparencia adopts a more low-profile, coalition-building approach which is also part of a targeted pro-accountability strategy. It concentrates on building project-specific partnerships with grassroots organisations of the rural poor, sharing information, and advising them on different options in terms of how to approach both government and MDBs.

Both approaches focus on providing reliable and credible information to other actors in civil society. They are therefore not primarily advocacy organisations; instead they try to facilitate constructive participation by a wide range of civil-society actors in the policy process.

Civil-society M&E units will choose widely varying methodologies and strategies for influencing policy, and there is a great deal of room for experimentation and South-South learning. Before that can happen, however, private foundation funders and international donor agencies need to decide whether independent M&E capacity-building is a worthwhile investment.

Notes

1 Operations Evaluation Department, 'Process Review of the FY95 Annual Report on Portfolio Performance (ARPP),' Washington: World Bank, Report No. 15113, 22 November 1995.

2 Operations Evaluation Department, 'An Overview of Monitoring and Evaluation in the World Bank,' Washington: World Bank Report No. 13247, 30 June 1994. See also the follow-up report, 'Monitoring and Evaluation Plans in Staff Appraisal Reports Issued in Fiscal Year 1995,' Washington: World Bank Report No. 15222, 29 December 1995, which found little change in terms of management support.

3 Operations Evaluation Department, 'Building evaluation capacity,' *Lessons and Practices*, World Bank, November 1994, p. 2. Here OED claims to support the building of evaluation capacity, but recognises that its record has been 'mixed' (p. 3).

4 A few World Bank analysts promote 'beneficiary assessments,' but they are marginal to most projects. See for example, Lawrence Salmen, 'The listening dimension of evaluation' in Operations Evaluation Department, *Evaluation and Development: Proceedings of the 1994 World Bank Conference*, Washington: World Bank, 1995. Most recently, see Deepa Narayan and David Nyamwaya, 'Learning from the Poor: A Participatory Poverty Assessment in Kenya', Environment Department Papers, No. 034, World Bank, May 1996. Partnerships between NGOs, the World Bank, and governments for the purposes of evaluation are just beginning to emerge. Overall, NGO collaboration was involved in 41 per cent of projects approved in FY 1995. Within this group, approximately 20 per cent involved some NGO role in evaluation (Operations Policy Group, 'Co-operation Between the World Bank and NGOs: FY 1995 Progress Report', March 1995 draft, p. 5). However, these NGO evaluations could have been confined to very small subsets of project activities. For discussions of monitoring participation, see Norman Uphoff, 'Monitoring and evaluating popular participation in World Bank-assisted projects,' and Christopher Ward, 'Monitoring and evaluation,' both in Bhuvan Bhatnagar and Aubrey Williams, eds., *Participatory Development and the World Bank*, Washington: World Bank Discussion Paper, No. 183, 1992.

5 See, for example, Lyn Squire, 'Evaluating the effectiveness of poverty alleviation programmes', in Operations Evaluation Department, *Evaluation and Development: Proceedings of the 1994 World Bank Conference*, Washington: World Bank, 1995.

6 See Samuel Paul, 'Evaluating public services: a case study on Bangalore, India,' in Operations Evaluation Department, *Evaluation and Development: Proceedings of the 1994 World Bank Conference*, Washington: World Bank, 1995.

7 For one such study, see Jonathan Fox and Josefina Aranda, *Decentralisation and Rural Development in Mexico: Community Participation in Oaxaca's Municipal Funds Programme*, La Jolla: University of California, San Diego, Center for US-Mexican Studies, Monograph Series 42, 1996. For more recent Spanish-language reports, contact Trasparencia at Avenida de los Maestros 91-8, Colonia Santo Tomas, CP 11340 Mexico, DF, +(52 5) 341-3184. http://www.laneta.apc.org/trasparencia/

■ **Jonathan Fox** *is Associate Professor of Social Science in the Latin American and Latino Studies Program at the University of California. This article first appeared in* Development in Practice*, Volume 7, number 2, in 1997.*

Strengthening unions:
the case of irrigated agriculture
in the Brazilian North East

Didier Bloch

About half of the Brazilian North East is occupied by the *Sertao*, a semi-desert area some three times the size of Great Britain, which is both very poor and densely populated. The region is, however, crossed by the San Francisco river, whose valley, especially around the towns of Petrolina and Juazeiro, has been the scene of huge socio-economic upheavals.

The first occurred in two stages, corresponding to the filling in 1979 and 1987 of two World Bank-funded hydro-electric dams: as a direct result, 100,000 people were displaced, some of whom became landless.

The second, more gradual, upheaval started in the mid-1970s with the decision to expand irrigated agriculture. Individuals and large private groups, attracted by the infrastructure put in place by the government, along with generous financial incentives, invested hundreds of millions of dollars along the banks of the San Francisco.

Two fruits, mangoes and grapes, soon experienced considerable success in both domestic and export markets. The grapes that are found in British, French, and German supermarkets at Christmas-time come from this part of Brazil. The vineyards provide significant employment: more than 15,000 labourers work there, the majority being permanent and female. The other labour-intensive crops, for example tomatoes and onions, tend to have a variable contingent of workers, depending on the period, paid by day or by season during harvests.

All these developments, along with the influx of small peasant farmers fleeing the terrible droughts that ravage the *Sertao* every ten years, explain why Petrolina and Juazeiro have seen an unprecedented growth in their populations and economies over the last two decades.

New union strategies

These transformations have forced the rural workers' unions (which in Brazil are organised by municipality) to rethink their strategy in the Sub-Medio San Francisco. Initially focused on small farmers, they had first to mobilise their efforts to help the victims of the big dams, demanding their resettlement on new lands. From the early 1990s, the more dynamic of these set up specific structures to defend the rights of the increasingly numerous salaried workers in irrigated agriculture. Two unions in the state of Pernambuco (Petrolina and Santa Maria de Boa Vista) effectively took up the defence of these wage labourers, despite the fact that on the other bank of the river, in the State of Bahia, their opposite numbers carried on with clientilistic policies focused on small farmers.

After being defeated in 1991 during the first attempt at negotiating with the owners of the irrigated farms, the two unions decided at the end of 1993 to start a big education and mobilisation campaign among the wage labourers. This time they benefited from two sources of support. On the one hand they had advisers, experienced lawyers and negotiators from the regional and national union federations. On the other, they received a small grant (US$6,300) from Oxfam (UK and Ireland), to finance an educational campaign on basic labour rights. This represented cash which they did not have, given the small number of workers actually unionised. The majority of the workers are essentially poor migrants from the arid zones of the *Sertao*, for whom wage labour and irrigated agriculture are completely new.

A large mobilisation process preceded the difficult negotiation phase. Information meetings were organised at people's places of work and living quarters, where the main demands of the workers were focused, as well as general assemblies in the two towns. Finally in February 1994, the first collective agreement in the San Francisco valley was signed: a significant occasion, which the Brazilian Minister of Labour attended in person. The agreement was valid for a year, and a new round of negotiation took place in February 1995, when new advances were made.

Improvements for the wage labourers

So what are the results a year and a half after the signing of the first accord? In terms of the direct benefits for the workers, the most important is without doubt the increase in wages. In 1995, the permanent workers were getting a minimum wage plus 10 per cent, which is around US$110 monthly; and a decrease in irregular employment (the employers registering their workers more than in the past, thus guaranteeing them their basic social rights). Overall, the working conditions have improved, even though they remain far from the ideal, as we shall see.

As far as the unions are concerned, the benefits are also visible. Following the campaign, the number of unionised wage labourers more than doubled, rising from 1,400 to 3,500, of whom 2,500 regularly pay their subscription. The unions have strengthened both their consituency and their financial autonomy. They also won free access to the farms at certain times for the union representatives; stable employment; and the right to two days' leave per month.

From Oxfam's point of view, a simple analysis of the ratio of costs (for Oxfam) versus the benefits (for the workers) demonstrates the multiplier effect of financing the campaign for the workers' rights. Following the 1994 campaign, about 20,000 workers each gained US\$6.47 extra each month. (The net monthly salary in 1993 was US\$64.70.) Calculating on the basis of 13 months' annual salary, that makes US\$1.68 million from financial support of US\$6,300, representing a multiplier ratio of 1:267. Of course, Oxfam is not the only factor in the campaign's success. Apart from the dynamism of the unions, the end of the terrible drought which assailed the North East between 1990 and 1993 also contributed to the reduction in available labour, and thus helped in the negotiations. Oxfam's support was necessary but not sufficient to achieving the package of results.

Finally, it is important to mention the increasing number of women who are engaged in union activity, becoming union representatives and indeed leading the strikes. Apart from the fact that they are in the majority in the vineyards, it is the women who are particularly affected by forms of abuse, ranging from sexual harassment by the overseers to the dismissal of pregnant women and the latters' exposure to the spraying of poisonous products. Here again, Oxfam has played an advisory role, insisting that gender questions have a special treatment at the very heart of the union.

A limited victory

Though there have been some concrete gains, there is still much to be done. Firstly, despite the support of the Federal Labour Office, the majority of the clauses in the accord are not respected. For example, the spraying of toxic chemicals continues to be carried out during work hours, and there is often no drinking water available, thus obliging the workers to drink the polluted water direct from the irrigation channels.

Secondly, it is the permanent workers who have most benefited from the accord, though these are on fixed-term contracts. However, the great mass of day and seasonal labourers are very difficult to organise, particularly as many live several hundred kilometres away, making the return journey between their home areas in the *Sertao* and the banks of the river each year. Thus the most numerous and the most exploited category, the seasonal workers (and very often their children) is for the moment beyond the reach of the union. An illustration of this is the dreadful labour fair that draws together several thousand labourers on the outskirts of Petrolina. The work these people do in the tomato and onion plantations has been classed as semi-slavery by a regional newspaper not given to exaggeration.

Finally, the accord takes in only one bank of the river, on the Pernambuco side. On the other, in the state of Bahia, the situation has hardly changed. Indeed, there could be a negative impact: lower salaries in Bahia could encourage new business concerns to give preference to establishing there in the future.

Limits of the development model

Over and above the question of employment, one is faced with the development model itself. On this, the union's stand is ambivalent. While calling for agrarian reform, it is not putting forward any concrete proposal that takes into account the specific situation of the riverine region.

Let us go back to the problem of the wage labourers: what is a monthly wage of US$110 worth? In Brazil, it is just about enough to buy a basic food ration, which covers only the minimum nutritional needs of a family of four. In other words, it is a miserable salary. The 40 per cent of families in Juazeiro (population 130,000) who live in poverty are testimony to that.

Further, the great majority of workers who are 'lucky' enough to get this wage work in the vineyards. Their work depends on the employment of a large number, five per hectare, of poorly qualified and ill-paid people. A simple calculation based on the rate of productivity (30 tonnes per hectare per year over two and a half pickings) demonstrates that there is little scope for increases in the workers' wages. A monthly wage of US$200 for the employees would mean no profit for the owners. Further, some would assert that this method does not allow for the simultaneous production of a large quantity and good-quality grapes, so that exports are limited to the months of November and December, when Brazil has a monopoly of the world market. As far as the domestic market is concerned, purchasing power is limited and it is unlikely that there will be a large increase in sales of an unessential product such as grapes.

In short, whether it be grapes or other products, apart from the climatic and financial conditions in the region, it is the low wages that make it attractive to business. The unions can go on attacking the low wages and employment conditions, but they will always come up against the 'economic imperative', unless they can come up with other suggestions for the way production is organised, or (better still) come up with new options that are both economically viable and socially just.

Finally, we should mention the serious ecological threats faced by the region. Among the worst are the salination of the irrigated areas resulting from poor drainage, the pollution of the river from fertiliser and pesticides and increasing waste from urban areas, and the silting of the river brought on by deforestation of the bordering areas. These phenomena are already advanced enough for some experts to be talking of the death of the river, in other words its loss of commercial viability (irrigation as well as fishing and energy generation) within two or three generations. The potential loss of productivity, and thus employment, due to the salination of the soils, should concern the unions.

Conclusion

If we are really talking about strengthening the unions of the Sub Medio San Francisco, this should include giving them access to a range of information about international business, the agri-food business, restructuring of world production and irrigation techniques, and their long-term impacts on the environment, thus encouraging them to get beyond the level of immediate labour issues. This would require promoting real networking with other unions and NGOs working in the heartland of the *Sertao*. In effect, the absence of a serious programme for the 12 million rural inhabitants of these semi-arid lands, and the resultant migration towards the river and large urban centres on the coast, constitute the fundamental problems of regional development.

Without a range of information that would allow them to participate in defining and implementing new directions for development, unions as well as NGOs risk being left in the wake of a development model that is led by global economic forces, by the business-owning class in Brazil whose sole motive is profit, and by a government that is little inclined to discussion, and from whom there is little hope of great efforts on the social or ecological front.

■ **Didier Bloch** *is a journalist and consultant to Oxfam-Brazil, and author of 'As frutas amargas do Velho Chico'. This article first appeared in* Development in Practice, *Volume 6, number 4, in 1996.*

The People's Communication Charter

Cees J. Hamelink

The development of the GII ... must be a democratic effort ... In a
sense, the GII will be a metaphor for democracy itself ... I see a new
Athenian Age of democracy forged in the fora the GII will create ...
The Global Information Infrastructure ... will circle the globe with
information superhighways on which all people can travel. These
highways — or, more accurately, networks of distributed intelligence
— will allow us to share information, to connect, and to
communicate as a global community. (US Vice-President Al Gore)

Highway Utopias

Development has never seemed so easy to achieve. An abundance of
Utopian scenarios promise sustainable development once digital
highways have been constructed. The deployment of new information
and communication technologies (ICTs) is to usher in a 'new civilisation',
an 'information revolution', or a 'knowledge society'.

This line of thought emphasises historical discontinuity as a major
consequence of technological developments. New social values will evolve,
new social relations will develop, and the 'zero sum society' comes to a
definite end, once ICTs have realised worldwide access to information for all.

The current highway Utopias forecast radical changes in economics,
politics, and culture. In the economy, the ICTs will create more
productivity and improved chances for employment. They will upgrade
the quality of work in many occupations, and also offer myriad
opportunities for small-scale, independent, and decentralised forms of
production. In the domain of politics, the decentralised and increased

access to unprecedented volumes of information will improve the process of democratisation. All people will be empowered to participate in public decision-making. In the cultural field, new and creative lifestyles will emerge, as well as vastly extended opportunities for different cultures to meet and understand each other; and new 'virtual communities' will be created which easily cross all the traditional borders of age, gender, race, and religion.

The essential vehicle to make these dreams come true will be the 'Global Information Infrastructure' (GII). The GII was launched by US Vice-President Al Gore in a speech at the 1994 conference of the International Telecommunication Union (ITU) in Buenos Aires. The proposal has received a good deal of international political and corporate support. The meeting of the G-7 in Brussels in February 1995 decided to move ahead with implementing this global infrastructure. Its Final Declaration stated that the global information society is expected to enrich people worldwide by providing, to developing countries and countries in transition, the chance 'to leapfrog states of technology'. Countries such as Canada, Japan, Singapore, and the European Union are intent on the rapid realisation of national information infrastructures.

The developing world has also shown considerable interest, as illustrated by the African region. Interest in ICTs was very prominent during the First African Regional Symposium on Telematics for Development (1995) and also at the 21st session of the Conference of African Ministers responsible for Economic, Social and Development Planning in the same year. The 1995 Cairo Workshop on the Role and Impact of Information and Communication Technologies in Development recommended that 'without proper national information and communication policies, strategies and implementation plans, countries will not be able to partake fully in the global information society'. Although most African countries are not known as hot-spots for ICT development, the United Nations Economic Commission for Africa (ECA) Conference of Ministers adopted on 2 May 1995 Resolution 795, 'Building Africa's Information Highway'. In this, African ministers for economic and social development requested that the ECA set up a high-level working group on information and communication technologies in Africa made up of African technical experts, with a view to preparing a plan of action. The High-Level Working Group (after meetings in Cairo, Addis Ababa, and Dakar) produced Africa's Information Society Initiatives: An Action Framework to Build Africa's Information and Communication Infrastructure. In May 1996, the plan was authorised by the Conference of

Ministers meetings at Addis Ababa. The May 1996 Conference on Information Society and Development (ISAD) in South Africa was the venue for launching this initiative, which by 2010 foresees for Africa an information society in which:

Every man and woman, schoolchild, village, government office, and business can access information through computers and telecommunications; Information and decision support systems are used to support decision making in all the major sectors of each nation's economy; Access is available throughout the region to international, regional and national 'information highways'; A vibrant private sector exhibits strong leadership in growing information-based economies; African information resources are accessible globally reflecting content on tourism, trade, education, culture, energy, health, transport, and natural-resource management; and Information and knowledge empower all sectors of society.

Big info-communications business is also taking a growing interest. Companies such as Time/Warner are making massive investments to secure a profitable place on the Information Superhighway. The GII project has a large number of 'computeropian prophets' such as European Commissioner Martin Bangemann, the Chief Executive Officers of companies such as AT&T, IBM, Microsoft, and American Express, media-tycoon Rupert Murdoch, authors such as Alvin Toffler, and US Vice-President Al Gore. The latter stated in his Buenos Aires address that the GII is a prerequisite to sustainable development. It will provide solutions to environmental problems, improve education and healthcare, create a global market-place, and forge a new Athenian age of democracy.

It is obviously true that ICTs can perform tasks that are indeed essential to democratic and sustainable social development. They can provide low cost, high speed, worldwide inter-active communications among large numbers of people, unprecedented access to information sources, and alternative channels for information provision which counter the commercial news channels; and they can support networking, lobbying, and mobilising. The 1995 Fourth World Conference on Women held in Beijing, for example, showed the benefits that women's groups could get from using ICTs. The overall experience of those involved in the Beijing electronic networking (despite all the real limitations) was that the low-cost and high-speed communications had improved organisational efficiency and facilitated access to up-to-date information. Southern non-government organisations (NGOs) indicated that the networks had allowed them to influence the conference agenda, to mobilise lobbies, and to counter commercial press coverage. The participants generally felt that the technology had strong empowerment potential. There are, however, serious obstacles in the way of realising this potential.

Economic factors

The introduction and use of ICTs do not take place in a social vacuum. This process cannot be separated from the emerging global communication order. The reality of this order is a global info-communications market that has yielded in 1997 over US$1.5 trillion in revenues, and that continues to feature a process of mergers and acquisitions which is very likely to lead to the control of the world's information and cultural supply by some four to six multi-media mega-conglomerates around the turn of the century.

Today's forerunner of the projected GII, the Internet, has begun to attract the attention of the major forces in this global market-place. The Internet, at present a public meeting place where more than 30 million PC users in some 150 countries exchange information, search databases, play games, and chat — and which has been guided by the rule of sharing information for free — has now been discovered as a major vehicle for commercial advertising. This raises the question: will the Internet (the Net) will remain an open, free, competitive, egalitarian public space? This is highly unlikely, since it cannot develop outside the current global economic order. It is fast becoming the new global advertising medium.

There is a great battle underway, with the future control of the world's largest network at stake. Money-making on the Net will require it to become an advertising medium. For companies to re-coup their enormous investments, advertising and sales will be essential. The competition to attract advertising dollars is already starting. As a result, a communicative structure that so far has been public, non-commercial, unregulated, uncensored, anarchistic, and very pluralistic may soon turn into a global electronic shopping mall.

It is difficult to understand how this transformation of the Net from a public forum into a commercial vehicle (much as happened in many countries with television) can contribute to the realisation of the empowerment potential of ICTs. In any case, if the GII project is predominantly driven by the search for profits, it is highly improbable that current inequalities in access to and use of ICTs will go away.

Political obstacles

An important political obstacle to the creation of open, public networks is the current global trend towards deregulatory policies. Their bottom line is that the introduction and use of ICTs should be largely, if not totally, a matter of market relations. The G-7 and the EU governments have reiterated that the GII will have to be constructed primarily through private investments.

Global and regional policy-making (primarily) addresses the removal of all obstacles in the way of the unhindered operation of the major ICT-investors on markets around the world. The policies of the World Trade Organisation (WTO) and International Monetary Fund (IMF) are instrumental in supporting the global commercial media system. They are not particularly helpful to the democratisation of the world's info-communications sector. A landmark in deregulatory policies is the 1997 WTO telecom agreement. This requires signatories (68 countries, representing 98 per cent of the US$600 billion telecom trade) to liberalise their markets to foreign competition. According to various governments, this will strongly facilitate the global Superhighway, but most probably as an infrastructure for transnational business, rather than necessarily as platform for public debate on social development.

The agreement has seriously compromised the chances for universal network access, since national policies may be considered anti-competitive if governments intervene in the market to guarantee universal service. According to industry spokesmen, the agreement will speed up the search for global alliances.

Info-telecom disparity

There seems to be general agreement in the scientific literature and in public policy statements that the gap in access to ICTs between the developed and developing countries in widening, and that this hinders the integration of all countries into the Global Information Society. The seriousness of the gap is clearly demonstrated by the figures for the world distribution of telephony.

- There are one billion telephones in the world and approximately 5.7 billion people. Today some 15 per cent of the world population occupy 71 per cent of the world's main telephone lines. Low-income countries (where 55 per cent of the world population lives) have fewer than 5 per cent of the world's telephone lines.

- High-income countries have 50 telephone lines per 100 inhabitants. Many-low income countries have less than one telephone line per 100; this ranges from Cambodia with 0.06 to China with 0.98 in 1992 (according to figures provided by the ITU/BDT Telecommunication Indicator Database).
- More than half the world's population have never even used a telephone!
- Fewer than 6 per cent of Internet computers are in Eastern Europe, Asia, Africa, the Middle East, Latin America and the Caribbean. Fewer than 4 per cent of World Wide Web users are in the Third World.
- In India there is one telephone line and 0.2 PCs for 100 people, compared with 49 lines and 15 PCs in Japan, and 63 lines and 21 PCs per 100 people in the USA.

The reality of the widening gap in ICT capacity raises the serious concern that the poorer countries may not be able to overcome the financial and technical obstacles which hamper their access to the new technologies. An obvious question regarding the former is whether the international community is ready to provide the massive investments needed for the renovation, upgrading, and expansion of networks in developing countries. To illustrate the scope of funds involved: it would take some US$12 billion to get half of the Philippines population on the Internet. To increase tele-density from 0.46 lines per 100 inhabitants to one per 100 in sub-Saharan Africa would require an investment of US$ 8 billion.

A particular funding problem also arises if the Internet is to be transformed into a global inter-active electronic highway. This demands a radical expansion of current band-width to transport all these signals. Simply to provide broad-band capacity to all US citizens would demand investments of several hundreds of billions of dollars.

In response to the challenge of the info-telecom gap, many public and private donor institutions have proposed plans to eliminate the disparity. Concern about the gap has inspired the World Bank, for example, to establish in early 1995 the Information for Development Program, charged with assisting developing countries in their integration into the global information economy. In 1995, the ITU established WorldTel: an ambitious project to generate private investments to bridge the global telecom gap by developing basic infrastructures. WorldTel aims to establish some 40 million telephone connections in developing countries in the next ten years, with an investment fund of at least US$ 1 billion.

AT&T plans that its Africa One project should have a fully operational optical fibre cable around the whole continent by 1999 to provide connections for all the major coastal cities. Siemens and Alcatel also have designs (Afrilink and Atlantis-2 respectively) to provide telecom connections, especially to West Africa. Both the International Satellite Organisation (IntelSat) and the Regional African Satellite Organisation are actively promoting the expansion of e-mail services for the continent.

Apart from the mismatch between these plans and the funds that are really required, there is also the critical issue of the appropriateness of the technologies to be transferred, and the capacity of the recipient countries to master them. Current discussion on 'the gap' provides no convincing argument that the technology owners will change their attitudes and policies towards the international transfer of technology. Hitherto, the prevailing international policies have erected formidable obstacles to the reduction of North-South technology gaps. Today, there is no indication that existing restrictive business practices, the constraints on the ownership of knowledge, and the rules on intellectual property rights that are adverse to developing-country interests are radically changing. There are as yet no realistic prospects that the relations between ICT-rich and ICT-poor countries will change in the near future.

The key actors in international ICT policy-making have expressed a clear preference to leave the construction of the Global Information Society to 'the forces of the free market'. It would seem that under the institutional arrangements of a corporate-capitalist market economy, the development of an equitable information society remains a very unlikely proposition.

An any rate, it may be questioned whether within the realities of the international economic order there *can* be any serious reduction of the disparity. It may well be an illusion to think that ICT-poor countries could catch up or keep pace with advances in the North, where the rate of technological development is very high and is supported by considerable resources. This is not to say that poor countries should not try to upgrade their ICTs. They should not, however, do this in the unrealistic expectation that those who are ahead will wait for them. The situation may improve for the poorer countries, but the disparity will not go away.

What should be done?

The most immediate political challenge today is the fact that the use of ICTs for sustainable development will be determined not by technology, but by politics. The realisation of their potential requires a re-thinking of the wisdom about current deregulatory policies, a re-thinking of the role of public funding, and a massive effort in training and education for the mastery of ICTs.

This political agenda is unlikely to be taken seriously if ICT policies are left to Princes and the Merchants alone. If market-driven arrangements are — for some time to come — the standard environment within which ICTs will be deployed, then the only force that could make a real difference are the ordinary people who buy on the market, and who have the (often unused and rarely recognised) power to say 'no'.

The realisation of the empowerment potential of ICTs should, therefore, primarily be the concern of civil-society organisations (CSOs). They need to mobilise and lobby for and with the ordinary men and women whose lives will be affected by the digital futures that are currently envisaged. Today there is only a very modest beginning of a global civil activism in the info-communications sector, connected with the People's Communication Charter, described below. These movements must urgently extend their reach by attracting the support of large public-interest organisations (labour unions, educational institutions, religious bodies) and intergovernment organisations such as UNESCO and ITU.

Since our cultural environment is as essential to our common future as is the natural ecology, it is time for people's movements to focus on the organisation and quality of the production and distribution of information and other cultural expressions. Mobilising the users' community, and stimulating critical reflection on the quality of the cultural environment, is a tall order. However, it can be done, and it is actually being done. An increasing number of individuals and groups around the world are beginning to express concern about the quality of media performance. A start has also been made with the creation of a broad international movement of alert and demanding media users, based upon what has been called the *People's Communication Charter*.

The People's Communication Charter

This Charter is an initiative of the Third World Network (TWN) in Malaysia, the Centre for Communication and Human Rights in The Netherlands, the Cultural Environment Movement in the USA, and AMARC — the World Association of Community Radio Broadcasters — based in Peru and Canada. In the early 1990s, academics and activists associated with TWN and its affiliated Consumers' Association of Penang (CAP) initiated a debate on the feasibility of a world people's movement in the field of communication and culture.

The TWN and CAP had already an impressive record in developing people's movements in such areas as reforming international trade and conservation of the tropical rain forest. They had proved capable of bringing the concerns of grassroots people in the South to the diplomatic negotiations of the Uruguay GATT multilateral trade round, and UNCED in Rio de Janeiro.

An obvious problem is that information consumers are seldom organised in representative associations. They are a diverse community, geographically dispersed and ideologically fragmented. The *People's Communication Charter* was seen as a first step in creating a constituency for concerns about the quality of the cultural environment. It provides a common framework for those who share the belief that people should be active and critical participants in their social reality, and capable of governing themselves. The Charter may help to develop a permanent movement concerned with the quality of our cultural environment. One idea is to organise an International Tribunal which would receive complaints by signatories to the Charter, and invite the parties involved to submit evidence and defence upon which the Tribunal could come to a judgment.

The Charter is not an end in itself. It provides the basis for a permanent critical reflection on those worldwide trends that will determine the quality of our lives in the third millennium. It is, therefore, important to see it as an open document which can always be updated, amended, improved, and expanded. In fact, since the Charter was presented on the Web (http://ww.waag.org/pcc), new ideas and suggested changes have been proposed and discussed. A critical moment in the history of the Charter was the founding convention of the Cultural Environment Movement in March 1996, when the first public ratification of the text took place. In June 1997, the governing body of the World Association for Christian Communication (WACC) endorsed the Charter, following much discussion by WACC members in its eight regions; and important amendments proposed by its central committee.

In 1998, the Charter will be on the agenda of the General Assembly of AMARC and of the Paris Convention of the Cultural Environment Movement. For the celebration of the 50th anniversary of the Universal Declaration of Human Rights (UHDR) in December 1998, initiatives are being developed to secure some form of acclaim for the Charter from the international political community.

Most important, however, is the goal of soliciting more support for the ideas that the Charter embodies from individuals and institutions worldwide. In August 1996, for example, it was displayed at the famous Dokumenta exhibition at Kassel in Germany, and was discussed and signed by many visitors. The web-site of the Charter is where such events and progress in widening support for it are publicised.

Beyond the text itself and its endorsement, the most critical element for the future of the Charter is obviously its implementation. In an open, democratic, people's movement this cannot be organised by some central governing body. Implementation is very much the concern of local and national groups, either newly formed or already established for other (or similar) purposes. The realisation of the people's right to communicate cannot be an homogeneous project, but will take different forms in different socio-cultural and political contexts. In one country, this may be the institution of an ombudsman's office to be responsible for the quality of the cultural environment; in another a national award may be given to the TV programme found most in violation of the Charter's principles; in some places a civil-society campaign to rescue public broadcasting may be necessary; elsewhere the focus may be on protecting children or defending the media interests of people with a disability.

This is really the business of ordinary people. It is also the ultimate test-case for the meaning of the People's Communication Charter. It only makes sense if people themselves eventually begin to be concerned about implementing it.

■ **Cees J. Hamelink** *is Professor of International Communication at the University of Amsterdam and Editor-in-Chief of the* International Journal for Communication Studies Gazette. *He is also Honorary President of the International Association for Mass Communication Research. This article was first published in* Development in Practice, *Volume 8, number 1, in 1998.*

Annotated bibliography

Writings on social action and development tend mostly to focus either on single issues, such as the environment or women's rights, or on examples of well-documented campaigns, such as the Chipko movement in India or the Anti-Poverty Campaign in Brazil. We have sought to take a broader focus, and to identify titles which explore elements that are common to the many expressions of contemporary social action taking place in the face of economic globalisation. Though reasons of space in this highly selective listing prevent us from including works by such names as Amilcar Cabral, Franz Fanon, Paulo Freire, or Mahatma Gandhi, we have sought to capture something of the diverse and rapidly changing ways in which civil society organises across boundaries, whether to push for certain goals or to resist forms of economic and cultural intrusion. These movements often take their inspiration from the thinking and example of leading social and political activists both past and present: it is not for nothing that the rebel movement in Chiapas which erupted in 1990, just as the North American Free Trade Agreement (NAFTA) was to come into force, takes its name from the 1910 revolutionary and pro-peasant leader, Emiliano Zapata. Yet the Zapatista movement is noteworthy also for its highly political and inventive use of electronic communication, which places its organisational methods and vision very firmly in the modern age.

The bibliography was compiled by Fenella Porter, Caroline Knowles, and Deborah Eade (respectively Reviews Editors and Editor of Development in Practice*), with input from Miloon Kothari.*

Books

Haleh Afshar (ed.): *Women and Empowerment: Illustrations from the Third World*, London, Macmillan Press, 1998.
The term 'empowerment' is critically analysed, and the various experiences and roles played by agencies, donors and recipients are explored, using case studies from Latin America, SE Asia, and the Middle East. Contributors note the value of communal activities and goals, and the way in which isolated groups who are engaged in political negotiations with the state are able to use links with the international empowerment agenda to strengthen their own position.

Sonia E. Alvarez, Evelina Dagnino, Arturo Escobar (eds.): *Cultures of Politics, Politics of Cultures: Re-Visioning Latin American Social Movements*, Boulder CO: Westview Press, 1998.
The cultural politics of social movements provides a lens for analysing emerging discourses and practices that are grounded in society and culture, the state, and political institutions, and for considering the extent to which these may either unsettle, or be co-opted by, prevailing neo-liberal strategies. The editors build on earlier work, notably that of Arturo Escobar and Sonia Alvarez, *The Making of Social Movements in Latin America: Identity, Strategy and Democracy* (1992), which examined the theory of social movements in the context of various contemporary expressions in Latin America (including feminism, urban popular movements, Christian Base communities, ecology movements, and indigenous movements). A leading post-development thinker, Arturo Escobar is also author of *Encountering Development: The Making and Unmaking of the Third World* (1995).

Samir Amin: *Spectres of Capitalism: A Critique of Current Intellectual Fashions*, New York: Monthly Review Press, 1998.
The author criticises current intellectual fashions that assume a global capitalist triumph by focusing on the aspirations of the destitute millions of the post-Cold War era. He examines in turn the changing notion of crisis in capitalism; misconceptions of the free-market model; the role of culture in revolutions; the decline of 'the law of value' in economics; the philosophical roots of post-modernism; how telecommunications affect ideology; and the myth of 'pure economics'. Other recent titles by this prolific author include *Capitalism in the Age of Globalization: The Management of Contemporary Society* (1997).

D. Archibugi and D. Held (eds): *Cosmopolitan Democracy: An Agenda for a New World Order*, Cambridge MA: Polity Press, 1995.
The end of the Cold War has led to major transformations in international and domestic politics. Contributors present ideas of national democracy and of a potential 'international' or 'cosmopolitan' democracy. The latter refers to political organisation in which all citizens worldwide have a voice, input, and political representation in international affairs, in parallel with and independently of their own governments. This model places the

pursuit of democratic values through popular participation in the political process at the centre, and relates this to the principles and institutions of human rights.

Bhagirath Lal Das : *An Introduction to the WTO Agreements* and *The WTO Agreements: Deficiencies, Imbalances and Required Changes*, Penang: Third World Network, 1998.

In the first of these companion volumes,the author explains the complex WTO Agreements, their background, the terms involved, and the implications of provisions that effectively extend world trade rules into areas not previously considered as falling into the economic sphere. In the second, he pinpoints the problems with these Agreements from the perspective of developing countries, stressing that only collective action by these countries will achieve the necessary changes in the regime now governing international trade.

Waldon Bello with Shea Cunningham and Bill Rau: *Dark Victory: the US, Structural Adjustment and Global Poverty*, London: Pluto, with the Transnational Institute and Institute for Food Development Policy, 1994.

A fiercely critical study of Western aid, arguing that re-colonisation of the Third World has been carried out through the agencies of the International Banks, echoing the Reagan agenda to 'discipline the Third World'. The consequences have been lower barriers to imports, the removal of restrictions on foreign investments, privatisation of state-owned enterprises, and a reduction in social-welfare spending, with disastrous consequences for people in the Third World. Bello has also written extensively on politics and economics in SE Asia, his most recent publication being *A Siamese Tragedy: Development and Disintegration in Modern Thailand* (with Shea Cunningham and Kheng Poh Li), Food First Books, 1998.

Amanda Bernard, Henny Helmich and Percy B. Lehning (eds): *Civil Society and International Development,* Paris: OECD and the North–South Centre of the Council of Europe, 1998.

In papers from a seminar on civil society and international development, contributors explore conceptual questions of civil society, and the role of external actors such as donors and NGOs, with perspectives from developing regions. Civil society is often a crucial manifestation of an associative impulse and is influenced by existing regimes and political resistance in its ideological, political, and social expression. A better understanding of the role, history, and traditions of civil society could provide useful practical insights into how to restore peace and resume the development process in regions plagued by violent conflicts, and also contribute to democratic processes and development elsewhere.

Roger Burbach, Orlando Nuñez and Boris Kagarlitsky: *Globalisation and its Discontents: The Rise of Postmodern Socialisms*, London: Pluto, 1997.

With the collapse of communism and the perceived triumph of capitalism, this book explores the crisis of social polarisation produced by globalisation. It links this exploration with the social movements that '[long] for liberation' from oppression and exploitation, including the organisation of collective identity around religion, nationalism, ethnic-minority rights, the environment, and women's movements. The book looks at the positive aspects of globalisation, asserting that with a common (even global) awareness, it becomes possible to end many of the forms of exploitation on which the capitalist system depends.

John Burbridge (ed.): *Beyond Prince and Merchant: Citizen Participation and the Rise of Civil Society*, New York: Pact Publications, 1997.
Contributors highlight the various historical roots of civil society, its diverse manifestations, and some of the new frontiers to be tackled. Through a series of extended case studies, the book describes the growth of civil society as people seek to address the root causes of deepening poverty, environmental destruction, and social disintegration. International networking and alliance building is, it is argued, leading to the formation of a globalised civil society with a shared vision of a world of diverse cultures and just and sustainable communities.

José Casanova: *Public Religions in the Modern World*, Chicago: University of Chicago Press, 1994.
The author considers the relationship between religion and modernity, and argues that during the 1980s religions from Islamic fundamentalism to Catholic Liberation Theology forced their way into the public scene. No longer content to administer pastoral care to individuals, religious institutions are challenging domestic political and social forces, raising questions about the claims of entities such as nations and 'markets' to be 'value neutral', and straining the traditional connections of private and public morality. Case studies from two religious traditions (Catholicism and Protestantism) in Spain, Poland, Brazil, and the USA are used to challenge assumptions about the role of modernity and secularisation in religious movements.

Manuel Castells: *The Information Age*: *The Rise of the Network Society* (Vol. 1), 1996 and *The Power of Identity* (Vol. 2), Oxford: Blackwell 1997.
The Information Age is concerned with trends of globalisation and identity, in the context of the information technology revolution and the restructuring of capitalism, which have given rise to 'the network society'. Characterised by the pervasive power of global capital, and interconnected media system, networking is a growing form of global social organisation, and has been accompanied by expressions of collective identity that challenge globalisation and cosmopolitanism. The nation-state is thus called into question, while powerful technological media are now used by various contenders to amplify and sharpen their struggle, as in the case for example of the Zapatistas' use of the Internet.

Volume 2 examines networks of identity such as religious communalism (including Islamic and Christian fundamentalism), and ethnic and territorial collective identity, which are elaborated into the broader theory of the Information Age. It also covers social movements against the New Global Order, the environmental movement, movements centred on issues of family and sexuality (such as feminisms, and the US gay community), the relationship between states and social movements, and the role of the media and 'electronic popularism'.

A. Chhachhi and R. Pittin: *Confronting State, Capital and Patriarchy: Women Organising the Process of Industrialisation,* London: Macmillan, 1996.

This book brings together contributors from an emerging international network of researchers/activists working on numerous women's and labour issues. The linkages between North and South, and the global nature of industrialisation and organising are overarching themes, and are demonstrated in chapters from Asia, Africa, and Latin America. These highlight the myriad ways in which women organise to confront state, capital, and patriarchal structures in the face of industrialisation, in particular socio-cultural and political settings. Despite local variations, there are macro-level similarities to contexts that are coming under the increasing influence of IMF/World Bank structural adjustment policies.

M. L. Dantwala, Harsh Sethi, and Pravin Visaria (eds.): *Social Change Through Voluntary Action,* New Delhi: Sage Publications, 1998.

Though focused on India, and with a series of case studies from the sub-continent, the essays in this volume examine the role of voluntary action in bringing about wider social-transformation goals. They do not assume, however, that NGOs have any special purchase on, or monopoly over, such efforts. Some contributors are indeed highly critical of the behaviour of NGOs, contrasting their radical and pro-poor rhetoric with their often low levels of accountability to their supposed constituencies.

Larry Diamond (ed.): *Political Culture and Democracy in Developing Countries,* Boulder CO: Lynne Rienner, 1993.

This book explores the complex and reciprocal interactions between a society's dominant beliefs, values, and attitudes about politics and the nature of its political system. Contributors examine specific cases and look at how these elements of political culture respond over time to social, political, and institutional changes. Issues addressed include whether political culture is cause or effect; how does one weigh its causal importance for democracy; what are the most important elements of a democratic political culture, and how do these elements evolve? Topics considered include historical and comparative perspectives; intellectuals, higher education and democracy; state elites and mass political culture; religion, political culture and democracy (Christian Democracy, Liberation Theology, and political culture in Latin America, Fundamentalism, ultra-nationalism, and political culture in the Israeli radical right; the Islamic movement and resource mobilisation in Egypt).

Jean Drèze and Amartya Sen (eds.): *Hunger and Public Action,* Oxford, Clarendon Press, 1989

The authors argue that famine is more commonly caused by human (in)action than by food shortages as such, and that famines do not occur in situations where governments are accountable to their citizens, and where public information systems are effective. Sen, an influential economist, philosopher, and Nobel laureate, is the author of many other seminal works, including *Poverty and Famines: An Essay on Entitlement and Deprivation*; *Inequality Re-examined*; *Choice;* and *Welfare and Measurement*. In particular, his work on capabilities, entitlements, and human development has been instrumental in shaping the annual UNDP *Human Development Report*.

Richard Falk: *On Humane Governance: Towards a New Global Politics*, Cambridge: Polity Press, 1995.
Economic globalisation is diminishing the political role of the nation-state, though the main market- and capital-driven forces that challenge it remain largely concealed as political actors. Variants of the politics of identity are also causing fragmentation and furthering the decline in governmental capacity in many states. Emerging forms of geo-governance are regarded as 'inhumane' on five political counts: that 20 per cent of the world's population lacks adequate food, shelter, health care, clothing, education, housing; that the most vulnerable are denied full protection of human rights; that there is no tangible, cumulative process towards abolishing war as a social institution; that there is insufficient effort to protect and restore the environment; that there is a failure to achieve transnational democracy and little progress in the extension of primary democratic practices of respect for others, of accountability, and participation in decision-making. The author calls for a commitment to 'humane' geo-governance, i.e. a set of social, political, economic, and cultural arrangements committed to rapid progress in these five areas. This will depend on dramatic growth of transnational democracy, the extension of primary democratic processes, a growing allegiance to global civil society, and the plausibility of humane governance as a political priority.

Jonathan A. Fox and L. David Brown (eds): *The Struggle for Accountability: The World Bank, NGOs, and Grassroots Movements*, Cambridge MA: MIT Press, 1998.
This book analyses policy reforms within the World Bank in favour of more rigorous environmental and social policies, and the subsequent conflicts over how and whether to follow them in practice — an international struggle for accountability that involves the Bank, donor and borrowing governments, public-interest groups, and grassroots movements. It asks how the Bank has responded to the NGO/grassroots environmental critique, with case studies to assess degrees of change, since even small changes in the behaviour of major institutions are significant to those affected. Secondly, it asks how far advocacy campaigns, often led by NGOs, represent the organisations of those most directly affected by Bank projects, and how accountable NGOs are to their own partners. The Bank is shown (to a small and uneven but significant degree) to be more publicly accountable as the result of protest, public scrutiny, and the empowering effect on inside reformers. It is argued that transnational NGO networks have gradually become more accountable to their local partners, partly because of more vocal and autonomous grassroots movements, and partly in response to the Bank's challenge to the legitimacy of international NGO critics.

Andre Gunder Frank: *ReOrient: Global Economy in the Asian Age*, Berkeley: University of California Press, 1998.

The author is widely known for his 1970s neo-Marxist theory of 'underdevelopment', which held that the economic surplus generated in Latin America and other Third World areas is siphoned off to the affluent capitalist nations, principally the USA. His recipe for Third World economic survival and revival was to 'de-link from the world economy'. In a spirited critique of contemporary 'Eurocentrics' such as Huntington, and drawing on a vast range of Southern intellectuals, the author argues that the rise of the West is a relatively recent and transient phenomenon that accompanied the economic decline of the East from the 1800s, and that the world is now set to revert to being centred, culturally and economically, in Asia. See also Frank's essay, co-authored with Marta Fuentes, 'Civil democracy: social movements in recent world history' in S. Amin, G. Arrighi, A. G. Frank, and I. Wallerstein (eds.): *Transforming the Revolution: Social Movements and the World System*, New York: Monthly Review Press, 1990.

Joe Foweraker: *Theorising Social Movements* London: Pluto, 1995.

Economic transformation and social upheaval intimately affect existing class, gender, and ethnic relations, creating diverse areas of challenge and change. Throughout Latin America, extensive political re-alignments and re-definitions are under way, even as social movements are challenging the traditional boundaries of 'politics' and its actors. The main debates and issues in contemporary social-movement theory are discussed in this context, with empirical reference to urban social movements and women's mobilisation ('with or without a feminist content'). While social-movements theory is necessarily drawn from particular experiences, the gap between theory and collective action appears to be growing. Major theoretical developments have emerged from western Europe and North America (where social action has declined), and the author questions the extent to which these 'travel', and their capacity to explain realities in Latin America, where social action is on the increase.

Anthony Giddens: *Beyond Left and Right: The Future of Radical Politics*, Cambridge: Polity Press, 1994.

Argues that the political radical, once viewed as standing on the left, opposing backward-looking conservatism, is now defensive, while the right has become radical in its support of allowing free rein to market forces, regardless of tradition. The author develops a new framework for contemporary radical politics, with the ecological crisis at the core, for a world in which modernity has reached its limits as a social and moral order. The end of nature, as an entity which exists independently of human intervention, and the end of tradition, combined with the impact of globalisation, are the forces now to be confronted, made use of, and managed. The author provides a powerful interpretation of the rise of fundamentalism, of democracy, the persistence of gender divisions, and the question of a normative political theory of violence.

Gustavo Gutiérrez: *The Power of the Poor in History: Selected Writings*, New York: Orbis Books, 1993.

A collection of eight essays by one of the leading intellectual proponents of Liberation Theology, a form of Christianity which inspired many social movements and pro-poor activists throughout Latin America during the 1970s and 1980s, a period during which much of the continent was under military rule.

John A. Hall (ed.): *Civil Society: Theory, History, Comparison*, Cambridge: Polity Press, 1995.

This book aims to clarify what is meant by 'civil society', in order to identify its usefulness as a descriptive as well as a prescriptive term. The analysis is comparative, historical, and theoretical, with a focus on the relationships between civil society and other social forces, notably nationalism and populism. The book defines civil society as a social value *and* a set of social institutions, noting that not every autonomous group creates or contributes to civil society, and that the notion that groups can balance the state is wrong. With case studies from Latin America, India, Turkey, and the Islamic world, the book asks where civil society has its foundation and its legitimacy.

Chris Hann and Elizabeth Dunn (eds): *Civil Society: Challenging Western Models*, London: Routledge, 1996.

'Civil society' has been enthusiastically and uncritically endorsed as a universal ideal of social organisation, despite its European origin and the fact that it fails even to do much to explain current social realities in Europe. Civil society is often presented as a private sphere and equated with the non-government sector. Contributors argue for a broader understanding that encompasses a range of everyday social practices, often elusive power relations, and the many material constraints which influence shared moralities and ideologies. Case studies from the USA, the UK, four former communist countries of Eastern Europe, Turkey, the Middle East, Indonesia, and Japan demonstrate the contribution which anthropology can make to current debate.

Jeffrey Haynes: *Democracy and Civil Society in the Third World: Politics and New Political Movements*, Cambridge: Polity Press, 1997.

Looking at 'Action Groups' as popular political, social and economic movements in Third World societies, and focusing on poor and marginalised groups within developing countries, the author argues that demands for democracy, human rights, and economic change were a catalyst for the emergence of hundreds of thousands of popular movements in Latin American, Africa, and Asia, including movements of indigenous peoples, environmental movements, women's movements, and Islamist action groups. These emerging popular organisations can be regarded as building blocks of civil society that will enhance the democratic nature of many political environments. The author speculates on the likelihood of their survival, once the regimes under whose jurisdiction they must live manage to exert control.

Richard Holloway: *Supporting Citizens' Initiatives: Bangladesh NGOs and Society*, London: IT Publications, 1998.

This book explains the role currently played by NGOs in Bangladesh. From being peripheral organisations, NGOs today have grown in importance and impact to play a major role in different developmental activities. Focusing on questions such as why Bangladeshi NGOs are praised throughout the development world and yet attacked in their own country, and why NGOs which take foreign donations are treated differently from the government, Islamic organisations and the business sector, the book contains lessons for all those concerned with understanding the relationship between the state and civil-society organisations throughout the developing world.

Samuel P. Huntington: *The Clash of Civilizations and the Remaking of World Order*, New York: Simon and Schuster, 1997.

In this controversial but influential account of the cultural fall-out of economic globalisation in the post-Cold War environment, the author holds that as people increasingly define themselves by ethnicity and religion, so the West will find itself ever more at odds with non-Western civilisations that reject its ideals of democracy, human rights, liberty, the rule of law, and the separation of church and state, as they have done throughout history. The principal threats to the West, Huntington maintains, are China and Islam; and his recommendation is that the West should abandon the attempt to establish universal values, refrain from intervening in non-Western cultures, and adopt a proactive form of isolationism.

Patricia Jeffery and Amrita Basu (eds): *Appropriating Gender: Women's Activism and Politicised Religion in South Asia*, London: Routledge, 1998.

The authors explore the paradoxical relationships between women and religious politics in India, Pakistan, Sri Lanka, and Bangladesh, where many women have defied feminists, religious nationalists, and nation-states alike in framing their own political demands. Feminist activism in South Asia has contributed both to raising people's awareness of gender injustices and to combating them directly. In part, politicised religion may be a response to the challenges so posed, and to secular changes in the wider economy. Despite being implicated in developments that are potentially deeply inimical to women's interests, the energies of many women have been successfully engaged in their support. Women's groups in the region have, however, been generally disturbed by the challenges that politicised religion poses for feminist activism and for women's rights. This comparative analysis permits an exploration of the varied meanings and expressions of gender identity in terms of time, place, and political context.

A. G. Jordan with William A. Maloney: *The Protest Business? Mobilising Campaign Groups,* Manchester: Manchester University Press 1997.

An examination of the support for an environmental group (Friends of the Earth) and a human rights group (Amnesty International) in the UK, asking why people join such organisations, what motivating factors are relevant, and whether the support for campaigning causes is an irresistible and growing wave or whether it is entering a period of stagnation. The book introduces the literature on the environmental movement, using different approaches to examine the concept of 'movement' and challenging the view of such organisations as 'new social movements', as this may imply that their ultimate political role is to enhance participatory democracy.

Margaret E. Keck and Kathryn Sikkink (eds.): *Activists Beyond Borders: Advocacy Networks in International Politics,* Ithaca, NY: Cornell University Press, 1998.
The contributors to this volume examine a type of pressure group that has been largely ignored by political analysts: networks of activists which coalesce and operate across national frontiers. They sketch the dynamics of emergence, strategies, and impact of activists from different nationalities working together on particular issues, such as violence against women. This work highlights a subset of international issues, characterised by the prominence of ideas based on ethical principles, and a central role for NGOs.

David C. Korten: *The Post-Corporate World: Life after Capitalism,* West Hartford CT: Kumarian, 1999.
Korten argues that capitalism is destroying life, democracy, and the market itself. Concentrated absentee ownership and footloose speculative capital, as embodied in global commercial corporations, are incompatible with a just, sustainable, and compassionate society. He holds that these values depend on favouring enterprises that are based on stakeholder ownership and rooted in their localities, involving workers, suppliers, customers, and local communities. Other well-known titles by the same author include *When Corporations Rule the World* (1995) and *Getting to the 21st Century: Voluntary Action and the Global Agenda* (1990).

David Lewis (ed.): *International Perspectives on Voluntary Action: Reshaping the Third Sector,* London: Earthscan, 1999.
Rather than considering NGOs separately from voluntary agencies, this book explores the similarities, differences and growing connections between the two types of organisation. The book is divided into two parts: Linkages and Learning, and Contrasts and Complementarities, and looks particularly at the contribution of North–South learning and exchange. Contributions draw on examples from the UK and the USA Bangladesh, Pakistan, and other contexts in both North and South, covering topics such as advocacy, legitimacy and values, evaluation, and governing bodies.

Stanford M. Lyman (ed.): *Social Movements: Critiques, Concepts, Case Studies,* London: Macmillan, 1995.
This compilation of classic and current analyses of social movements includes discussions on the various disciplinary approaches, topical debates, and criticisms of the literature on social movements, as well as case studies on the Townsend Movement (which sought pensions for the elderly during the US Great Depression), the Iranian Revolution, the collective protest over AIDS, and environmental reform. The book concludes with three essays on the future of social movements, reflecting perspectives from the USA and Europe.

Greg B. Madison: *The Political Economy of Civil Society and Human Rights,* London: Routledge, 1998.

A comprehensive analysis that looks at the concept of civil society and the relationship with democracy/democratisation and human rights, and its political 'rebirth' following the end of the Cold War era. It centres on three dimensions (the moral-cultural, the political, and the economic), arguing that these are closely interrelated yet autonomous, synergistic, and based in a rationality of dialogue and discourse. The author concludes that the sure way to achieve international justice is to build civil societies worldwide. Although the analysis is based on the idea of the nation-state, an appendix looks specifically at the application of these ideas to international issues of democracy and development.

Brendan Martin: *In the Public Interest? Privatisation and Public Sector Reform,* London: Zed Books in association with Public Services International, 1993.

Since the early 1980s, public-sector reform worldwide has been characterised by privatisation, commercialisation, and deregulation. However, privatisation and economic structural adjustment have failed to deliver better public services or improved economic prospects. The author argues that it is vital for unions, citizen groups, and policy makers to move beyond simple 'public vs private' dichotomies in combining financial efficiency, democratic responsiveness, equity, and effectiveness in accordance with public demands.

Philip McMichael: *Development and Social Change: A Global Perspective,* London: Sage, 1996.

The author offers a basic introduction to the history of the failed 'development project', putting it into context as a transnational project designed to integrate the world, and used as an organising principle in the Cold War era. Part Three addresses 'the Globalisation project', examining its relationship with development and the economic system, and its organising power of labour. Part Four looks at social responses to globalisation, focusing on movements such as fundamentalism, environmentalism, feminism, and 'cosmopolitan localism'. The central message is that the style and scale of politics are changing and new issues of human rights are complicating the 'tidy image' of development, and exposing the integrated nature of the forces that currently constitute 'development'.

Maria Mies: *Patriarchy and Accumulation on a World Scale: Women in the International Division of Labour* (2nd Edition), London, Zed, 1999.

In this classic text, arguing that feminist analysis must transcend the divisions created by a capitalist patriarchal system between Northern and Southern women, Mies explores the state of the women's movement worldwide, the history of colonialist processes, and the relationship between women's liberation and national liberation struggles. She calls for a feminist perspective that transcends the international system of gender roles and the gender division of labour, and looks forward to a society where the liberation of one set of people is not based on the exploitation of another.

Manaranjan Mohanty and **Partha Nath Mukerji (eds.):** *People's Rights: Social Movements and the State in the Third World*, New Delhi : Sage Publications, 1998. Contributors examine the role of social movements as a democratic assertion of people's rights. Rather than locating rights in the individualist tradition of Western liberalism, these are viewed as an affirmation of the political condition of human existence that involves a struggle against class exploitation and social oppression. Case studies from Africa and Asia illustrate the dilemmas faced by social movements, and challenge the supposed dichotomy between class politics and social movements.

J. J. Pettman: *Worlding Women: A Feminist International Politics*, London: Routledge, 1996.
The author offers a feminist overview of International Relations, arguing that this is a male-gendered sphere, though women are players (albeit largely invisible) in the world that International Relations seeks to explain. Drawing on Southern feminist scholars such as Mohanty, Afshar, Kandiyoti, and Moghadam, and the growing visibility of women and feminist transnational organising, Pettman puts forward a 'feminist international politics' which would address international political identities, the gendered politics of peace and war, and the international sexual division of labour; and suggests a notion of an international political economy of sex. A concluding review of current experience looks at the possibilities and problems of transnational feminisms.

R. S. Powers and W. B. Vogele (eds): *Protest, Power and Change: An Encyclopaedia of Non-violent Action from ACT-Up to Women's Suffrage*, New York: Garland Publishing, 1997.
An encyclopaedia with case studies of non-violent struggle, methods of non-violent action, and profiles of people and organisations who have contributed through their arguments or their actions (or both) to advancing the knowledge and practice of non-violent struggle. The editors have sought to be representative rather than exhaustive, and to present the diverse applications of non-violent action, as well as cases that they hold to be valuable. They acknowledge that the contents are biased towards the twentieth century and examples from the USA. The central purpose is to provide a standard reference work for a domain of human behaviour that has been well studied but incompletely identified. Non-violent action is defined here as a range of methods for actively waging conflict without directly threatening or inflicting physical harm. This locates non-violent action within the realms of social conflict and identifies it as a distinctive form of conflict behaviour — one that eschews violence and physical force.

Mady Schutzman and Jan Cohen-Cruz (eds): *Playing Boal: Theatre, Therapy, Activism*, London: Routledge, 1994.
Boal's work has influenced theatre artists, social workers, educators, political activists, and scholars worldwide, encouraging spectators to become spect*actors*: active participants rehearsing strategies for change. This book examines the

techniques in application, and looks at the use of Theatre of the Oppressed exercises by practitioners and scholars in Europe and North America. It explores the possibilities and problems of these tools for 'active learning and personal empowerment, cooperative education and healing, participatory theatre, and community action'.

Christine E. Sleeter: *Multicultural Education as Social Activism*, Albany NY: State University of New York Press, 1996.

Connecting multicultural education with issues of power and struggle, this book explores what multicultural education means to white people, given the prevailing inequality in racial power relations. It examines connections between race, gender, and social class, particularly for white women. While taking a feminist perspective, the author is also wary of the power that white middle-class women exercise in defining what count as gender issues. The author argues that, since multicultural education was born in political struggle and cannot meaningfully be disconnected from politics, the quest for schooling for social justice is a political goal rather than a technical issue.

Jackie Smith, Charles Chatfield and Ron Pagnucco (eds.): *Transnational Social Movements and Global Politics: Solidarity Beyond the State,* Syracuse, New York: Syracuse University Press, 1997.

From developing an environmental policy for the EU, to mobilising around the UN special sessions on disarmament; and from transnational strategies of the service for peace and justice in Latin America, to cooperative accompaniment and Peace Brigades International in Sri Lanka, this book describes the powerful dynamics at work in an emerging global civic culture. It lays the ground work for continuing cultural development, rather than the destruction of culture through development. Particular emphasis is given to the importance of the UN, and the constituencies being developed by international NGOs — particularly international communities of ethnic and inter-faith groups, and the development of the capacity for global civic action.

Matthias Stiefel and Marshall Wolfe: *A Voice for the Excluded: Popular Participation in Development — Utopia or Necessity?* London: Zed Books in association with UNRISD, 1994.

The outcome of an UNRISD research programme to examine the interacting transformations (political, economic, and other) which bear upon the prospects for popular participation, this book presents concepts of participation prevalent in the 1970s and 1980s and several case studies of participation among rural workers, urban wage workers, and the urban poor; the institutionalisation of participation; and the transformation from social movements to national movements. It also considers the ways in which grassroots movements, governments, inter-government organisations, and NGOs confront or evade the relevance of popular participation, and how participation is changing in the 1990s.

UNRISD: *States of Disarray: The Social Effects of Globalization*, UNRISD: Geneva, 1995.

Prepared as part of the run-up to the 1995 UN Social Summit, this has now become a classic, translated into most major languages. It lays out the key trends that define globalisation — the spread of liberal democracy, the dominance of market forces, the integration of the global economy, the transformation of production systems and labour markets, the speed of technological change, and the media revolution and consumerism — and links these to other trends, such as migration, crime, war and ethnic conflict. A final section outlines the challenges posed by globalisation for citizenship, social action, and human rights; and recommends ways in which to subject global forces and institutions to regulation and public scrutiny.

Paul Wapner: *Environmental Activism and World Civic Politics*, Albany NY: State University of New York Press, 1996.

Transnational environmental activist groups such as Greenpeace, the Worldwide Fund for Nature (WWF), and Friends of the Earth play a central role in the way the world addresses environmental issues. This book provides a systematic and theoretically informed study of strategies through which, in addition to lobbying governments, activists operate within and across societies and via transnational social, economic, and cultural networks to alter corporate practices, educate vast numbers of people, pressure multilateral development banks, and shift standards of good conduct. Wapner argues that. since this takes place outside the formal arena of inter-state politics, environmental activists practise 'world civic politics'; they politicise global civil society. The book throws world civic politics into sharp relief and draws out wider conclusions concerning NGOs in world politics.

Peter Waterman: *Globalisation, Social Movements and the New Internationalisms*, London: Mansell, 1998.

The Communist Manifesto's 'workers of the world unite!' inspired generations of unionists and socialists. But internationalism became nationalism, the chains were not loosened, and the wars were lost. This book examines the decline of socialist and proletarian internationalism. It reconceptualises labour internationalism in Europe and the Third World, and looks at the international nature of the new radical-democratic social movements (such as women's movements and feminism). Waterman argues for a 'new global solidarity that relates to a radicalised, globalised, informatised, and complex capitalist modernity ... that addresses multiple global social problems and democratic movements'.

Ponna Wignaraja (ed.): *New Social Movements in the South: Empowering the People*, London: Zed Books, 1993.

Contributors identify various social movements and people's responses to crises – poverty reproducing itself, the ecological crisis, gender conflicts, human-rights conflicts, and the inability of state structures to mediate these tensions — and how such responses also attempt to protect the South from penetration by external forces which further intensify these internal tensions. Popular responses are taking the form of new social movements, people's movements, and experiments, and this book concentrates on those that have elements of sustainability and which promote development and democracy in new terms. The book thus provides an overview of the new thinking on social movements, and the nuances within it, that is emerging under different socio-political circumstances.

M. Wuyts, M. Mackintosh and T. Hewitt (eds.): *Development Policy and Public Action*, Oxford: OUP in association with the Open University, 1992.
Treating development policy as an activity of many types of public institution — public action — contributors move from 'public vs private' dichotomies, question the rigid boundaries of traditional concepts of the public sphere, expand the notion of public action, and explore the negative results of structural adjustment, while also emphasising the potential for new forms of social organisation that might emerge to bring about change.

Journals

Alternatives: A Journal for Social Transformation and Humane Governance: published quarterly by Lynne Reinner. ISSN: 0304-3754. Editors: Saul H. Mendovitz (World Order Models Project), D. L. Sheth (Centre for the Study of Developing Societies), and Yoshikazu Sakamoto (International Peace Research Institute).
An alternative to coventional international politics journals, providing a forum for feminist, post-colonial and post-modern scholarship in international relations, with articles on the theoretical and practical implications of global change. Contributors consider emerging new forms of world politics, challenging the ethnocentrism of much modern social and political analysis, and emphasise the possibilities of a humane global polity.

Development in Practice: published in five issues per volume by Carfax Publishing Ltd on behalf of Oxfam GB, ISSN:0961-4524, Editor: Deborah Eade.
A forum for practitioners, policy makers, and academics to exchange information and analysis concerning the social dimensions of development and humanitarian work. As a multidisciplinary journal of policy and practice, it reflects a wide range of institutional and cultural backgrounds and a variety of cultural experience. Other relevant titles in the Development in Practice Reader series include *Development and Patronage* (1997), and *Development and Rights* (1998).

The European Journal of Development Research — Journal of the European Association of Development Research and Training Institutes (EADI): published twice-yearly by Frank Cass & Co, ISSN:0957-8811, Editor: Cristóbal Kay. An academic journal that reflects the wide diversity of disciplines and approaches to development represented among the 150 member agencies of EADI. Relevant thematic issues include *Globalisation, Competitiveness and Human Security —* *Papers from the Vienna Conference of EADI, 1996,* and *Development and Rights: Negotiating Justice in Changing Societies.*

Development: published quarterly by Sage on behalf of the Society for International Development, ISSN:1011-6730,. Editor: Wendy Harcourt.
Aims to be a point of reference for the dialogue between activists and intellectuals who are committed to the search for alternative paths of social transformation towards a more sustainable and just world. With a strong emphasis on local–global links running through the journal, its 1997 volume focused on globalisation and civic engagement.

Organisations concerned with social action (postal addresses at the end of the bibliography)

The Anti-MAI Coalition: The anti-MAI Coalition is a broad-based, multi-centred coalition whose programme and main international and regional partners can be accessed via Third World Network, and at the following websites: Public Citizen Global Trade Watch: <www.tradewatch.org>
ATTAC: http://www.attac.org/

CIVICUS (World Alliance for Citizen Participation): An international alliance of organisations dedicated to strengthening citizen action and civil society worldwide, particularly where freedom of association is under threat. CIVICUS believes that citizen action is a predominant feature of the political, economic, and cultural life of all societies, and that private action for the public good can take place either within the civil sphere or in combination with government or with business. A healthy society needs an equitable relationship among its citizens, their associations and foundtions, business and government. Recent publications include Rajesh Tandon and Miguel Darcy de Oliveira (coords.) (1994) *CITIZENS: Strengthening Global Civil Society*; and Leslie M. Fox and S. Bruce Schearer (eds.) (1997) *Sustaining Civil Society: Strategies for Resource Mobilisation* . Web: http://www.civicus.org/

Focus on the Global South: Established in 1995, Focus on the Global South is dedicated to regional and global policy analysis, linking micro-macro issues, and advocacy work. E-mail: admin@focusweb.org

FoodFirst Information and Action Network: The first and most prominent international organisation to work in the field of economic human rights, as codified in international law. It promotes economic and social rights, particularly the right of all human beings to adequate food, within international civil-society arenas and at the UN; and challenges violations of such rights through letter campaigns and other activities. Its international secretariat in Germany supports national sections in three continents. Web: http://www.fian.org/

Habitat International Coalition (HIC): An international alliance of 350 CSOs and NGOs from 70 countries working primarily on housing rights, forced evictions, and human settlements, concentrating on issues around the recognition, defence, and realisation of the human right to adequate housing. Its three committees work at various levels through training, alliance-building, using the UN system, research and fact-finding: Housing and Land Rights Committee (India), the Women and Shelter Network (Tanzania), and the Housing and Environment Committee (Senegal). E-mail: <hic@mweb.co.za>

International Confederation of Free Trade Unions (ICFTU): General Secretary: Bill Jordan. One of the largest workers' bodies in the world, representing 124 million members in 143 countries and territories, ICTFU works extensively on trade union rights as well as on wider issues of equality, jobs and working practices, and multinational enterprises. It has representative status at the UN and publishes widely on its areas of interest. International Confederation of Free Trade Unions (ICFTU): General Secretary: Bill Jordan. Web: http://www.icftu.org/

International NGO Committee on Human Rights in Trade and Investment: An international alliance of CSOs working to ensure that the international human-rights perspective, principles and provisions are no longer ignored in international and regional economic policy and practice, through advocacy work at the UN and at global and regional economic forums, research and publication work. Information on activities of the NGO Committee and its main documents can be found at the web-site of the People's Decade of Human Rights Organisation (PDHRE): http://www.pdhre.org/. The Committee can be contacted via Latin American and Caribbean Committee for the Defence of Women (CLADEM), Fax: 51.1.4635898; E-mail: cladem@chavin.rcp.net.pe

North-South Centre of the Council of Europe — The European Centre for Global Interdependence and Solidarity: Set up in 1990 in Lisbon. It has its roots in the European Public Campaign on North–South Interdependence and Solidarity, launched by the Council of Europe in 1988. Its aims are to raise public awareness of issues of global interdependence and solidarity and to advocate pluralist democracy and respect for human rights as fundamental elements of sustainable development. http://www.nscentre.org/

The North–South Institute: Though focusing much of its work on Canadian foreign policy, NSI's research supports global efforts to strengthen international development cooperation, improve governance, enhance gender and social equity in globalising markets, and prevent ethnic and other conflict. The results of this research are shared through publications, seminars, and conferences. The Institute collaborates closely with the International Development Research Centre (IDRC) and with the International Institute for Sustainable Development (IISD) in Canada. Web: http://www.nsi-ins.ca/

People-Centred Development Forum is an international alliance of individuals and organisations dedicated to the creation of just, inclusive, and sustainable human societies through voluntary citizen action. Its Founding Director is David Korten (see under 'Books'). The Forum's activities and publications convey the basic message that transformational change to reduce current levels of inequality and exploitation is not only possible but essential to human survival. Web: http://www.iisd1.iisd.ca/pcdf/

The Third World Network: An international network of organisations and individuals involved in issues relating to development, Third World, and North–South affairs. It conducts research on economic, social, and environmental issues pertaining to the South, organises and participates in seminars; and provides an international platform for Southern perspectives. **TWN** publishes a wide range of books as well as the daily *SUNS (South–North Development Monitor)*; *Third World Economics*; and the monthly magazine *Third World Resurgence* (an African edition, *African Agenda,* is published by Africa Secretariat of TWN; and a Spanish-language edition *Sur* is published by the Third World Institute).

The Transnational Institute is an independent fellowship of researchers and activists worldwide who work on major issues of poverty and injustice focusing especially on the global economy, peace and security, and democratisation. Recent publications (all co-published with Pluto Press) include John Cavanagh, Daphne Wysham and Marcos Aruda (eds.): *Beyond Bretton Woods: Alternatives to the Global Economic Order;* Susan George: *The Debt Boomerang: How Third World Debt Harms Us All*; David Sogge (ed.): *Compassion and Calculation: The Business of Private Foreign Aid*; and (co-published with International Books) Kees Biekart: *The Politics of Civil Society Building: European Private Aid Agencies and Democratic Transitions in Central America*. Website: http://www.worldcom.nl/tni/

UN Non-governmental Liaison Service (NGLS) is concerned with the entire UN development agenda and works with NGO and NGO networks worldwide, both facilitating their access to and providing information about the UN system, and acting as a communication channel for the UN agencies to the NGO sector. It publishes regular bulletins (in English and in French), such as *Go Between* and several occasional publications and series. Materials are usually available free of charge on request.

Addresses of publishers and other organisations

Blackwell Publishers, 108 Cowley Road, Oxford OX4 1JF, UK.
Fax: +44 (0)1865 791347.

Carfax Publishing Company, PO Box 25, Abingdon OX14 3UE, UK.
Fax: +44 (0)1235 401550.

Centre for the Study of Developing Societies, 29 Rajpur Road, Delhi 110054, India.

The Clarendon Press, Walton Street, Oxford OX2 6DP, UK.

Cornell University Press, 512 E. State St. PO Box 250, Ithaca NY 14851, USA.

EADI Secretariat, 24 rue Rothschild, 1202 Geneva, Switzerland. Tas: +41 22 738 5797.

Earthscan Publications, 120 Pentonville Road, London N1 9JN, UK. Fax: +44 (0)171 278 1142.

Focus on the Global South, CUSRI Wisit Prachuabmoh Building, Chulalongkorn University, Phayathai Road, Bangkok, Thailand. Fax: +66 (2) 2559976

FoodFirst Information and Action Network, PO Box 102243, D-69012 Heidelberg, Germany. Fax: +49 6221 830 545.

Frank Cass, Newbury House, 900 Eastern Avenue, Newbury Park, Ilford, Essex IG2 7HH, Fax: +44 (0)181 599 0984

Garland Publishing, 717 Fifth Avenue, Suite 2500, New York NY 10022–8102, USA. Fax: +1 (212) 308 9399.

Habitat International Coalition (IIIC) Secretariat, PO Box 34519, Groote Schuur 7937, Cape Town, Republic of South Africa. Fax: +272 1 447 4741

International Confederation of Free Trade Unions (ICFTU), 155 boulevard Emile Jacqmain, 1210 Brussels, Belgium. Fax : + 32 (0)2 201 5815.

International Peace Research Institute, Meigaku, Kamikurata 1518, Totzukaku, Yokahama, Japan 224.

Kumarian Press, 14 Oakwood Avenue, West Hartford CT 06119 2127, USA. Fax: +1 (860) 233 6072.

Macmillan Press, Houndmills, Basingstoke RG21 6XS, UK. Fax: +44 (0)1256 842084.

Manchester University Press, Oxford Road, Manchester M13 9NR, UK. Fax: +44 (0)161 274 2234.

Mansell Publishing, Wellington House, 125 Strand, London WC2R 0BB, UK. Fax: +44 (0)171 240 7261.

The MIT Press, Massachusetts Institute of Technology, Five Cambridge Center, Cambridge MA 02142, USA.

Monthly Review Press, 122 West 27th Street, New York NY 10001, USA. Fax: +1 (212) 727 3676.

North–South Institute, 55 Murray, Suite 200, Ottawa, Canada K1N 5M3. Fax: +613 241–7435.

The North–South Centre, European Centre for Global Interdependence and Solidarity, Avenida da Liberdade, 229–40, 1250–142 Lisbon, Portugal. Fax: + 351 (0)1 353 1329.

OECD, 2 rue André Pascal, 75775 Paris, Cedex 16, France. Fax: +33 (0)1 452 47943.

Orbis Books, Box 302, NY 10545–0302, USA. Fax: +1 (914) 941 7005.

Oxfam Publications, Oxfam, 274 Banbury Road, Oxford OX2 7DZ, UK. Fax: +44 (0)1865 313925.

Oxford University Press, Walton Street, Oxford OX2 6DP, UK. Fax: +44 (0)1865 56646.

Pact Publications, 777 UN Plaza, New York NY 10017, USA. Fax: +1 (212) 692 9748

Pluto Press, 345 Archway Road, London N6 5AA, UK. Fax: +44 (0)181 348 9133.

Polity Press, 65 Bridge Street, Cambridge CB2 1UR, UK.

Lynne Rienner Publishers, 1800 30th St, Boulder, Colorado 80301, USA. Fax: +1 (303) 444 0824.

Routledge, 11 New Fetter Lane, London EC4P 4EE, UK. Fax: +44 (0)171 842 2302.

Sage Publications, 6 Bonhill Street, London EC2A 4PU, UK. Fax: +44 (0)171 374 8741.

Sage Publications India, M 32 Greater Kailash Market I, New Delhi 110 048, India. Fax: +91 (0)11 647 2426.

Simon and Schuster, 1230 Avenue of the Americas, New York NY 10029, USA.

Society for International Development (SID), Via Panisperna 207, 00184 Rome, Italy. Fax : +39 6 487 2170.

State University of New York Press, State University Plaza, Albany NY 12246, USA.

Syracuse University Press, 1600 Jamesville Ave, Syracuse NY 13244–5160, USA. Fax : +1 (315) 443 5545.

Third World Network, International Secretariat, 228 Macallister Road, 10400 Penang, Malaysia. Fax: +60 (0)4 226 4505.

Third World Network, Africa Secretariat, PO Box 8604, Accra-North, Ghana. Fax: +233 (0)21 773857.

Trans-National Institute, Paulus Potterstraat 20, 1071 DA Amsterdam, The Netherlands. Fax: +31 (0)20 673 0179.

University of California Press, 2120 Berkeley Way, Berkeley CA 94270, USA. Fax: +1 (510) 643 7127.

University of Chicago Press, 5801 Ellis Avenue, 4th floor, Chicago, IL 60637. Fax: +1 773 202 9756.

UN Non-governmental Liaison Service (NGLS), Palais des Nations, 1211 Geneva 10, Switzerland. Fax: +41 (0)22 917 0049. OR United Nations, Room FF-346, New York: NY 10017, USA. Fax:+1 (212) 963 8712.

UNRISD, Palais des Nations, 1211 Geneva 10, Switzerland. Fax:+41 (0)22 917 0650.

Westview Press, 5500 Central Avenue, Boulder, Colorado 80301–2877, USA. Fax: +1 (303) 449 3356.

World Order Models Project, 777 UN Plaza, New York NY 10017, USA.

Zed Books, 7 Cynthia Street, London N1 9JF, UK. Fax: +44 (0)171 833 3960.